Gambling, Freedom and Democracy

Routledge Studies in Social and Political Thought

Gambling, Freedom and Democracy

Peter J. Adams

Routledge
Taylor & Francis Group
New York   London

First published 2008
by Routledge
270 Madison Ave, New York NY 10016

Simultaneously published in the UK
by Routledge
2 Park Square, Milton Park, Abingdon, Oxon, OX14 4RN

Routledge is an imprint of the Taylor & Francis Group, an informa business

Transferred to Digital Printing 2008

Typeset in Sabon by IBT Global

Library of Congress Cataloging in Publication Data
Adams, Peter J., 1956-
Gambling, freedom, and democracy / Peter J. Adams.
p. cm. — (Routledge studies in social and political thought)
Includes bibliographical references and index.
ISBN-13: 978-0-415-95762-5 (hardback : alk. paper)
1. Gambling—Government policy.   2. Gambling industry.   I. Title.
HV6710.A33 2007

338.4'795—dc22   2007016116

ISBN10: 0-415-95762-1 (hbk)
ISBN10: 0-203-93509-8 (ebk)

ISBN13: 978-0-415-95762-5 (hbk)
ISBN13: 978-0-203-93509-5 (ebk)

Contents

Preface

This is no ordinary book about gambling. Democracy is too weighty a topic and freedom is too close to the heart of most people for it to be treated lightly. This book sets out to pry open an area of discussion and debate that, if it is to be believed, will have significant implications for the future of democratic systems. It looks beyond the immediate scene and poses questions regarding where the modern engagement with gambling might lead. It presents the case that there is something intrinsic in the nature of commercial gambling that cuts deep into the heart of what we understand as democracy and it does so in a way that threatens its very function.

At first it must seem strange to link a minor pleasure like gambling to major issues like freedom and democracy. How can the small activities of placing a bet, having a flutter, or taking a punt possibly interact with these grander systems? However, the issue here is one of scale. When gambling consumption is low, threats to democracy are minimal. As democracies heat up their investment in gambling, they move progressively into territories where the economic and social impacts of gambling become more difficult to manage, a territory where they have the potential to influence and change the overall shape of social relations. The book is intended, therefore, as a cautionary piece. It needs to be read with one eye on the current scene and, more importantly, the other eye looking into the future. It asks this question: What are some of the long-term effects of the current warm embrace, the modern love affair that Western-style democracies have taken on when they embarked on a program of high-intensity, commercialized gambling? It concludes that there is strong reason to be concerned, and it offers up a range of ways in which nation states might choose to protect their democratic systems from predictable harms.

The writing of this book was driven by a series of firsthand exposures to the ways in which governments, the gambling industry, and local interests interconnect in their common pursuit of revenue generated by gambling. From 1993 onward I was progressively drawn into change processes occurring in New Zealand at the interfaces of these three intersecting communities of interest. At first I was persuaded into the naive belief that these interests would be moderated by the broader interests of social well-being. It did not take long for me to realize that these main players were more interested in how to achieve increased revenue while minimizing potential opposition. As time went on, the coalition among government, industry, and local developers appeared more and more formidable. Over the course of a decade, gambling consumption in New Zealand rose tenfold and the extent of these alliances appeared only to deepen. This put my colleagues and me in an increasingly difficult position. Our challenges to the expansion were unpopular and propelled us with increasing frequency into conflict with members of this triumvirate.

When one has strong experiences, particularly a series of them, it sometimes takes a few years to process them and decipher what they all mean. This book was written partially as a response to the strong emotions I felt during this time; it was written partially as a way of capturing some of the understandings that were formed from what I was privileged to observe; it was partially driven by fascination, indignation, and pride. The pride part relates to what a small bunch of us over an 8-year period were able to achieve in playing an influential role in our government adopting a public health approach to gambling (to be explored later in this book). However, this achievement came at enormous cost to us and our relationships, with several of those involved suffering enduring negative effects. The effort all culminated in a crisis in September 2002 when, as Chair of the Problem Gambling Foundation of New Zealand, I faced the collapse of the organization as a consequence of pressure from the media, government, and gambling industry figures. The crisis also threw into relief how the intersecting interests of these three players are capable of combining into a potent force, and this highlighted for me the need to look more closely at how they interrelate. Fortunately, the Problem Gambling Foundation survived this period of crisis and continues to operate strongly to this day.

ACKNOWLEDGMENTS

In putting this book together, I want to declare my wholehearted gratitude to my partner Judith for her patience throughout, and also to our four children, who might not have known what I was up to at the time but lived with the effects in terms of time away and preoccupations. I want to acknowledge the contribution of Ralph Gerdelan for his ideas and commitment to what we were trying to achieve in the early years. I am also grateful for the support and encouragement of Charles Livingstone in Melbourne; David Korn and Phil Lange in Toronto; and my colleagues Fiona Rossen, Lana Perese, Robin Shepherd, Maria Bellringer, and Lisa Campbell, who worked together with me at our Centre for Gambling Studies at the University of Auckland. I would also like to acknowledge the support of several people who with courage and love helped me through times when the going got tough, particularly Robert Brown, John Raeburn, Cynthia Orme, Samson Tse, Helen Warren, Peter Smith, and my wider family.

1 Introduction

In the first decade of the new millennium, several affluent economies have already experienced 20 years of unprecedented rises in gambling consumption. Details in specific countries are not easily obtained and there are large variations in how national consumption data are reported. For example, some calculate net expenditure on gambling differently by excluding reasonable operational costs, but others are affected by inflated estimates of what it takes to deliver the product.[1] Despite these variations, gross estimates give some idea of the scale of current annual consumption. At the upper end, the Canadian theorist, John Ralston Saul (2005) estimated that worldwide expenditures on gambling total around $900 billion per year.[2] This estimate is most likely an exaggeration, but it highlights the absence of data on global expansion. A more accurate guess could be inferred from official consumption figures, including an estimated expenditure in 2004 in the United States of $78.6 billion,[3] a Canadian expenditure of $12.4 billion (Statistics Canada, 2005),[4] a combined $14.2 billion in Australia and New Zealand,[5] and around $15 billion in the United Kingdom (U.K. Gambling Commission, 2005–2006).[6] These figures together add up to an annual consumption of more than $110 billion. However, the figures leave out the considerable amounts of money that are expended in unofficial and illegal gambling (e.g., sweepstakes, raffles, poker among friends, etc.), as well as unrecorded amounts spent on Internet gambling. When these are combined with less documented but rising levels of gambling in other parts of Europe, Latin America, east Asia, and central Asia, it would be reasonable to expect the annual global expenditure on gambling to be reaching levels above $300 billion. These are high amounts, particularly when they are contrasted with other leading global expenditures. Although gambling does fall well short of the highest expenditure, where in 2003 an estimated $950 billion was spent globally on military equipment and armaments, it does rank at a similar level to another leading global expenditure of an estimated $364 billion in 2001 on pharmaceuticals (Pan America Health Association, 2004).

What differentiates gambling from other large expenditures is the rate at which it is increasing. For example, in the South Pacific, gambling expenditure in Australia increased from $4.7 billion in 1990 to $10.5 billion by

2000 (an adult per capita increase from $242 to $505), and in New Zealand, gambling expenditure rose from $0.4 billion in 1991 to $1 billion by 2001 (an adult per capita increase from about $100 to $234). From this increased consumption governments are deriving progressively higher revenues. For example, in 2003 the Canadian government received revenue of $5.1 billion, which was greater than the $5.0 billion received from alcohol and tobacco combined (Marshall & Wynne, 2004). As the global proliferation of commercial gambling continues, it is not unreasonable to expect that over the next 10 years gambling could rank with the highest expenditures in the world.

In most cases, the expansion of consumption is associated with the progressive commercialization and resultant increases in the availability of higher intensity forms of gambling, most important, the introduction of new "continuous" forms of betting. The more traditional noncontinuous forms of gambling such as race betting and lotteries involve significant time delays between placing a bet and knowing the outcome. Continuous forms of gambling, such as casino table games and electronic gambling machines (EGMs), involve very short delays between betting and its outcome, enabling rapid and repeated betting within a short period of time. In many countries, continuous forms of gambling are eclipsing noncontinuous forms. For example, gambling expenditure on EGMs has risen markedly over the last decade in Australia, the Netherlands, and New Zealand to over half the respective total gambling expenditure.[7] Casinos and EGMs have spread steadily in availability throughout most of the United States and Canada. With the fall of the Iron Curtain, European countries in transition are exploring the revenue capacity of continuous forms of gambling to finance aspects of their development. For example, joint venture partnerships are establishing casinos in Slovenia, Hungary, Poland, and the Czech Republic. Many Asian nations are also intensifying their relationships to gambling. Japan has a long, established relationship to a skill and luck-mixed EGM called *pachinko*, which is now in widespread use throughout their communities. Large casinos are becoming a more prominent feature in places such as the Philippines and Macao. With its dramatic economic growth, the government of mainland China is beginning to seriously explore the potential of new forms of gambling (Gu, 2000; Hulme, 2005).

It would be expected that with such dramatic shifts in financial and leisure investment, responsible governments would seek to carefully monitor what rapid proliferation might mean for their communities. The change is bound to have major implications for social and financial transactions. However, despite the rapidity of the modern expansion, remarkably little is known yet about how the scale of this increase will affect the way people live in the long term. The majority of research effort to date has focused on population prevalence studies. Little investigation has occurred into the impact of high-intensity gambling on families and communities. Few studies have explored the broader social and economic changes. Little is understood about how the design of new forms of continuous gambling could be varied to reduce their harm potential. Research is only beginning on the addictive processes associated with new forms of gambling and little is understood about effective interventions (Jackson et al., 2000; Raylu & Oei, 2002). The international research on gambling simply lacks adequate information to predict how gambling and social systems will interact 20 years into the future. What is worse, none of the countries embarking on rapid proliferation have assembled adequate processes to monitor the consequent social and economic changes that will occur. It is as if governments around the world have collectively chosen to embark on an unprecedented social experiment—a bold experiment—with little idea of the medium- or long-term consequences of what they are pursuing. How are we to make sense of their bold undertaking? How will it impact the social and economic systems of those who get involved, and what will the long-term effects be on political systems and the foundations of democracy itself? These are concerns that I seek to address in this book.

ECOLOGICAL DEGRADATION

The current international proliferation of gambling can be productively compared to the expansion of other commercial operations that involve the large-scale exploitation of primary resources. Primary extractive industries such as the mining of precious metals, the logging of primeval forests, or the netting of ocean fish species focus efforts on converting a primary resource for which there is a demand into a unitized and transportable product for distribution and sale. Commercial gambling closely resembles these extractive processes. Gambling operations directly exploit systems of financial transaction within a particular context. As with the natural environment, the processes of extraction for gambling interact with a range of interlocking systems. These systems include those that underpin the patterns of social interchange, those that incorporate language and cultural practices, those of legal transaction, those of friendship and kinship, and those complex networks of social involvement that spread across localities and territories. For example, the first installment of a set of EGMs in the main hotel of a small town will connect immediately with the flow of money within that town and affect patterns of social and leisure activity. In time, through consequent increases in debt and problem gambling, family systems will be affected and legal issues will emerge in the form of increases in property crime. In a similar fashion to the way mining and logging interact with the complex systems of the natural world, the introduction of commercial gambling connects into the social and political ecologies within a broader context.

To illustrate this comparison, consider the effects of commercial logging on the primeval forests of Indonesia's outer islands of Kalimantan. Prior to

1967, little of these extensive tropical forests had been disturbed. They had grown there for millions of years, developing complex networks of vegetation and animal life. Their complexity spread across and between different levels that involve systems in the soil, in the undergrowth, in the growth of trees, and in the overhanging canopy. After 1967, with incentives and encouragement from government, an emerging logging industry focused its efforts on the clear-logging of vast tracts of tropical forest. At the beginning of his long rule as leader of Indonesia, President Soeharto faced a range of severe economic and political problems and logging offered a convenient source of much needed revenue and assisted in his drive to centralize his political power base. There was also pressure for agricultural land to feed Indonesia's rapidly growing population. Logging began in earnest in 1967, and the harvest doubled between 1970 and 1975. At its high point in 1979, gross foreign exchange earnings were $2.1 billion and the country was the world's leading exporter of tropical logs with 41% of market share (Osgood, 1994). After the 1980s, the industry shifted to value-added wood products, particularly tropical plywood, and by the late 1980s Indonesia was producing 79% of the global supply. Following this, the pulp and paper industry began to take off and by 2001 it was the largest income generator in the Indonesian forestry industry. What had been one of the most biologically diverse ecosystems on the planet was progressively peeled off the land, leaving little that recognized its economic, biological, and environmental value. Few were ready for the rapidity and scale of this deforestation and it has had serious ongoing consequences, not only in the local context, but also for the global environment. The loss of old-growth forests has led to degradation of a unique biodiversity. The increase in forest fires has polluted the air with toxic fumes and ash, which in turn have made significant contributions to the greenhouse gases that are raising global temperatures.

The social and economic networks in which people build their lives resemble in many ways the interlocking complexities of the natural world. In the tropical forest, major changes to the upper tree canopy of will affect lower vegetation, which in turn affects insect life, which then affects animal life, which then affects lower vegetation, and so on. With groups of humans, changes in the social ecology of a particular community will entail changes within other connected systems. For example, the introduction of new ways of spending money will interact with financial and social systems in ways that have knock-on effects in terms of leisure time and patterns of social involvement. This is particularly the case with gambling. Commercial gambling, as essentially an extractive industry, does not establish its own base and contributes little to establishing the primary resources on which it draws. It progresses by plugging into and exploiting systems of social and economic transactions that already exist. It introduces little into community systems in terms of new materials and new investments. Instead, it latches onto the broader social ecology of human interaction and engages people in changes to the way they spend their money and time.

FEATURES OF EXTRACTION

The parallel with large-scale commercial logging helps identify five salient features that can be usefully transferred into understanding the modern expansion of commercial gambling. The first feature relates to the commercial nature of extractive industries in their early phases of development; the second feature focuses on the development of new methods and technologies for extraction; the third feature focuses on the creation of a frontier society that services the expanding industry activity; the fourth feature focuses on the importance of the relative size and scale of commercial activity; and the final feature describes how resistance to the initial expansion is compromised by the naivete of resident populations.

Commercialization

The nature of primary extraction changes radically when the strategies and disciplines of larger commercial operations are applied. The isolated woodsman felling trees to meet a small local demand for firewood and building materials will have minimal impact on large forests, and business growth will most likely remain very modest. Once a commercial organization moves in, it brings with it the capacity to organize the extraction process on a larger scale. Managers and developers cast their gaze wider than the local scene. In reviewing the needs of more distant markets, they identify a major commercial opportunity and in response they organize new transport systems, enlist an appropriate workforce, and apply the most up-to-date methods of extraction to ensure the constant delivery of wood products to the places that need them. Obviously the new operation will initially require significant investment capital, but this is soon recovered because in the early phases of extraction the target raw material is easily accessed and felling is unimpeded by resistance from a knowledgeable public or a government keen on regulation. The organization, its operations, and its profits grow quickly and the scene soon attracts other similar organizations seeking a share in the success. As with any commercial operation in a competitive environment, attaining significant growth and profit quickly become critical for survival, for without them the organization would be at risk of losing the confidence of its shareholders and being swallowed by its competitors.

As with commercial logging, the main vehicle for the modern expansion of gambling has been the emergence of larger, profit-driven commercial organizations that bring with them the investment capital that enables them to achieve jumps in the scale of exploitation. What started out in many contexts as small-scale forms of gambling such as card games, raffles, and church bingo are quickly eclipsed by new and more potent forms offered by larger and commercially more astute firms. They bring with them investment capital that enables them to achieve wider distribution and promote consumption on a scale unimagined by the small local providers. Their commercial success is soon noticed by other organizations that move in to vie for a place in the market by developing increasingly varied and attractive gambling products. As in forestry, increases in competition magnify the importance of the commercial drive for profits. Survival and success grows increasingly dependent on achieving a competitive edge in the market through new products or innovations in forms of delivery. However, the nature of these organizations is not limited to large private firms. In many situations, such as in Canada and the Netherlands, the dominant commercial organization is the government itself, but the dynamic remains the same. Governments run their forms of gambling to maximize a financial return to their own stakeholders, the public. Their products, such as lottery tickets, often compete with those of private organizations, and they, too, seek to create a product niche by introducing new products and forms of delivery.

Refinements in Methods of Extraction

The invention and subsequent widespread use of the gas-powered chainsaw enabled fewer workers to fell increasingly larger tracts of forest. This then led to increases in the commercial viability of larger scale operations. Other devices enabled similar increases in capacity: the helicopter for surveying and improving access, the bulldozer for clearing, new logging trucks and log hoists for handling, and the wood-chipper for reprocessing. Along with the gadgets came refinements in the methods of extraction. For instance, new methods and materials for constructing roads increased vehicle access deep into forested regions; improved techniques for controlled burn-offs enabled widespread clearances; the processing of logs into wood chips simplified handling; and the constantly improving network of road, rail, and sea transport systems ensured that wood products would reach their markets. In a parallel fashion, the rapid growth in commercialized gambling has to a large extent been driven by refinements in technology and methods of extraction. Improvements in telecommunications have enabled the marketing of increasingly grander national lottery products. They have also enabled horse gambling to move beyond the racetrack into shops and people's living rooms. The extensive use of television, radio, and other media has improved the immediacy of each event. The combination of Internet and credit card technologies has opened up new frontiers for product development, such as the arrival of Internet virtual casinos. However, beside these refinements, the impacts of improved technology are perhaps best illustrated in the evolution of the EGM. The EGM has done for gambling what the chainsaw did for forestry. It has enabled widespread and intensive engagement with the product. The EGM is best seen as a gambling supply console. It has evolved into a complex and flexible delivery platform upon which a range of technologies can be employed to maximize consumer engagement and enjoyment.

In constructing an EGM, innovative designers have a considerable amount to play with. They can change the size of jackpots, vary the odds of winning, change the ratio of wins to losses, vary the speed of each bet and the number of bets per button press, change the way money is loaded into the machine and the way it pays out, as well as varying the look, the feel, and the sound of the machine. Their designs invariably call on two critical types of technology, electronic technologies and psychological technologies. For example, electronic technologies allow several bets to occur simultaneously and for the results to be displayed (in poker-style EGMs) on lines of symbols across the screen. On many EGMs, consumers can bet on more lines than are available on the screen, and EGMs can be programmed to display only those lines that come closest to a win. The psychological effect of showing only the near misses reinforces the impression that the person gambling is on the verge of a major win, and this encourages the gambler to keep playing.[8] This combination of electronic design features with strategies to exploit their psychological impact is a potent mix. New refinements are in constant development, and the intelligence now built into modern machines is steadily improving their engaging qualities and enabling machines to adapt their responses to the patterns of behaviors specific to individual players.

Superimposed Frontier Environments

In large extractive operations such as forestry the workforce required can quickly grow in size to proportions that eclipse the small long-term resident population in the area. The new arrivals coalesce around the nodes of industry activity. They include forestry workers, loggers, transport workers, mechanics, engineers, and mill workers. Some bring their skills from far-away places, others drift in from adjacent regions and pick up the necessary skills as opportunities arise, and others are drawn from the local community and acquire their abilities by filling in for labor shortfalls. Those involved directly in primary extraction comprise only one part of the new population. Their needs drive the formation of a second-tier workforce, people from differing backgrounds providing a wide variety of services that support the infrastructure base for the primary workforce. These people construct places to live; run shops for supplies; provide opportunities for rest and relaxation; and provide access to banking services, health services, mail services, schools, and so forth. Added to both these workforces are the friends, family members, and various hangers-on who choose to follow into the territory. In this way a frontier society begins to take the form of a network of small communities that spin off the activities involved in extraction.

The current early phase in the expansion of commercialized gambling creates a network of people whose lives are intricately connected and reliant on the success of the new industry. Hotel bars containing EGMs dispersed across a suburban landscape resemble the scatter of small logging teams working in different parts of a forest. Casinos resemble the large-scale mechanized logging operations that intensively exploit a confined area.

Whether concentrated or dispersed, both these forms of extraction call for a labor force with specialized skills and one that quickly becomes reliant on the income generated by the new economic activity. For example, casinos require specially trained croupiers; they require machine operators and maintenance workers; they need specialized managers and accountants; and they also require teams of bar workers, entertainers, security officers, restaurant workers, cleaners, and so forth. Behind the workforce involved in primary extraction develops another workforce associated with ancillary industries. People in this second-tier workforce provide a wide range of services that include accommodation, legal services, transport, recreation, and regulatory services. For example, a new easy access finance industry typically emerges in the form of specialized lending institutions, pawn shops, and associated services such as debt collecting agencies and informal networks of loan sharks. Although both tiers of this emergent workforce are unlikely to eclipse the resident population (except in destination venues such as Las Vegas), its presence spreads progressively throughout the complex social ecology that makes up that community. Over time most people in the resident community find themselves personally connected, through family or friends, with someone who has a role in part of this industry. Consequently, large portions of the resident population form connections to the extractive industry and thereby find themselves with an investment in its future success.

As with most frontier societies, the institutions, systems, and processes that support orderly transaction are at an early phase of development. Initiatives can happen quickly, sometimes with a level of randomness, or even lawlessness, because few of the regulatory systems that minimize risk and ensure fairness are in place to moderate the boom-and-bust pattern of growth. Within frontier logging towns the occupants can live hard and variable lives. They are likely to have little investment in the long-term development of their communities; housing is often makeshift and functional; they move frequently to new locations according to demand; and the very poor often live side-by-side with those who have been recently elevated to the absurdly rich. This dynamic but transient character permeates all levels of the workforce. The emergent ancillary industries have a similar frontier character. For example, the rough life of a logger involves multiple risks to health; consequently, a makeshift ancillary industry can form that provides rudimentary health and rehabilitation services to the inevitable groups of those with injuries. In a parallel fashion, an undesirable by-product of increased gambling consumption is the associated rise in presentations of problem gamblers. The community and the industry, embarrassed by the suffering the new pastime has created, support the formation of new organizations—small frontier towns—set up to provide basic intervention services, predominantly counseling, to reduce the scale of the problem. The emergence of this ancillary workforce is explored in more detail in Chapter 8.

Impacts of Scale

Gambling, as with other primary extractive industries like logging and mining, has varying impacts, depending on the manner and scale of the operation. The small-scale logging of trees from primeval forests is unlikely to damage the forest ecology as a whole. The indigenous people of Kalimantan have exploited forest resources for thousands of years, but their modest demands were easily accommodated by such a vast natural expanse. In some ways their use of forest resources was incorporated into the ecological balance that sustained the forest environment. Similarly, small-scale commercial milling and mining operations might initially have some impact in terms of destruction and pollution, but their impact is localized and in time natural vegetation regenerates and the former ecology is restored. The real threat to the natural ecology occurs when larger commercial organizations invest in methods and technologies of extraction that involve wholesale and widespread exploitation of a natural resource. The impact of these is not absorbed because the large scale and ongoing nature of the exploitation prevents recovery from taking its course. Once large tracts of the Kalimantan forests were removed, their delicately balanced ecologies were delivered a fatal blow, and forest systems progressively collapsed, making the regeneration of large portions of the forests impossible.

Gambling in the form of strategies for the collective manipulation of chance has a long history, with roots that stretch back into the origins of most cultures. As civilizations encountered the enjoyment derived from games of chance, they incorporated them progressively into practices associated with leisure and socialization. For example, in 17th-century England, all manner of betting—on horse races, card games, number games, and even stakes on births, deaths, and marriages—was incorporated into the activities of people coming together and sharing in ritual and social intercourse.[9] In this way gambling can be viewed as comprising part of the social ecology, a positive contributor to the glue that binds us as communities and societies. As such, it poses little threat to the integrity of social and political structures, but this positive value is challenged as the scale of consumption leaps to new levels. The widespread commercialization of gambling elevates the activity from having a minor influence to having a major influence on patterns of social involvement. As discussed earlier, within the short span of the last two decades, most major Western democracies have experienced tenfold increases in gambling consumption. In the largest states of Australia, Victoria and New South Wales, income from gambling is approaching one sixth of state government revenue. The sheer scale of such increases and their long-term consequences for community well-being require closer examination. Added to this, and undoubtedly driven by commercial imperatives, low-intensity forms of gambling with few social impacts are being eclipsed by higher intensity forms with lower potential for social engagement. For instance, the social involvement generated by people mixing and mingling at racetracks contrasts with what are typically low levels of social interaction on lines of EGMs in hotel bars. It is not gambling per se that poses a risk to social and political ecologies; rather, it is the scale of the increase that motivates the focus in this book.

Naivete of Resident Populations

A feature of the commercial exploitation of natural ecologies has been the relative naivete of the inhabitants of the vicinity to understand or respond quickly enough to prevent the long-term impacts of wholesale exploitation. A resident population with little previous experience or understanding of the consequences of large-scale commercial logging is likely to initially view the logging as similar to their own modest felling, only larger. They accordingly assume that although they see large areas of trees disappearing, the forests will have the capacity to regenerate and sustain the felling and recover as they always have. Furthermore, the increases in exploitation tend not to happen all at once. It is an incremental process, so the initial logging draws little attention and locals remain unaware that as the market is established, the capacity for growth will mean further leaps in production. They might also assume that their government would not allow levels of exploitation to harm the long-term future of their nation.

The rapid expansion of commercial gambling has for many nations caught their populations napping. The time lag between first deregulating the gambling environment and eventual public recognition of the social and economic downsides creates a window of opportunity for high-intensity gambling to gain an enduring foothold in a nation's economy. For countries such as Canada, New Zealand, and more recently countries in transition in eastern Europe, gambling had in the past been heavily regulated and people had learned to perceive gambling as a benign enjoyment with few negative consequences. They had grown accustomed to government agencies that enforced tough regulations and took direct roles in restricting gambling to less potent forms. The public does not need to know too much about gambling because the size of associated problems is minimal. They assume that any changes to the regulatory environment must have been made for the correct reasons and with public interests at heart. As governments loosened the noose of regulation around gambling opportunities, their previous role as public protector was tipped on its head. With the public continuing to assume high standards of protection, governments began to explore the potential of gambling to generate easy tax revenue. Their publics, naive to the risks, tolerated each progressive liberalization falsely assuming that governments have fully examined potential harms and that negative consequences will continue at previous tolerable levels. They were unaware that their leaders were taking them on a new adventure with very little understanding of its long-term consequences. Whatever protests were raised, their misgivings were effectively managed through media campaigns that emphasized the benefits of gambling (this will be explored more fully in Chapter 5). People are reassured that the proliferation is for the public good. It might not be until well into the proliferation that sufficient public concern is expressed to worry governments, but by this time the commercial base for high-intensity gambling is well established and public health advocates have little chance of introducing significant changes.

GAMBLING IN A POLITICAL ECOLOGY

Another dimension in the comparison of the current expansion of gambling with the logging of tropical forests concerns the impact on the political ecology of such events. As mentioned earlier, the large-scale logging operations in the outer islands of Kalimantan required the assembly of a complex network of services. These services involved a range of developments that included teams of specialist professionals, bureaucrats, and consultants to help design the systems of extraction, build new roads and port facilities, and construct factories to process the wood into ply. Local small-scale forestry operations were actively discouraged and quickly eclipsed by the larger commercial operations. For some locals the new industry delivered the hope of full employment and prosperity. As they engaged in the commercial activity, their incomes grew and they found themselves enjoying more and more influence within their changing communities. For others the developments shattered patterns of life that had taken centuries to evolve and their sense of influence in the community steadily diminished. These people might attempt to resist the change by protest, dissent, or disengagement, but next to the accelerating fortunes of their participating kin, they found themselves progressively impoverished and marginalized and their resistance was largely ignored. From the midst of those benefiting from the expansion of logging in Kalimantan emerged a network of new bosses (or *bapak*), whose complex systems of patronage ensured that traditional structures of authority were replaced. Added to this, lucrative illegal logging activities flourished, partially ignored by government and military officials. This enabled gang networks to take root and establish their practices of extortion and intimidation, further ensuring little protest from those who might question the expansion (Human Rights Watch, 2003).

Meanwhile, new systems of political influence were evolving. A triangle of alliances formed among business leaders, central government, and external stakeholders overseas. Business leaders such as Mohamad "Bob" Hasan and his plywood cartel APKINDO, and Prajogo Pangestu and his company Barito Pacific Timber obtained concessions through connections to the Soeharto family to log vast areas of forest. Barito Pacific Timber worked on 5.5 million hectares of primeval tropical forest, employing more than 50,000, people and grew to become the world's largest exporter of tropical plywood. Pangestu secured these concessions by making substantial "donations" to charities and social programs connected to Soeharto's, family thereby ensuring ongoing patronage, but reinvesting practically nothing in reforestation or rehabilitation programs (Dauvergne, 1997). The central state played its part by imposing formal legal processes of ownership of the forests over the previous complex but legally poorly defined forms of traditional ownership. This enabled them to transfer ownership of vast areas of forest to the large corporations. In return, income from increases in tax revenue and patronage enabled Soeharto's government to continue in the process of centralizing its power base through the policies of the "New Order," thereby securing its 32 years of rule. Although central government prospered, the logging operations were devastating to the rural poor and those who were traditionally dependent on forests for their livelihood (Barr & Setiono, 2003). In turn, central government and local industry leaders worked cooperatively to engage with commercial leaders in Japan and Singapore who controlled the main overseas markets for wood products. All three parties strove together to ensure they maintained access to high volumes of cheap plywood and obstacles to expansion were reduced to a minimum.

It is difficult to be precise about how much of the power play of the deforestation of Kalimantan is reflected in the political dynamics of the expansion of gambling, but some general observations can be made that are at least suggestive of a strong similarity. Local gambling industry leaders tend to be influential players, and their operations quickly eclipse traditional forms of gambling. They typically rely heavily on developing points of influence with central government and on forming alliances with local sympathizers. They often make use of charities to advance their reputations, but invest minimally in monitoring and correcting the social disruptions they cause.[10] Although their operations require a substantial workforce, in many situations the workforce moves in from other places and local employment can find itself disrupted as spending patterns are diverted away from traditional forms of entertainment.[11] People who challenge the expansion can find themselves marginalized through the combined efforts of the gambling providers, government officials, and local entrepreneurs. Local providers will often work in close consultation with larger organizations, particularly international gambling corporations, and these relationships play a critical role in managing resistance. Governments in turn find themselves generating increasing revenues from taxation of gambling, and this engages their interest in managing negative public or community responses. They also benefit from the various forms of charitable funds generated by the industry. Working together, industry leaders, government, local stakeholders, and international corporations all share an interest in continued growth and in combining their efforts in countering any potential threats to its advance.

A democratic society relies on the proactive and optimistic participation of its citizens in its political structures and processes. People in a well-functioning democracy feel that they have a say, that their viewpoints matter, and that their voices will have some influence within the interacting systems that comprise their immediate political ecology. The extent to which they have confidence in these processes has implications well beyond the occasional opportunities to vote. It extends to a person's willingness to participate in public debates, his or her interest in supporting protest movements and in participating in government pressure and lobby groups. Furthermore, such confidence relies on a person's ability to embrace divergent cultural practices, to hear alternative viewpoints, and to engage respectfully in dialogue and negotiation. Variations in the extent of democratic assertiveness also span the micro to the macro level of social involvement. At the individual level democratic processes are reflected in the degree of equality and respect operating within intimate relationships. For example, a woman enduring violent and controlling behavior from her husband will find her freedoms compromised in a wide variety of ways and as a consequence she will feel her choices have little place in shaping her home environment. At a neighborhood level, democratic processes are reflected in the extent to which a person maintains interaction and involvement in shaping the local environment. Participation in local attempts to keep the environment clean or reduce crime is likely to increase a person's sense of connectedness and influence within that particular context. In a similar fashion, perceptions of choice are reinforced by the extent to which a person participates in policy and planning at community, regional, and state levels.

The perceptions people have of their freedom to participate in a political ecology are critical to the vigor and integrity of any democracy, but these perceptions are also very fragile. Real or perceived threats to participation can come in many shapes and sizes. A person might come to fear the consequences of participation. For example, in many totalitarian regimes those who voice dissent can realistically anticipate incarceration, or in some contexts execution. People might come to view some freedoms as less important in the face of more urgent matters. For example, the perceived threats from outside powers will increase a public's willingness to tolerate reductions in personal liberties, as can be observed in Guantanamo Bay recently in the U.S. War on Terror. Some might perceive that their views are unlikely to have influence either because they feel outnumbered or they feel that certain subsectors have a much larger say than themselves. They might also perceive that other more powerful forces from both inside and outside their society (e.g., economic factors) are the central drivers and that their own aspirations impact little on what really happens. Although these perceptions can play a significant role in discouraging democratic participation, the main challenge—and the one that will occupy much of this book—is derived from perceptions based on moral integrity and consistency. Once people choose to benefit in one domain from morally questionable occurrences in another domain, they find their ability to express strong positions severely compromised. For example, people who enjoy eating beef are likely to find it difficult to confidently challenge butchery practices with animals. They might find these practices abhorrent, but their complicity in eating meat makes it difficult to credibly maintain a position. In response to others pointing out the inconsistency, they might find themselves toning down their perspective, avoiding the topic, or simply remaining silent. Similarly, as more and more people are drawn into the web of relationships and benefits associated with the modern proliferation of commercial gambling, it becomes more difficult for them to speak their views and contribute to the broader ethical debates.

This book sets out to examine in detail the various ways in which the current expansion of gambling has implications for democratic systems. It proposes that in the long term, democracies that permit high-intensity gambling face challenges in preserving the integrity of their political ecologies. The book is organized into five pairs of chapters. The first two (Chapters 1 and 2) provide a broad outline of the intrusions of high-intensity commercialized gambling into a political ecology, then illustrate how this works at an individual level. The second pair of chapters (Chapters 3 and 4) explores the different arrangements governments and communities develop with gambling funding and examine how these relationships potentially distort democratic functions. The third pair of chapters (Chapters 5 and 6) turns to portrayals of gambling in public media and examines the way gambling industries position and then reposition themselves to advance their public image and then examines in detail the advertising strategies the gambling industries employ to engage and sustain high levels of consumption. The fourth pair (Chapters 7 and 8) switches the focus to examining the evolution of two types of services, research and helping services, and their relationships to the expansion of gambling. The final three chapters (Chapters 9, 10, and 11) explore how organizations in prudent democratic nations could put into place measures that protect their democratic systems and individuals within them from subtle degradation.

2 Subtle Degradation

This book asserts that the current rapid proliferation of gambling throughout the majority of Western-style democratic nations poses, in the long term, a range of threats to the vibrancy and integrity of the very base that supports their democratic structures and processes. In the previous chapter gambling was compared to other primary extractive industries that, when they are organized on a large-scale commercial basis, have the capacity to create rifts in ecological connectedness and thereby threaten their viability. Commercial gambling is introduced into an already well-established system of financial exchange. This system is intimately connected to systems of social interaction and political involvement. Widespread gambling, therefore, has the capacity not only to impact on patterns of financial transactions, but also to affect ways in which people relate socially and politically. As with the processes of tropical deforestation, the rapid expansion of commercialized gambling poses threats to a political ecology in three important ways. One way relates to the shared interests of governments and gambling industries in the revenues derived from gambling. A second way relates to the broadening opportunities for gambling industries themselves to link globally and build up formidable collective influence. A third way, and the focus of this book, relates to the ways in which benefits from gambling can subtly compromise the integrity of those with key roles in a democratic society and thereby lead to a progressive degradation of a political ecology.[1]

INDUSTRY–GOVERNMENT ALLIANCES

Powerful alliances between gambling industry providers and sections of government can operate in ways that deny the public a genuine say in the nature and extent of gambling within their communities. The opportunity for such alliances stems from the convergence of interest for both parties in the significant income available from increases in gambling consumption. Governments are lured by the prospect of convenient and sizable taxation revenues and gambling industry providers are drawn in by opportunities to influence regulation in ways that sustain and open up new and lucrative markets.[2] Both parties need each other to achieve access to the bonanza. These industry–government alliances can propel liberalization in ways that override the wishes of the majority of the population. For example, the licensing of casinos in Australia and New Zealand has on the whole proceeded in spite of majority opposition from local communities.[3] In many jurisdictions the industry and government collude in maintaining high levels of gambling naivete within a population. This can be achieved by preventing or delaying funding for public education and media campaigns and by ensuring research activity is kept to a minimum.

Gambling Industry Globalization

A second way in which democratic systems can be threatened relates to the opportunities for a globally interconnected gambling industry to marshal the linkages and resources to influence the choices of targeted governments and their publics. The processes and strategies used have been well documented with the expansion of the tobacco and alcohol industries. These include strategies such as target marketing to vulnerable populations, strategic commissioning of research, saturation promotion of international brands, technical refinements of products, and coordinated political lobbying.[4] These have had the net effect of diminishing the ability of populations to make informed decisions about the extent of their alcohol or tobacco consumption. When it comes to the emergent global networks of the gambling industry, it makes sense to expect that what has worked so effectively for tobacco and alcohol producers is highly likely to emerge in similar ways as gambling providers strengthen their interconnections and form transnational groupings that lobby governments on common interests.

Internal Threats

Although the two threats to democracy already mentioned are worthy topics for enquiry, this book shifts attention away from the macro processes of government–industry alliances and industry globalization in favor of a narrower focus on the potential for gambling monies to subtly compromise the ability of individuals to participate in democratic systems. The focus will be less on the macro processes of global or societal power, and more on the individual processes of perceived power. The book will progressively argue that people at any level in society can find themselves influenced in ways that diminish their confidence in asserting their views about gambling and in doing so downgrade their capacity to function proactively in democratic systems. The rising availability of proceeds from gambling engages more and more people in a web of benefits and privileges that in their minds and in the minds of others progressively compromises their ability to openly question the way gambling is being provided. Individuals fulfilling a wide range of roles find themselves tangled in dilemmas between the duties of their position and their moral stance on gambling. They respond to these dilemmas in a variety of ways, but a common response is to withdraw from the debate altogether and thereby effectively endorse the interests of gambling expansion. This degradation of their confidence to participate in democratic processes applies initially to gambling alone, but over time could arguably extend to their willingness to participate in democratic processes as a whole.

Internal Threats and Moral Jeopardy

The threats to democracy through these forms of subtle degradation are driven at an individual level by situations that place people at risk of making choices that compromise them morally. These situations of moral jeopardy increase the likelihood that people will encounter significant moral dilemmas, dilemmas that could lead them to violate their own or their communities' understanding of moral codes of behavior. As will be explored in later chapters, contexts of moral jeopardy are created by groups of people (networks, communities, organizations) but enabled in a broader frame by power relationships among government authorities, gambling providers, and local community stakeholders. Putting this another way, authorities, providers, and developers prepare the field and set the rules, key groups of people (e.g., politicians or journalists) establish the context and set the norms for moral behavior, and the individuals within the context experience the dilemmas and deal with the consequences. For example, the rapid proliferation of EGM gambling in the Australian state of Victoria has increased the range of ways community organizations find themselves connected to funding derived from gambling and thereby create an increasing range of contexts in which their employees encounter moral dilemmas.

Morality is a broad term that encompasses ethical, practical, and perceptual issues. Morality evolves according to the norms generated over time through the influences of history, culture, and material resources. It embraces what a particular society at a particular point in time deems acceptable and unacceptable. These perceptions are never fixed and can vary considerably over time. For example, the morality of drug use (e.g., with tobacco and heroin) has changed radically over the last century. The rising levels of consumption of commercialized gambling in Western-style democracies are relatively new and the way in which this is perceived from a moral perspective is changing and likely to keep changing. During the first half of the 20th century, temperance and church organizations effectively challenged the morality of all gambling and were in many situations effective in ensuring that gambling remained highly regulated. The last two decades have seen a challenge to this interpretation of morality, with a resultant liberalization of gambling availability, only to find that commercial proliferation has introduced a whole new range of moral concerns.

As gambling consumption rises, people with key democratic responsibilities are increasingly subject to influences associated with the profits from gambling. These influences are typically subtle, difficult to detect, hard to measure, and problematic to report on. For instance, politicians are unlikely to speak openly about the extent to which financial contributions from gambling industry sources might influence their approach to gambling policy. Open discussion would jeopardize their credibility both with the public and with their colleagues. Similarly, gambling counseling agencies are unlikely to admit that receiving funds from gambling industry sources influences whether they would speak out about the impacts on clients. Such an admission would affect their credibility with clients and with the broader community. Their understandable reluctance to discuss these issues openly creates problems in monitoring the extent to which they are having an influence.

INDIVIDUAL EXAMPLES OF MORAL JEOPARDY

Because open disclosure of moral dilemmas is problematic, discussion here seeks to point out the risks to democracy by presenting a set of hypothetical scenarios. The scenarios focus on people in five different contexts: academic and research bodies, the media, community agencies, politicians, and government agencies. The scenarios have been composed to illustrate the different ways key people are faced with situations of moral jeopardy and democratic distortions rather than providing definitive evidence of their occurrence. They are based on the author's 14-year involvement in the gambling field, an involvement that has enabled many opportunities to discuss these issues with people in different roles and to ask them about their perceptions of the risks posed by links to gambling funding sources. Hypothetical narratives such as these have been used effectively in other fields to help highlight issues on sensitive topics.[5] They are used to assist discussion on areas of perception and morality that in normal circumstances are difficult to explore. They present a case for protecting democratic systems based on the plausibility of the risk.

Academic and Research Bodies

Universities have a major responsibility in modern democracies to support independent and critical academic scrutiny of changes and trends in social systems. Universities are also under enormous financial pressure to deliver quality teaching and research programs. Tension persists between their duty as "conscience of society" and their need within a competitive research environment to establish stable funding. In the following scenario,[6] Jason finds himself caught in this tension:

Jason has worked for 13 years in a university department of psychology. He had twice applied unsuccessfully for promotion to associate professor. At the conclusion of each promotion round he was told his research profile was not strong enough to qualify. During the last 5 years he has been working with the support of the racing industry to develop an interesting series of small studies on the cognitions of heavy track gamblers use when planning their betting. The racing industry funders were happy for him to publish the results as long as he acknowledged their contribution. Their funding had provided for two research assistants and for any material or equipment costs. More recently, two representatives from the racing industry visited him to state how pleased they were with his work and to convey their willingness to fund a considerably larger 3-year project. Jason is flattered by their comments and excited by the prospect of a larger project. He could begin comparing the cognitive repertoire of heavy and infrequent track gamblers. He could look more at the interplay between cognitions and perceptions of luck and skill. The research design opportunities would be enormous. He asks the racing representatives what they expect in return. They state that because the funding would, of course, be of a greater magnitude, they would prefer some control over what gets published and they would be particularly interested in research into cognitions that might have some relevance to marketing their product.

Jason is faced with a difficult and common dilemma. On the one hand, combined with the pressure to increase his research productivity, he is attracted by the opportunity to apply his hard-earned research knowledge and skills. On the other hand, the stronger a relationship he develops with gambling providers, the more his work will be seen by others as influenced by the commercial interests of the industry. His research output will also come to rely more and more on their continued support, and he will over time adapt his focus in ways that are unlikely to jeopardize future funding.[7]

Media Professionals

The media play an important role in democracies by presenting information and issues to the public that enables citizens to form views and make informed decisions. As with universities, media outlets such as television and newspapers also seek to protect their major sources of revenue, and for most of them commercial advertising is a vital contributor to revenue. The person in the following scenario is caught in the tension between the role of public informer and maintaining a viable business.

A reporter, Melanie, is working late one night to meet the deadline for the morning edition of a daily newspaper. A press release is relayed by a subeditor to her computer: "Casinos Targeting Local Asians." She pauses a moment to ponder the various angles she might explore of such an issue. She could interview local Asian community representatives, she could examine casino practices regarding incentives such as free drinks and meals for Asian customers, she might enquire into the revenue casinos derive from Asian customers . . . But hold on. Putting energy into this area would be pointless if the editors were to chop it down and bury it deep into the back pages, or, worse, if it was rejected outright. Melanie is aware how during the last 4 years her newspaper has derived increasing advertising income from gambling providers, particularly from the local casino. Many of these advertisements declare recent contributions by gambling providers to public good activities such cultural, charity, and sports events. The newspaper now regularly runs a half-page and sometimes a full-page advertisement for the local casino. She had seen her editor express increasing anxiety regarding threats to this income. This came to a head when 6 months ago she was involved in a series of four articles reviewing the debate between pro- and antigambling expansion lobbies. As the flow of letters to the editor subsided, the editor had received a letter of concern from a casino executive, claiming that the newspaper's coverage was biased and as a result likely to affect the casino's business. The editorial the next morning extolled the virtues of the casino to the local economy and the editor spoke to the staff encouraging them to focus more on problem gamblers and discouraging any focus on the role of gambling providers.

What should Melanie do now? By not pursuing the article, she is surely preventing public access to information on the issue. Even so, the newspaper still has the occasional informative article. There are plenty of other issues that are less troublesome and less likely to complicate advertising revenue.

Community Agencies

Sports clubs, charities, church and school committees, work social clubs, and hobby groups, from small local groups to large national nongovernment organizations, these all comprise the intricate web of interconnections that provide the base for social involvements. It is often through interactions in community groups that people form their views on social issues. Consequently, financial influence at a community level could go a long way in shaping public views on gambling. The person in the following scenario is feeling the pressure exerted by industry contributions to community development.

Robert is employed by a church organization to coordinate a community project focused on youth at risk. He believes passionately in the positive impact of this project both for the many marginalized young people he encounters and for his community as a whole. He has applied each year for funding from a local gambling machine trust (a collective of several hotels with gambling machines that are required by law to distribute a percentage of income for community benefit). The amount awarded to his youth project has increased each year to such an extent that he is unsure whether the project could continue without the money. He has had little personal exposure to gambling or to problem gambling. He is aware that increasing numbers of young people in his community regularly play gambling machines. He has also heard the government is currently conducting a fundamental review of gambling policy. In response to this, a member of the local gambling machine trust contacts him to speak about fears that the community benefit monies could be moved from local to central distribution. He is naturally concerned that the fruitful relationship he has built up with the trust will no longer continue and he would be forced to compete nationally with dozens of similar projects. He immediately considers volunteering to compile a submission to government opposing the central distribution and praising the work of the gambling machine trust. He pauses. He has difficulty seeing himself as an advocate for communities while promoting the interests of something that people claim will harm his community.

In choosing to promote the interests of gambling machine providers, Robert places himself in a conflicted position. He can no longer speak out credibly to question youth exposure to machine gambling. It would be inconsistent in one breath to praise their contribution and in another to criticize them. In this way the local gambling provider not only gains an advocate but also manages to effectively silence potential criticism. The charitable contributions of the gambling industry to public good activities quickly translate into community support for their developments and their recognition as responsible community benefactors.

Politicians

As elected representatives of the people, politicians have clear obligations to respond to threats to public well-being. This is not an easy task. The choice of the wrong issue could mean an early exit from the political arena. Judgment and skill are required in choosing social issues that are likely to attract public support and avoid unnecessary conflict with other sources of power and influence. In the following scenario, a politician finds himself caught between the interests of the public and the influence of gambling provider contributions to political funds.

Bill was first elected into parliament 20 years ago. His party is currently the major partner in a coalition government, but, due to a series of internal spats, it is now scoring poorly in public opinion polls. During the last election he won by a very slim majority and he remains concerned that he might not be reelected. A collective of local hoteliers who own the majority of the EGMs in his electorate had contributed a reasonable sum to his last electoral campaign. They have also been very receptive to his suggestions as to suitable charities and other community groups they should fund with community benefit profits. This has endeared him to many organizations. A few days ago a group of local community leaders approached him regarding concerns about the spread of gambling machines throughout his electorate. They presented alarming figures on increases in problem gambling, crime, and social disruption. Bill understands the issues and is sympathetic to their arguments. He promises to do what he can in parliament, but he stops short of openly challenging the expansion. It would be political suicide. Without the gambling machine money he would have very little chance of reelection, and, furthermore, his party would not welcome him, complicating what they receive from gambling providers. Stirring up concern about gambling would most likely lead to central party bosses withdrawing any financial support for his campaign.

Bill recognizes that alone, as one politician, there is little he can do in terms of advancing public disquiet about gambling. Discussion with his colleagues produced little. They feel similarly vulnerable. Progress would really require a collective and concerted response within the party.

Government Agencies

Multiple parts of the machinery of government are capable of forming key linkages with the activities of the gambling industry, particularly under conditions of managed expansion. The executive of government and its departments of finance and treasury will have a keen interest in the revenue it generates. In addition, many governments have their own agencies that directly provide gambling products for public consumption (e.g., state casinos and horse racing). Departments that manage development and regulation of the industry will derive increasing leverage and kudos from successful growth. Departments that respond to potential harm (e.g., health, justice, social welfare) in seeking to develop remedial programs will be mindful of how gambling revenue contributes to their other programs. The following scenario epitomizes the individual dilemmas faced by civil servants when they become part of these gambling industry linkages.

Karen has worked for the last year as a policy analyst for the government agency in charge of gambling policy, regulation, and enforcement. Another section of the same agency runs the national lotteries. She had previously worked in a government department in charge of social welfare. She has strong ambitions to perform well and advance in her public service career. Unfortunately with increasing competition from other products the profits from lotteries are declining. Huge efforts are being made to increase participation—expensive TV advertising campaigns, promotion of large sports events, new lottery products, and special bonus events—but participation continues to drop. The managers in her agency are becoming increasingly worried, particularly because the profits have enabled them to fund a variety of cultural, sporting, and charitable activities and they are concerned about the public response to a dip in funding. Karen's current task involves reviewing legislation on gambling advertising. She is providing the detailed analysis for the review committee of the large number of submissions from a broad range of stakeholders that include community, government, and gambling provider organizations. She is personally persuaded by the submissions that a compulsory advertising code should be introduced but is concerned about her own agency's response. The most aggressive marketing occurs in the lottery advertising that comes from her agency. Clearly, advocating for tougher advertising standards will lead to tension with other parts of the agency and she is unlikely to receive support from her immediate superiors. It would be easy to bury her position in weaker recommendations.

As with previous scenarios, Karen faces a difficult choice. If she stands up as one individual to contest positions of convenience to the organization, she risks being moved sideways and thereby being replaced by a more compliant and perhaps less knowledgeable official. If she remains silent, she violates her own sense of integrity. She is tempted to remain and console herself that her weakened recommendations are at least a step in the right direction, even though she knows the suggestions will be ignored.

EFFECTS OF DEGRADATION

Each of these individuals—Jason, Melanie, Robert, Bill, and Karen—shares a common moral dilemma. On the one hand, they occupy positions of influence that could enable increased public responsiveness to the societal impacts of gambling. On the other hand, the small part they could play in strengthening the financial relationship of their organization to the gambling industries in turn reduces the organization's credibility and capacity to act on behalf of the public. Should they choose the former, they jeopardize financial gains for the organization; should they choose the latter, they risk distortions of public awareness. They are each caught in a tangle of benefits and risks that pull them in both directions. These positions of moral jeopardy create confusion and uncertainty in ways that are likely to result in inaction.

On closer inspection, the balance in this dilemma is not evenly weighted. The incentives in favor of the industry are typically more immediate and attractive than incentives to serve the public. For example, the researcher,

Jason, will receive stronger and more immediate recognition within the university for scoring a large research grant than he would for making a stand on refusing industry funds. A few colleagues might admire his resolve, but in the context of the broader university community, his ethical stance is likely to pass unnoticed. This contrasts with the highly visible presence of the products from industry funding. On the flip side and in a similar way, the disincentives to serve public interests are also typically stronger than those affecting industry involvements. For example, should the reporter, Melanie, choose not to write about casino targeting of Asian clients, her decision is unlikely to be challenged. Even if questioned, she could easily rationalize it in terms of stronger stories elsewhere. It is hard to imagine her compliance sparking a formal investigation or a public scandal; it would be unlikely to attract even passing comments from colleagues. In contrast, an article critical of the industry is likely to prompt immediate and stern responses from the editor, casino executives, and possibly the newspaper ownership.

With incentives and disincentives favoring linkages with gambling provider interests, individual compliance with organizational and industry involvements becomes a more probable event than attempts to challenge such connections. Individual people within this interface will feel pressure to make choices that strengthen the involvements and build collectively toward more powerful societal effects. The researcher diverts energy from understanding impacts, the reporter avoids conveying information to the public, the community worker allows good work to reinforce the public image of a gambling provider, the politician misses opportunities to champion issues, and the government worker translates industry favor into policy recommendations. Each act in itself is small and largely untraceable, but taken collectively, they add to the accumulating momentum of gambling expansion and to the cumulative effect of public misinformation and consequent missed opportunities for informed decision making.

The role of modern democratic governments in these processes is complex. They certainly play a pivotal role in protecting the public from gambling-related harm, but, in most nations, governments are also major recipients of gambling revenues. As this revenue increases, their focus on the public good competes with their interest in the funds. The balance between these opposing interests can reach a point where the need for money outstrips duties of public protection. Consequently, it is important that any government that embraces rapid expansion of gambling also recognizes that its democratic structures are being placed at risk. In an environment of managed expansion, this calls for strategies that not only weed out blatant distortions but also set up procedures to counteract the less visible, low-grade threats.

3   Governments

Why have so many democratic governments during the current expansion of commercial gambling participated so wholeheartedly in liberalizing gambling regulations and thereby neglected to protect their publics from the impacts? A straightforward answer to this question is that they do so because of the money. There is simply too much potential revenue for governments to collect with minimal effort for them not to proceed down this path. A more complex response to this question recognizes that "governments" are not single entities. They are made up of complex aggregations of agencies, communication systems, informal networks, and of course individual people working in their confined contexts and subject to their own aspirations and vulnerabilities. Ascribing motivation and intent to the system as a whole is problematic because systems are not volitional entities; it is the people operating within them that experience the motivations. When the whole mechanism of government systems moves in one direction, it makes more sense to consider that there are a range of processes coinciding at varying levels that enable this movement to occur and that individuals positioned at these various levels find themselves drawn in and subject to the momentum that surrounds them. In this chapter I aim to explore how governments as complex systems, despite resistance by some individuals within, end up as active players in gambling expansion. This description parallels the roles governments play in the frontier of other newly discovered extractive industries, such as mining, logging, or petroleum exploration, where the interests of the site of production and the people around are often secondary to the interests of development.

PATTERNS OF PROLIFERATION

Although gambling has evolved in varying ways in different countries, when viewed as a whole, a general pattern of proliferation is discernible, particularly in the more affluent democratic nations of Western Europe, North America, and Australasia. The pattern can be divided into a sequence of four general phases: emergence, regulation, liberalization, and normalization.

The enjoyment derived from associating material reward with games of chance can be traced back into early human society. This *emergence* phase can be traced back to the tombs of early Egyptian, South American, and African civilizations in which archaeologists have uncovered primitive gambling devices resembling dice that provide evidence that gambling in various forms was incorporated at a very early stage into the customary practices of many ancient cultures.[1] Over time societies began to appreciate that alongside the obvious enjoyment from gambling they also faced a range of worrying impacts. They started to recognize that overindulgence could contribute to disruption of family, community, and societal systems.[2] They noticed how various forms of corruption and crime clustered around locations of high gambling intensity. They began to explicitly identify a type of person who, despite the strongest advice and support, continued resolutely to squander all their own and other people's wealth on gambling. In response, subsectors of these societies started to question the unrestrained availability of gambling, and slowly social institutions—church organizations, civic authorities, and governments—evolved ways to protect their constituencies from excesses.[3]

For most countries over the last century, well-developed frameworks of restrictive legislation have formed the base for shaping gambling environments. During this lengthy phase of *regulation,* governments take care to prevent any accelerated growth. They permit some noncontinuous forms of gambling under reasonably controlled conditions, horse race betting being the most common form. They permit local community groups to fund-raise using small-scale, low-stakes forms of gambling such as raffles, housie, and bingo. Some governments, alert to the growth and success of illegal numbers games, set up their own national lotteries, but many other countries, such as the United Kingdom and Canada, chose to delay the introduction of national lotteries until fairly recently.[4] High-intensity forms of gambling such as occurs in casinos were either banned or confined to destination venues such as Las Vegas, where the inconvenience of distance moderated excess.

The ensuing phase of *liberalization* has occurred in most affluent nations over the last 20 years. It is during this phase that organized commercial gambling is established on a state-wise and interstate basis. Individual governments progressively liberalize the availability of both continuous and noncontinuous forms of gambling. For example, in the United States the frontier for the licensing of table games in casinos shifted, first, from destination venues to locations on riverboats and Indian reservations, and then moved progressively closer to venues adjacent to major populations.[5] In Australia, electronic gambling machines (EGMs) (another continuous form of gambling) were initially licensed in New South Wales sports clubs for the purpose of fund-raising. The financial success of these whet the appetite of proprietors, state governments, and prospective punters and the machines soon become available in hotel bars throughout all but one Australian state.[6]

The timing of gambling *liberalization* in many countries has coincided internationally with a major shift in economic thinking. In the mid-1980s, Western democracies had embraced a program of radical economic reforms that had ushered in an extended period of liberalization of marketing and regulatory regimes. Top-heavy government management was seen as a major impediment to the productive forces of markets and businesses. Governments reformed their role and in the process sought to remove many of the constraints on gambling, thereby opening the doors to a liberalized gambling industry. This was totally congruent with the economic rationalism of the period. Draconian government regulations were holding back an industry that was capable of stimulating local economies, increasing employment, boosting tourism, and increasing tax takes for government without additional strain on personal income tax.

The liberalization in gambling legislation and consequent increases in its availability opens the door to unprecedented increases in consumption. This period of *normalization* is characterized by gradual social acceptance of high levels of gambling. Government interest in gambling revenue consolidates and is viewed as a means of supplementing their direct taxation base. Gambling opportunities spread widely throughout communities and people within them have become familiar with their presence. People progressively build more of their lives around its presence: Many are employed in related occupations; gambling venues are present in most drinking, eating, and entertainment venues; television and other media virtuously promote gambling as family entertainment; and sports, charity, and community organizations grow accustomed to gambling providing the financial base for their activities.

As discussed in Chapter 1, the time lag between the beginning of liberalization and public recognition of the social and economic downsides creates a window of opportunity for high-intensity gambling to gain a foothold into a nation's economy. This lack of awareness can be further managed by employing some of the profits in media campaigns on the benefits of gambling. People are reassured that the proliferation is for the public good. It might not be until well into the normalization phase that sufficient public concern is expressed to worry governments, but by this time the commercial base for high-intensity gambling is well established and public health advocates have little chance of introducing significant changes.

ROLES WITHIN GOVERNMENT

Perhaps more than with any other dangerous consumption, governments have played a critical and active role in the global expansion of commercialized gambling. Without proactive government, support for the proliferation of gambling would not have occurred at the same rate or on the same scale.

Goodman (1995) examined the processes of gambling expansion within the United States and made the following observation:

> One of the most surprising findings of our research is that we didn't come across a single popularly based organization that lobbies for more gambling. Many other government prohibitions—such as laws against the smoking of marijuana—have inspired popular legalization movements. But not gambling. In fact, when given a chance to make its views known, the public usually rejects gambling . . .
>
> So if it's not the public, who is behind the push for more gambling opportunities? Two parties are almost entirely responsible; legislators in search of easy answers to tough economic problems, and the gambling industry itself. (p. x)

His point here is that the pressure to change the regulatory environment to favor gambling proliferation has not been driven by public attitudes. Industry entrepreneurs would undoubtedly provide some pressure by courting a freer environment in which to operate, but their influence is dependent on the extent to which governments are open and willing to embrace their influence. The critical ingredient for change has to have been a willingness by people at different levels of government to put aside concerns about harm and to embrace the opportunities for them that an expanded gambling market offers.

The Incentives for Governments

As noted earlier, the primary incentive for government to embrace the proliferation of commercial gambling is that it provides a highly attractive form of revenue with minimal investment in infrastructure and product development. For many governments the revenue is heaven sent to rescue and help underwrite economic and social development without increasing direct taxation. The scale to which modern democracies have engaged in this process is extraordinary. Over the 20-year period between the early 1980s and the early 2000s, annual per capita gambling expenditure in Australia rose threefold from around $146 per person to over $454 per person (AusStats, 2000–2001; Tasmania Gaming Commission, 1999). In New Zealand the increases were even more dramatic over the same period, with annual per capita expenditure rising twelvefold from around $26 per person to $318 per person.[7] Even allowing for inflation, these heady increases give us some idea why different parts of government are responsive to the potential of gambling proliferation. Similar steady increases have occurred in European nations such as Spain, Germany, the Netherlands, and Sweden.[8] With each increase in consumption there is a corresponding increase in government revenue from gambling. For example, in Canada over the decade of the 1990s, expenditure on gambling rose more than threefold from about $2.2

billion to more than $7.9 billion, and government revenues rose more than thirteen-fold from less than $0.4 billion to more than $4.8 billion.[9]

In the early liberalization phase of global proliferation, governments have put little in place to protect the public and inform them of the risks from gambling. Following long periods of tight regulation and low consumption, politicians and their officials parallel public perceptions by treating gambling as a low-risk activity. They understandably display little appreciation of the potential harms associated with opening up the volume and range of gambling products. Officials look outward at the behavior of other governments and there they are reassured by relaxed attitudes to loosened regulations with few attempts to manage the harms. At home they face a variety of pressures. Their own population is beginning to access gambling provided by adjacent states with more liberal policies. They are constantly lobbied by industry representatives claiming improvements in employment and economic opportunities. They see how easily a new government revenue stream can be turned on without much capital investment and they interpret liberalization to be a normal and enlightened approach, part of an improving free-market economy. They are persuaded by the hype and lack any other reference point on which to gauge their own management of the sector.

Underlying the role governments play in promoting economic development is the more fundamental role of protecting the welfare of citizens. Governments have a fundamental duty to protect public interests. It is their responsibility to ensure that, during a period of change, systems are established that manage the negative impacts. It is conceivable that in time negatively affected individuals and communities will hold governments accountable for their lack of attention to protecting them from harm. So far most governments embarking on liberalization have taken few precautions with respect to impacts: The addictive potential of intensified gambling is not being examined, new product testing is not occurring, little is put in place to monitor impacts on vulnerable populations, and public information on risks is negligible. Furthermore, once a process of liberalization has been initiated, it is very difficult to reverse the trend. Providers of the different types of gambling gather strength by competing for market share. Their businesses plug in and become part of the network of businesses that drive the economy. Employees within the various industries build their own and their families' lives around the income, and community organizations come to rely on proceeds. By the time officials realize the implications of liberalization, its momentum is typically too strong to reverse. Governments naive to the impacts could find themselves decades later facing public outcry regarding the harms with little opportunity to backtrack on mistakes.

Gambling Roles and Responsibilities

The participation of government in gambling proliferation is mediated by the various roles individuals and collections of individuals adopt within their systems. These roles and associated responsibilities emerge and consolidate as the importance of gambling to government grows. Table 3.1 describes these roles as they emerge through each phase and as the scale of gambling consumption requires increasing government involvement.

The phases of liberalization and normalization are of most interest for the discussion here because it is during these phases that the expansion of commercial gambling occurs and is consolidated. They are also the two phases in which governments take on the most roles and responsibilities and are therefore when role blurring and conflict are most likely to occur.

Emergence Roles

In the early stages of the presence of commercialized gambling, which in many economies lasts for decades, governments, reflecting the public they serve, are unlikely to have consolidated a strong interest in the contribution

Table 3.1 Key Functions of Government in Commercial Gambling Expansion

	Government Role	Function	Phase
1	Public monitor	Observe developments and intervene as problems emerge	Emergence
2	Law maker	Put in place the regulatory framework that determines the environment in which gambling occurs	Regulation
3	Law enforcer	Enforce regulations	Regulation
4	Gambling provider	Develop government-associated industries, often lottery products, sometimes racing and casinos	Liberalization
5	Gambling promoter	Actively support positive public views on the benefits of increased gambling consumption	Liberalization
6	Revenue collector	Ensure government maximizes its return from gambling	Liberalization
7	Policymaker	Develop overarching policy framework with clearly defined principles	Normalization
8	Harm alleviator	Develop robust and integrated services, spanning public health to treatment	Normalization
9	Honest broker	Provide an impartial base for decisions regarding sector development, regulation, and knowledge	Normalization

of gambling to their own revenue base. As government officials gradually hear about the new activities and watch with curiosity, and perhaps some concern, as the new forms of commercialized gambling emerge, they begin to think of how they should respond.

Government as Public Monitor

Because consumption is low at this stage, problems, too, are at a relatively low level and unlikely to have crossed over the threshold into prompting governments to any special reaction. Gambling might emerge in the form of community-run numbers games (housie, bingo), raffles, card games, and informal betting on horses.[10] Over time the provision of these informal forms of gambling becomes more organized and makeshift organizations emerge to manage their provision. However, the numbers of problem gamblers are low, and few people are aware of the risks associated with frequent gambling; consequently, government agencies maintain a watching brief.

Regulation Roles

The regulation phase emerges as a response to problems that result from unmanaged gambling expansion. Examples of unmanaged gambling environments include the development of numbers games by crime syndicates in United States during the 1930s and the early casinos in the United Kingdom during the 1960s,[11] both of which led to gambling links to organized crime. The visible signs of illegal practices, such as corruption and extortion, alert governments to the need to take an active role in managing gambling expansion.

Government as Law Maker

Public outcry over the excesses associated with unfettered expansion pressures governments from merely monitoring the emerging situation into actively developing a framework of legislation to manage the growth. At this stage the revenue potential of gambling is unlikely to be fully realized; consequently the legal framework tends to be fairly restrictive, with gambling limited to particular venues and purposes. As permitted forms expand and pressure increases for new types of gambling, more and more laws are passed that enable the often ad hoc construction of a complex web of regulations. For example, prior to 2002 gambling in New Zealand was managed under three statutes: the Racing Act 1971, the Gaming and Lotteries Act 1977, and the Casino Control Act 1990. As commercialized gambling began to expand, these acts came under considerable pressure. Not only were they based on different principles and objectives, but the responsible minister was forced to introduce a range of amendments that helped build a very complex and unwieldy legal framework.[12]

Government as Law Enforcer

The laws in a regulatory framework are only as good as the ability to enforce them. The enforcement of gambling laws is complex, particularly as the range of products and the technologies associated with them evolve. Some enforcement tasks, such as gambling-related fraud and corruption, can be enforced effectively by the police, but in most jurisdictions, gambling law enforcement is on the whole viewed as a specialist role requiring expertise across a broad range of disciplines. This applies particularly to enforcement associated with probity, licensing, surveillance, complaints, promotion, and electronic monitoring. Accordingly, most governments opt to locate enforcement in specialist government agencies often embedded in larger ministries or departments. For example, in the Australian state of New South Wales, the Department of Gaming and Racing provides most aspects of gambling policy formulation, regulation, enforcement, and harm minimization.

Liberalization Roles

Liberalization begins when governments identify increased gambling consumption as leading to significant increases in its tax revenue. By this stage gambling consumption is typically already on the rise and the extent of gambling has fostered widespread commercial interest.

Government as Gambling Provider

In many jurisdictions, such as in Canada and the Netherlands, governments opt on behalf of their public to become the main providers of gambling, with all profits channeled back into services to improve the welfare of the public. However, in most jurisdictions, governments are not the main provider, but one of many. Such governments are likely to enable independent providers to develop venue-based forms of gambling such as casinos and EGM bars, but would tend to maintain a controlling stake in transregional gambling such as lottery products and track betting. In both systems—governments as a dominant (or even monopoly) provider or as one provider among many—they risk an intensified interest and subsequent reliance on gambling revenue, as well as the temptation to manage regulations in a way that protects or advantages its own products.

Government as Gambling Promoter

Once governments enter the marketplace they seek, along with all other providers, to protect their investment and maximize their profits. One way they do this is by enabling media advertising of gambling products, while not enabling the equivalent promotion of messages informing the public of gambling-related harm. Typically the promotion of their own products receives fewer restrictions than independent products.[13] However, promotion is not limited to advertising. Gambling-oriented government agencies might produce their own promotional booklets and brochures, they might speak out in support of liberalization, and politicians and government officials could attend and visibly endorse gambling promotional events. (Their complicity in gambling promotion is discussed more when examining industry constructions of freedom in Chapter 5.)

Government as Revenue Collector

The primary driver for governments during liberalization is gambling revenue; accordingly, considerable effort is put into ensuring and protecting the systems required for tax collection. As revenue increases, government agencies involved in finance—including cabinet members—become increasingly aware that revenue from this source reduces their reliance on revenue from other sources. Threats to gambling revenue and associated increases in other taxation take on political consequences. For example, very few politicians would consider measures that significantly reduce gambling consumption because it could entail significant increases in personal income tax.[14] Furthermore, as gambling revenue increases, efforts are made to plan management of the resource in such a way that the income is protected in a long-term sustainable fashion. This explains the anxiety many governments express regarding Internet betting, whereby consumption increases but because it is provided in other jurisdictions, the means by which to derive income is uncertain.

Normalization Roles

Normalization occurs as the public becomes more acutely aware of the negative impacts of the rapid expansion of gambling. In this phase the focus shifts from growth to sustainability. Accordingly, government seeks to stabilize the environment for the long term by both protecting consumption and ensuring the negative consequences are visibly managed.

Government as Policymaker

The first major task in normalization is to develop a comprehensive, integrated policy framework for the long-term management of gambling. The previous ad hoc measures that were cobbled together to manage the rapid changes in gambling availability are tidied up under a set of unifying principles and objectives. The cleaning-up process typically involves a lengthy examination of the current scene, which results in acceptance of the bulk of what currently exists with attempts to reduce some of the more flagrantly exploitive and unpalatable aspects of the industry. In this way normalization does not challenge the central parts of gambling expansion; rather the process serves to consolidate and organize the bits that already exist.

For example, during its liberalization phase, the New Zealand government undertook 6 years of continuous "review" of gambling before finally passing its Gambling Act 2003. This act provided a comprehensive framework for gambling policy and legislation, thereby laying the foundations for its longer term normalization.

Government as Harm Alleviator

As discussed in more detail in the next chapter, gambling is associated with a broad range of impacts that include rises in problem gambling, family distress, mental health issues, criminal offending, and economic disruptions. These impacts are accentuated as liberalization drives consumption up. Earlier on, although governments are aware that gambling creates harm, through a combination of low public awareness, lack of research, and a government's own preoccupation with revenue, the level of harm is tolerated alongside a few token attempts at prevention and remediation—enough to smooth the rough edges driving public concern. The funding for these responses is derived from a range of mechanisms that include direct industry funding and voluntary or compulsory levies from providers. These amounts typically comprise a very small proportion of overall industry or government income from gambling.[15] With normalization, government recognizes that it has a longer term role in setting up systems for managing harm. It takes a more and more active part in directing investment into harm minimization strategies and in the design and management of related programs.

Government as Honest Broker

In the latter stages of normalization, the need for this, the ninth role, occurs precisely because there has been such a proliferation of roles. Government might attempt to manage role conflicts through declaration processes, intra- and interagency separations, and process monitoring, but to maintain creditability in the face of rapid increases in revenue, some place of independence is required to ensure the network of roles retains its integrity.[16] The honest broker role becomes increasingly important in providing independent assessment of the levels of harm, in deciding proportionally how much revenue is invested in prevention and remediation and in moderating between different branches of government with interests in revenue.

ROLE CONFLICT

As the phases of proliferation unfold, as each emergent role asserts itself as the top priority of the moment, the need to fulfill the other roles is not replaced; instead, they get added to the list. For instance, during normalization the need for remedial services for problem gamblers becomes a priority, but it is unlikely to diminish government expectations of sustained tax take. In terms of government relationship to gambling industries, the nature of the various roles takes two opposing directions: gambling development versus gambling control. Gambling development includes the roles of promoter, provider, and revenue collector. The gambling control roles include law maker, enforcer, harm alleviator, and honest broker. During regulation the balance is tipped in favor of control. During liberalization the balance favors gambling development. In between, in the normalization phase, governments attempt to create an infrastructure of control in a way that does not jeopardize future development. Also by the normalization phase, government will be faced, to some degree or other, with managing all nine roles. The complexity of this is enormous, and challenges both the structures and the individuals within them. The role of harm alleviator clashes with the earlier and ongoing role of government as promoter and provider of gambling. The opportunities for role conflict are widespread and significant.

Similar to the ways other extractive industries expand, relationships with government agencies can play a crucial role in the speed and extent of industrial development. As discussed earlier, the rapid exploitation of primeval forests in places like Indonesia and Brazil has relied heavily on levels of passive and active support from within governments. At one level, governments acknowledge their role in protecting their nation's animal and plant life and in preventing degradation of their natural environment. However, they also see a strong role in ensuring that the economy progresses and they recognize the critical part they play in fostering the ongoing expansion of their economy's industrial base. The conflict inherent between these two directions, the drive to conserve and the drive to expand, is constantly present. Unfortunately, benefits derived from conservation activities lead more slowly to tangible rewards, hence the roles associated with protection and prevention are often subordinated to the roles associated with progress and development. In a parallel fashion, roles associated with imperatives to develop commercial gambling coexist with roles associated with preventing and protecting the public from harm, and the tangible benefits associated with increases in gambling revenue are often far too enticing to allow (social) conservation issues to stand in the way. The following sections explore some of the ways governments manage these conflicts.

Agency Responses to Role Conflict

While some governments have chosen to place their key roles with gambling in differing agency locations, many others have opted to bundle various roles into the same agencies. For example, in the Canadian province of Ontario, the Ministry of Economic Development and Trade plays a leading role in the development of gambling policy, regulation, enforcement, and harm minimization, leaving the Ministry of Health and Long-Term Care to manage remedial responses.[17] Similarly, in the United Kingdom, the Department of Culture, Media, and Sport plays a leading role in gambling policy, regulation, and enforcement (in conjunction with their Gambling Commission) and an indirect role with remedial responses through links with the Responsibility in Gambling Trust.[18] The situation in the United States varies considerably between different states. For example, the California Gambling Control Commission manages or supervises most functions in that state, whereas in other states (e.g., Louisiana and Georgia) the roles are spread among different agencies. In many states of Australia, the Treasury takes a leading role in policy formulation, regulation, and enforcement. In New Zealand, the Department of Internal Affairs leads the development of gambling policy, regulation, enforcement, and harm minimization, with remedial responses now based the Ministry of Health.[19]

Because most of these countries are in late-stage liberalization or early-stage normalization, the number of agencies involved varies.[20] Consequently the various government agencies involved are forced to juggle different arrangements that help them adjust to the differences between their respective functions. Figure 3.1 depicts the main ways in which government agencies attempt to manage role conflicts at different stages of gambling expansion. In the early phases of expansion, the imperatives for managing role conflicts are less acute because the scale of concern is low. The same people (or small teams) are often required to manage multiple roles by declaring the conflicts and taking steps to ensure activities associated with these roles are clearly marked and kept separate. As the stakes rise, so this weak form of role separation leads to credibility problems both in terms of

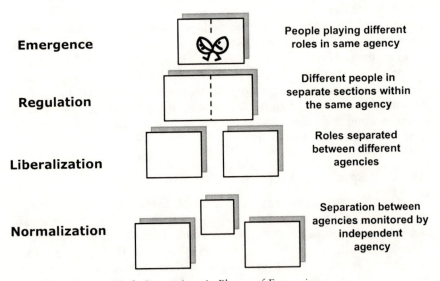

Emergence	**People playing different roles in same agency**
Regulation	**Different people in separate sections within the same agency**
Liberalization	**Roles separated between different agencies**
Normalization	**Separation between agencies monitored by independent agency**

Figure 3.1 Common Role Separations in Phases of Expansion

internal systems and in terms of external perceptions.[21] During the regulation phase, government agencies tend to seek stronger role delineation by creating internal divisions or Chinese walls within their operations whereby a subteam with one role operates separately from a subteam with another role, and the people belonging to each subteam do not overlap. However, as the liberalization phase gathers momentum, these separations are again challenged from within and without. It becomes increasingly tempting for one part of an agency to use gambling revenue to reduce demands for funding on other parts of that agency. For example, the pressure on governments to provide social services can be mitigated by setting up systems of charitable gambling funding, thereby reducing the need to draw on tax revenue. However, in the public eye, such arrangements lack credibility, particularly when they involve transfers within the same agency. Liberalization requires stronger visible separation and expectations rise that different roles will be managed by different agencies. This separation is particularly important in managing those roles associated with gambling expansion and those associated with moderating harm. With large amounts of revenue at stake, it becomes increasingly difficult to see how one agency can credibly manage both functions.[22] This is further compounded during the normalization phase when the number of roles has expanded to nine and gambling revenue interests are perceived to override other concerns. Arrangements not only require agency separation, but the public also needs reassurance that some independent processes exist to monitor and promote this separation. This can be achieved by commissioning an independent agency to investigate and report on processes and breaches.

Personal Responses to Role Conflict

As discussed in the previous chapter, it is the subtle degradation of democratic duties at an individual level that provides the strongest threat to a political ecology. In essence, gambling involves a transfer of money, typically from the hands of the many to the hands of the few. As each transfer occurs, government punches the ticket and ensures its financial claim on each transaction is protected. With increases in consumption, revenue also increases, thereby enabling the accumulation of financial resources at various nodes across the government sector. Individuals associated with these revenue nodes find themselves progressively connected in various ways to the processes of power and influence that access to resources creates. As the liberalization phase unfolds, whether by design or as a matter of course, it becomes increasingly difficult for government employees associated directly or indirectly with gambling to avoid being affected in some way by what they are handling. They find themselves progressively caught up in a private world where their own ambitions and the expectations associated with their work role become intertwined. Furthermore, surrounding each revenue node is a circle of potential inducements that have the capacity to gently draw the officials into and persuade them of the beneficence associated with gambling monies.

The part inducements play in the behavior of government employees is a sensitive area, and few individuals, agencies, or gambling providers are likely to openly describe these processes. The following considers the various possibilities open to those providers interested in maximizing their leverage. Gross examples are evident in the past when gambling expansion has occurred in an unrestrained fashion.[23] However, the patterns of current expansion are managed far more closely and it is the cumulative effect of subtle, hidden, and private processes, not the gross examples, that are of more concern. The purpose here of discussing inducements is to explore some of the possible routes by which government employees might find themselves drawn in by role conflicts. The discussion does not intend to imply that this is necessarily the case in each government context, but to point out how such processes could operate, particularly as the scale of gambling revenue increases.

Financial Inducements

An option in generating support for gambling liberalization is to create processes that enable individual politicians and government officials to benefit financially from their involvements. In less democratically developed nations, this is likely to be a common practice, but in democratically developed nations the offering of bribes and other direct inducements would be a hazardous option, particularly in contexts where a vigilant media is keen to expose political corruption. In these contexts financial inducements might require more subtle and indirect administration. An alternative option to receiving direct bribes is to make use of customary practices associated with gifting. The presentation of a gift or a prize is a well-established practice in most cultures as a means of one person or group to honor or recognize the achievements of another person or group. These practices occur commonly in sports, science, commerce, and the arts. Refusal of a gift in some circumstances could be interpreted as a rejection of a person's respect and therefore perceived as a direct dishonoring of the giver. In this way the return of the gift of a racehorse to a group of politicians would be seen as ungracious and provide some justification for keeping it. Another similar practice relates to the granting of workplace privileges. Employers often seek to foster employee professional development and loyalty by providing support for learning and travel, so it is reasonable for government agencies to access such funds for scholarships, travel grants, and exploratory business trips. For example, gambling funding sources are often used to fund exploratory missions for government officials and politicians (and sometimes their families) to visit overseas jurisdictions to explore regulatory systems that might or might not have anything to do with gambling.

Profile Inducements

Funds derived directly or indirectly from gambling sources are also useful in improving the profile of both individuals and agencies. Government agencies are typically hierarchical structures with staff promotion based on successful administration. The revenue of an expanding gambling sector brings to agencies involved and those managing them an increase in relative status. This applies particularly in the liberalization and normalization phases, where the need for new policy frameworks increases the range of roles and functions required within relevant agencies and more people are brought on to meet the expanding needs for research, consultation, document preparation, and legal processes. This increased activity boosts agency profile and by association the leading figures within the agency. A related strategy is to improve the profile of both an agency and associated politicians by influencing the distribution of charitable gambling funds. A politician's constituency kudos can be improved by providing funds for favored charities or charities linked to his or her public profile. This could work in a number of different ways. Government agencies could advise or facilitate the manner in which gambling providers provide charitable donations or sponsorship. Alternatively, charitable funding committees managed by government agencies could develop sensitivity to the constituency issues of key politicians. For example, a politician who has made a public stand regarding road safety would have his or her profile enhanced if local road safety campaigns received significant funding.

Influence Inducements

Another possibility occurs with appointment processes. As gambling moves through its regulation and normalization phases, increases in the range of agency roles require increasing numbers of new official appointment, committees, boards, and working groups. For example, when governments take on the role of providing comprehensive problem gambling services, they typically require advisory groups to oversee developments and accreditation boards and processes, each of which require the appointments of chairs, secretaries, and carefully thought-out membership. For the management of funds, those responsible often require purchasing agents, secretariats, auditing, and monitoring services. People in these positions—as well as those wanting to be in these positions—will be alert to attitudes and behaviors that might jeopardize their prospects and will act carefully to avoid missing out. A further influence inducement, particularly for employees positioned higher in government hierarchies, is the capacity of gambling to facilitate involvement with the rich and powerful. As the consumption of gambling grows, gambling industry providers grow in scale, become more organized, and progressively become more significant players within the commercial sector. For example, casino bosses can become business leaders and provide politicians and senior government officials with entrees into circles that enable or support their personal or collective ambitions.

Cooperation Inducements

Inducements that enable cooperation tend to occur at higher levels within government. During the phases of liberalization and normalization, the numbers of gambling providers multiply and they gradually see the benefits of forming cross-sector organizations to represent their interests in dealing with government. With increased membership, their investment in managing government relations similarly increases. As EGM proliferation unfolds, their increased financial muscle assists government agencies in recognizing that industry organizations have an important role in determining the nature of gambling environments. To be effective, government agencies find themselves increasingly tied into negotiations and bartering with gambling provider stakeholder groups to implement policy objectives. For example, a government might be keen to introduce centralized computer-linked online monitoring for all EGMs, but its introduction will require a high degree of cooperation from EGM providers. An organization that might represent EGM providers could then negotiate the cooperation of its members on the basis that it enables them access to something else, such as using the system for linked jackpots.

As mentioned earlier, the purpose of identifying these four varieties of inducement is to indicate their potential to influence individuals working in government agencies and to link increases in this potential to increases in the volume of gambling consumption. As greater amounts of revenue are collected, the potency of these inducements increases and role conflicts become more probable. Governments during liberalization and normalization that ignore this potential are likely to generate environments of high moral jeopardy within their own structures that are likely in time to become sites for the subtle degradation of democratic functions and perhaps leading to corruption scandals.

A CULTURE OF PERMISSIVENESS

The main threat posed by the blurring of roles and the unmonitored conflicts of interest is that a culture of permissiveness will evolve and gradually permeate those parts of government with some association with gambling. For example, during the liberalization phase in New Zealand, a relatively small agency of government, the Department of Internal Affairs, provided the majority of roles for managing gambling: It devised policy, it set the rules and enforced them, it monitored outcomes, and it managed responses to harm. During that time I found myself connecting to this agency at a variety of levels and I was repeatedly disappointed at the extent to which its employees chose to favor the interests of gambling expansion and were unwilling to seriously consider the impacts of gambling-related harm. This played out in various ways. For instance, up until 2002, it was unusual for any EGM operator to be investigated, and venue operators themselves reported being provided with considerable warning before license inspectors arrived. My observations of the behavior of officials at that time led me to conclude that they considered gambling to be a fairly benign activity with relatively few harmful consequences. The prevailing attitude took this form: "OK, gambling causes harm, but it is not really that bad compared to other issues such as illicit drug use and violent crime, and besides, the potential benefits to communities far outweigh the few who encounter harms." Such a view is consistent with pursuing, at best, a passive approach to law enforcement and, at worst, an active promotion of gambling. With limited involvement from other government agencies, these permissive attitudes discouraged any processes that might involve questioning or challenging their procedures. With this as a backdrop, it is difficult to accept that a small government agency that has a strong investment in the collection of gambling revenue can at the same time credibly set policy, set the rules, and manage enforcement. While this agency has in more recent years adopted a more active stance on regulation and enforcement, it still juggles a variety of conflicting roles.

Governments have a primary duty to protect their own democratic foundations from distortions and degradations. This chapter has highlighted ways in which government agencies and the individuals who inhabit them might find themselves participating in roles associated with gambling that at least blur and most likely compromise their duty to protect the integrity of government systems and protect the interests of the public. It has illustrated some of the permissive practices that people within the government sector could find them drawn into and how these can spread into a culture of permissiveness that can have degrading consequences for the political ecology of a nation. With global warming to the attractiveness of gambling revenue and with gambling providers better equipped and increasingly motivated to maximize their influence on relevant policy, it is at times difficult to conceive of how government agencies could avoid these influences. These forces are unlikely to diminish in the future. A pragmatic response would be to shift attention away from pointing the blame at those who blatantly transgress within the system and to focus on determinants in the environment. This shift would involve developing protective strategies for the new environment, rather than relying on strategies of the past. Later in the final three chapters, strategies are examined that governments might adopt to protect their agencies from the types of subtle degradation that undermine their contribution to the systems and processes of democracy.

4 Communities

The vibrancy of a democracy is evident in the extent to which its citizens and its community organizations actively participate in its democratic structures and processes. In previous chapters I have argued that the widespread proliferation of commercialized gambling cuts across the social and political ecologies resulting in unforeseen and long-term impacts to the cohesion of family and broader social networks. The following chapter considers the relative payoff to communities of the expansion of commercialized gambling. It first summarizes the main forms of harm to communities. It next reviews the potential benefits and examines in more detail ways in which communities benefit financially from gambling. It argues that financial benefits from gambling can be a double-edged sword. For the purposes of this chapter, the term *community organization* refers to a broad range of organizations that all share a common purpose in seeking to improve the quality of life of their members or the people they serve. Such organizations include nongovernmental organizations (NGOs), not-for-profit societies and trusts, civil society organizations, government and quasi-government organizations, community well-being organizations, health service organizations, and academic and research organizations.

COMMUNITY HARMS

Similar to the impacts of other dangerous consumptions with addictive potential (e.g., tobacco and alcohol), the impacts of gambling are complex and diverse. By plugging into systems of financial transaction, gambling interacts with individual lifestyles and patterns of social connection. Because the phases of liberalization and normalization are relatively recent, the evidential base for understanding the impact of large-scale commercialized gambling on communities is at an early stage. Despite the paucity of monitoring data, overview information is available that gives some idea of likely downstream effects. The following sections summarize key areas moving from striking impacts to the more subtle and diffuse.

Problem Gambling

The most obvious impact visible in the medium term is the rise in prevalence of problem gambling.[1] Problem gambling is a multileveled behavioral disorder that varies in intensity and that by definition involves a range of major and sustained impacts on a person's quality of life.[2] In many ways, it resembles alcohol abuse and dependence, but it also carries aspects of other behavioral disorders such as obsessional thought processes, dissociative mental states, and reduced impulse control. Left unchecked, problem gambling will incur sustained impairments to a person's social and occupational functioning as well as severe economic impacts to that person's immediate social environment. Measurement of the occurrence of problem gambling in the adult populations of the United States and Canada averages a 12-month prevalence rate of 2.9% and a lifetime prevalence of 5.4% (Shaffer et al., 1997). At the more severe end, Level 3 pathological gambling, 12-month prevalence averages 0.9% and lifetime prevalence is 1.5%. As a general trend, nations with higher gambling consumption will record higher rates of problem gambling, although this is moderated by factors such as length of exposure, public awareness of risk, and the intensity of product promotion.[3] Problem gambling is strongly linked to a range of indicators of social distress. In North America where nearly a third of younger people gamble weekly, their involvement with gambling outstrips their participation in smoking, drinking, and taking other drugs (Gupta & Derevensky, 1998; Shaffer, Hall, Vander Bilt, & George, 2003), and 10% to 15% of younger people are at risk of problem gambling (Jacobs, 2000; Shaffer & Hall, 1996). Problem gambling also cooccurs at high rates with other mental health concerns, particularly depression, anxiety, suicide, and substance abuse (see Cunningham-Williams, Cottler, Compton, & Spitznagel, 1998; Specker, Carlson, Edmonson, Johnson, & Marcotte, 1996). Other indicators of disruption from problem gambling include family dysfunction and violence (Bland, Newman, Orn, & Stebelsky, 1993; Lorenz & Yaffee, 1986), bankruptcy (Gernstein et al., 1999), and criminal offending (Abbott & McKenna, 2000).

Intervention strategies specifically designed to address problem gambling are in their early stages of development and to date have borrowed heavily from approaches to alcohol and drug addictions (see Jackson et al., 2000; Raylu & Oei, 2002). Common intervention strategies involve adaptations of psychological and counseling approaches such as cognitive or "thinking therapies" that engage gamblers in improving their sense of self-efficacy while reducing their false beliefs and false attributions regarding their influence over gambling outcomes. Other common approaches involve motivational strategies that assist problem gamblers in consolidating their commitment to change and applications of the 12 steps of Alcoholics Anonymous to forming the recovery fellowship of Gamblers Anonymous. Because for most contexts the expansion of gambling is at an early stage, these approaches are still being evaluated and refined, and the service frameworks on which they are being delivered remain relatively rudimentary.

The relationship between problem gambling and profits from gambling highlight the primary extractive nature of gambling expansion. In an analysis of past survey data, the Australian Productivity Commission (1999) estimated that although problem gamblers represent a small proportion of players, they account for about one third of commercial gambling expenditure, contributing to a higher 42.3% of spending on EGMs. An analysis in Ontario, Canada of prospective diaries indicated that about 35% of Ontario gambling revenue is derived from moderate and severe problem gamblers, with even higher proportions for gaming machines and horse racing (Williams & Wood, 2003). Furthermore, a study of casino gambling in the United States estimated that 52% of casino revenue comes from problem or pathological gambling (Grinols, 2004; Grinols & Mustard, 2006). These observations led the Australian Productivity Commission (1999) to observe:

> Overall, problem gamblers, while small in number, have a cumulatively large impact because they spend around 19 times more than recreational gamblers. The implication is that of the $10.7 billion [U.S. $8.4 billion] of gambling expenditure by Australians in 1997–98, around $3.6 billion [U.S. $2.8 billion] comes from problem gamblers. (p. 742)

This highlights how a large proportion of gambling revenue should be seen as having been extracted from people who are experiencing issues with controlling their consumption and that this revenue is linked to struggles in dealing with the suffering and chaos associated with gambling. It suggests that this form of extraction relies heavily on preying on the weak and vulnerable.

In terms of the various phases in which commercial gambling has expanded, during the regulation phase, where low-potency noncontinuous forms of gambling keep rates of problem gambling to low levels, intervention services where they do occur are low-key affairs, perhaps attached as a small part of another service. During liberalization, the prevalence of problem gambling is rising but the general public remains unaware, so little interest is shown in intervention services and what develops tends to be poorly coordinated and inadequately funded. During the normalization phase, gambling intervention services tend to be seen as an essential part of a gambling regulatory framework, but also tend to be focused primarily on the severe end of problem gambling, with little developed in the way of prevention, early intervention, and community development. As will be discussed in Chapter 8, this preoccupation with advanced pathology runs the risk that organizations providing interventions for problem gambling become incorporated as part of what is required to continue the extraction activities associated with frequent commercial gambling.

Community Impacts

The negative impacts of gambling are not confined to problem gambling. Regular nonproblematic gambling can contribute to a variety of worrying trends. For example, regular gambling can divert parental energy away from family life, thereby reducing input into such areas as family recreation and care of children.[4] Frequent gambling also correlates highly with other behaviors that pose risks to health such as heavy alcohol use and smoking (National Opinion Research Center, Gemini Research, The Lewin Group, & Christiansen/Cummings Associates, 1999). For members of low-income families, even a moderate investment in gambling might tip the balance between managing rent or mortgage payments and facing destitution. The loss of a financially stable home environment contributes to family conflict; it impacts the emotional development and educational prospects of children and propels movement between locations that contributes further to the fragmentation of local communities (Dyall & Hand, 2003; McGowan, Droessler, Nixin, & Grimshaw, 2000).

Economists researching gambling have explored the ways in which gambling could be considered to function as a form of regressive taxation (see Pickernell, Brown, Worthington, & Crawford, 2004). By *regressive* they mean instead of the burden of taxation being differentially lighter on people of lower income, the revenue collection results in placing a higher burden on those who can least afford it. The research here is at an early stage and remains controversial, but investigations from several different angles are drawing similar conclusions. Some researchers have identified higher engagement of people of low income in most forms of gambling. For example, the concentration of EGMs has been recorded as significantly higher in low-income compared to higher income communities.[5] Added to this effect, people with lower incomes have less to lose, are more financially vulnerable, and are therefore more likely to suffer negative effects from gambling losses. As mentioned earlier, other researchers have identified how a large proportion of revenue from gambling is collected from the activities of problem gamblers.

Added to the diffuse effects of gambling on social disconnection and access inequities is the level to which communities feel empowered to determine whether and to what extent gambling occurs in their territories. Particularly during liberalization and normalization phases, communities often find they have very little influence over the manner in which gambling is entering their midst. At one stage gambling was confined to a limited number of premises; then, in what seems like a fairly short period, lottery products are available on every street corner, bars are installing increasingly potent EGMs, and casinos are being built nearby. As occurs with the industries that extract resources from natural ecologies, alliances among governments, gambling providers, and local entrepreneurs frequently support processes that lead to overriding or dismissing the wishes of local communities. For example, in proceedings that enabled the introduction of six new casinos into New

Zealand, several opinion polls indicated that the majority in each relevant community were opposed to them being licensed. Later, community leaders were shocked to find that central government had failed to provide any means by which community opinion could have a bearing on the outcome and accordingly all licenses were granted. Similar experiences with communities having a limited say have been reported in the expansion of gambling in the United States, Canada, and Australia.[6] An increasing amount of social science research has identified community empowerment as a critical dimension to the strength and resilience of communities in responding to threats to their health and well-being (Labonte, 1990; Laverack, 2001). Consequently, this disempowering of communities in determining the nature of their gambling environments could arguably be seen as contributing negatively both to their capacity to respond to specific harms from gambling and their capacity to actively build up their general strength and resilience.

Vulnerable Populations

What can a specific population expect when its gambling reaches saturated levels? As with tobacco, once initial markets reach saturation, commercial imperatives drive gambling industries to seek out new opportunities and realize new markets. These new markets tend to span out in two directions: first, new markets within the current population and, second, untapped markets in foreign locations. The task of engaging new consumers within the current population often relies on the development and marketing of a new product (we look at this in more detail in Chapter 6). During the regulation phase for many countries, the typical gambler would tend to be a middle-aged man with a passion for horse betting. During liberalization and normalization, a greater range of products have become available that appeal specifically to populations such as youth, older people, women, and people of different ethnicities. For instance, the increasing presence of casinos in major urban centers is drawing in higher numbers of immigrant Chinese to play at casino tables (Petry, Armentano, Kuoch, Norinth, & Smith, 2003; Wong & Tse, 2003). Increased availability of gambling machines in clubs and casinos has engaged more women in regular gambling, and the introduction of interactive game technologies and sports betting are increasing the participation of young people. These new users understandably have little awareness of the risks associated with these new products.

The marketing of new forms of gambling to targeted populations has been particularly damaging to First Nation peoples. Indigenous communities in North America and the South Pacific have had little previous exposure to commercial gambling and typically have low awareness of the risks. For Maori (the indigenous people of New Zealand), during the regulation phase their communities made use of noncontinuous forms of gambling, such as cards and housie or bingo, to fund communal projects like the building of meetinghouses.[7] Locally organized gambling events also provided important opportunities for families and communities to reconnect in an atmosphere of enjoyment and sharing. During the current phase of liberalization, the availability of continuous forms of gambling is enticing gamblers away from local events in favor of bulk gambling in larger commercial establishments. The investment of time and money is drawn out of the community with little benefit filtering back to local groups. Because most Maori families have a poorer capital base than the remainder of the population, and additionally with little previous experience of continuous forms of gambling, negative impacts have rapidly emerged. For example, in 2001 national statistics on problem gambling services recorded rates of Maori women seeking services as high as six times the proportional rate among the remainder of the population (Problem Gambling Committee, 2003). A similar pattern of poor preparedness, asset loss, and increased problem gambling can be observed for other First Nations people (see McGowan et al., 2000) and can also be observed with people migrating from nations with lower to higher gambling intensity.[8]

COMMUNITY BENEFITS

In contrast to the range of potential harms, gambling also delivers a range of tangible benefits to communities. These benefits by their nature sustain the ongoing interest and support of large numbers of people in the further growth of gambling opportunities. The benefits can be roughly divided into five categories: (a) individual enjoyment, (b) social connection, (c) economic stimulus, (d) employment, and (e) community benefit funding.

Individual Enjoyment

By far the largest benefit from gambling is the fun it creates. The extra dimension of financial risk lifts a game from an amusing pastime to an activity charged with excitement and anticipation. The Australian Productivity Commission's (1999) review of gambling industries examined a broad range of potential benefits from gambling and concluded, "The benefits from liberalization of the gambling industries come primarily from the satisfaction that consumers obtain from the ability to access what for many is a desired from of entertainment" (p. 51). As with other forms of entertainment, fun from gambling can be seen as contributing to the pleasure and meaningfulness of daily life with benefits including reprieve from work drudgery, relaxation, and reductions in stress.

Social Connection

Gambling has traditionally provided a means for bringing people together. Many gambling contexts provide a focus for strong and enjoyable social interaction: a day at the racetrack, crowding around a table at a local bingo hall, workmates at home upping the ante in a game of poker, discussions in staff canteens about which horse to place bets on, friends rubbing shoulders around a roulette wheel, or people chatting in a line to purchase a lottery ticket. The value of these opportunities contributes undeniably to those patterns of involvement on which communities are created and within which individuals construct their identity and maintain their well-being. Although it is important not to lose sight of the positive value gambling can play in enhancing community connectedness, a feature of the trend to commercialization has been a parallel trend favoring forms of gambling with lower levels of social interaction. For example, in most jurisdictions, more socially oriented forms—such as track betting or informal card games—are steadily becoming eclipsed by the more solitary activities of scratch cards and EGM gambling. This trend also appears to be leading to the ultimate form of socially disconnected gambling where frequent gamblers can choose to stay in their bedrooms and gamble for hours on the Internet. In this way gambling as a reason for people to come together is now moving toward a reason for people to remain on their own.

Economic Stimulus

Various claims are made that expanded commercial gambling provides general impetus to development of local economies. It does this by attracting tourists and other visitors to spend in that locality, by providing a focal point for other entertainment businesses such as restaurants and cinemas, and by injecting money into the region as a consequence of its own activities.[9] The merits of these claims are difficult to assess because most research has been conducted with either direct or indirect support of gambling industries with an interest in advancing their activities in that locality.[10] Furthermore, these claims run into difficulty when claims of economic growth are contrasted with the estimates of the growth that could have occurred if the same investment had been put into alternative activities. For example, Pinge (2000) monitored the economic activity associated with EGMs in Bendigo, a town of 81,000 people about 150 km north of Melbourne. With access to financial records in EGM venues and other businesses, he was able to build up an economic model that contrasted spending on gambling with spending on alternative activities such as manufacturing and retail.[11] He estimated that at the time of the study the opportunity cost of gambling amounted to $4.2 million lost to output, $5.9 million lost in household income, and a loss of 237 jobs resulting from the switch to gambling activities in the region. He concluded:

> The adoption of EGMs in Bendigo has had a significant negative impact on the region . . . subject to similar findings in other regions, such a situation should not be allowed to continue and governments must act on

an industry that not only imposes its burden on lower income groups, but also on particular communities (p 21).

As he acknowledged, this type of study needs to be conducted in other locations before claims regarding the real economic benefits of gambling can be assessed.

Employment Within and Around

Associated with providing stimulus to stagnant economies is the claim that commercial gambling contributes positively to employment in a region. This is not only evident in the large numbers of people employed within gambling venues, but also in ancillary and related businesses such as bars, restaurants, machine manufacturing and maintenance, businesses that include lottery products, and so forth (Austrialian Productivity Commission, 1999). The Australian Productivity Commission (1999) looked closely at this claim and concluded:

> The gambling industries employ a large number of people in Australia, but the net production-side benefits of liberalization have been small when account is taken of the substitution effects and the alternatives available for gambling spending. Benefits in terms of employment and activity in the gambling industries are largely offset by declines in industries that have lost the consumers' dollar to gambling. (p. 51)

Again, the contribution to employment is not as straightforward as it would seem. Had money invested on gambling been spent differently, a range of other employment opportunities could have emerged.

Community Benefit Funding

The final major way communities benefit from gambling is through the disbursement of proceeds from gambling into community activities. *Community benefit funding* refers to a variety of arrangements that enable communities and the individuals and organizations within them to benefit financially from gambling. Differing nations (and differing states for those in federal systems) have adopted varying approaches to the extent to which gambling is used as a specific mechanism for raising revenue. Some jurisdictions (e.g., many states in the United States and Australia) regard gambling as a heavily taxed commercial activity with revenue absorbed into their consolidated funds. Other countries (e.g., the United Kingdom, Canada, and New Zealand) have strong traditions where community benefit funding is identified as one of or the primary purpose for permitting gambling.[12] Under the latter arrangement, increasingly larger amounts of available funds, particularly from EGM providers, engage more and more community organizations in seeking gambling funds for their activities. For example, in New Zealand, a small country of 4 million people, gambling industries generate somewhere in the vicinity of $400 million to $600 million per year for community organizations.[13] This is a significant contribution, and its extent has led the majority of community organizations into receiving gambling funding in some form. For those that do not, ongoing difficulties in survival persist.

RISKS FROM COMMUNITY BENEFIT FUNDING

As discussed earlier, the benefits derived from gambling can be seen to cut in both positive and negative directions. For instance, although communities are likely to initially benefit from increases in gambling-related employment, such increases engage and commit a portion of a community's workforce in an area of activity that could have been deployed in other ways. Similarly, the economic investment in gambling could arguably come at the cost of other and potentially more productive sectors of investment.[14] This question remains: Could the social and economic investment in gambling have been committed in other ways with far better long-term outcomes for communities concerned? The double-sided nature of benefits from gambling is most strongly evident when it comes to community benefit funding. It is easy to understand how poorly funded community organizations are attracted to this considerable and easily accessible source of revenue, particularly when government contributions grow increasingly more difficult to obtain. The catch is that once an organization receives its first amount of funding from a gambling industry source, a precedent is set that, for many, will lead to the acceptance of further funding, thereby laying the foundations for a relationship of reliance and dependency.

There is a complex array of ways in which money becomes available to community organizations from gambling activity. The following sections examine five of the most common of these arrangements.

Direct Industry Contributions

In this arrangement, private commercial gambling operators choose to provide direct funding to community organizations for clear community-good purposes. For example, in Australia in the year 2003–2004 casinos claim they contributed $31.6 million to community organizations and charities (Australian Casino Association, 2006). Because gambling providers are profit driven, their contributions are understandably driven mainly by commercial imperatives. For example, during its first few years of operation, a casino might seek the goodwill of adjacent community trusts (e.g., churches, charities, and performance venues) by donating generously to their development projects. Such contributions can vary according to the perceived strategic importance of the recipient to the donor's business. For example, high-profile Asian events might receive generous sponsorship if the donor considers Asian patronage important. The following scenario provides a typical example.

> The large casino in the center of Sydney (200 gaming tables and 1,500 gaming machines) contributes approximately $8 million annually to a Casino Community Benefit Fund managed by a secretariat to which community organizations apply for funding. The applications are then processed by an independent trust, with the main recipients being "researchers, counselors and experts who run rehabilitation programs for people who need assistance" (Star City Casino, 2006). The Casino Community Benefit Trustees form a statutory committee of eight representatives from a range of welfare, government, and community organizations. They allocate the funds to applicants and report on progress directly to the state Minister of Gaming and Racing (Casino Community Benefit Fund Trustees, 2005).

In terms of community benefit, direct contributions by a gambling provider comprise the least desirable arrangement because they involve a strong and moderately direct or semi-direct relationship of the recipient organization with a gambling provider. Within this relationship, the contribution is unlikely to occur anonymously because the donor is seeking an association primarily for the purposes of improving its public profile. Community recipients are consequently likely to perceive a strong obligation to those who provided the funds. They might even develop a concern that any open questioning or criticism of the activities of the donor organization will threaten positive branding effects and consequently jeopardize future funding. Furthermore, this form of charitable funding, which predominates in the United States, has resulted in severely lower rates of funding than in jurisdictions that have adopted other arrangements.

Community-Administered Contributions

With this arrangement, community organizations run their own gambling operation for the primary purpose of raising money to fund their own activities. Often this is on a small scale and involves low-salience forms of gambling such as raffles or bingo (housie). However, in some jurisdictions, organizations are permitted to offer more salient forms, such as EGMs and casino table games.

> In the United States, tribal authorities have gradually come to view reservation casinos as a means of funding economic development within Indian communities. Following the passage of the Indian Gaming Regulation Act in 1988, increasing numbers of tribes have opened casinos on reservation land. The size of these ventures has varied enormously from

a small, barely profitable venue with a few EGMs and table games, to the much larger commercial venues with many machines and tables, plus the provision of accommodations, other entertainment, and marketing that draws large numbers of patrons into the venue. Those reservations positioned close to locations with large populations are those more likely to attract sufficient external investment to establish the larger, more lucrative casinos and consequently it is their tribes that have derived significant economic benefits and development opportunities from this source.[15]

Although on the whole this arrangement occurs on a relatively small scale, these organizations often end up targeting their own constituencies.[16] For example, people attending church-run bingo evenings are most likely to be friends and families of local parishioners. Similarly, EGMs in venues such as sports clubs, tribal venues, or war veteran organizations will on the whole be accessed by their own membership, often a membership (older, younger, and poorer) already identified as vulnerable to gambling-related problems. Besides engaging their own constituencies, the other main drawbacks to this arrangement are the manner in which it normalizes and legitimizes gambling at a grassroots community level and the way in which organizations with a concern for the poor and underprivileged in their communities are discouraged from speaking out about gambling.

Government-Administered Contributions

In this arrangement, government manages the provision of gambling and disperses profits to the community in the form of funding grants. The most common example is the various forms of national and state lotteries. In the United Kingdom and New Zealand and many of the states in Australia, Canada, and the United States, lottery products are either provided by the government or by a commercial subsidiary under supervision of government, with disbursement of the profits administered directly by a branch of government.

In the United States 37 states offer a range of lottery products (weekly or biweekly draws, scratch cards, TV keno, etc.), the profits from which they distribute to a broad range of community and other charitable causes. The Georgia State Lottery allocates what players spend into the costs for operators in providing the products, a tax of 35% for the state government, and the remainder to charitable purposes. Georgia's lottery is unique in that it allocates all its charitable funds to three educational areas: Helping Outstanding Pupils Educationally (HOPE) College Scholarships, universal prekindergarten, and education infrastructure. Over a 5-year period (1994–1999) it expended more than $3 billion, roughly distributed evenly among these three recipients. Since its inception the fund has remained stable, popular, and successful in achieving its goals, and is being explored as a model in other states (described by Rubenstein & Scafidi, 2002).

The chief risk with this arrangement is that the agency that administers the funding begins to benefit itself from dispersing the money: It begins to derive direct and indirect benefits from the activity and thereby risks building a reliance on that source. The strongest temptation for governments is to use such funds to support community services that they would have had to fund out of a personal income tax base. In Georgia, the lottery investment in educational infrastructure (technology and construction) reduces the load for state funding in these areas. However, reliance on these funds to support educational initiatives has been challenged in a number of ways. For example, in an analysis of this fund, Rubenstein and Scafidi (2002) concluded that this form of funding is "regressive," meaning that it relies heavily on people with low incomes:

> Consistent with numerous other studies, we find that spending on lottery products is highly regressive. We also find that higher income households tend to receive a higher level of benefits from lottery-funded programs than do lower-income households, though these benefits represent a higher proportion of income to lower-income households. (p. 236)[17]

Other temptations for governments include the taxation benefits they receive, the ability to implement favored development priorities, and enhancement of a positive political profile. In addition, their interest in ensuring lottery products maintain a share of the gambling market often entails them maintaining a lead and privileged access to advertising and other promotional opportunities. As with community-administered contributions, the involvement of government in the provision and promotion of gambling products contributes further to the normalization and acceptance of gambling as a low-risk part of everyday life.

Government-Brokered Contributions

In response to perceptions that direct industry funding allows the industry too much leeway to influence outcomes, some governments have sought to establish their own independent organizations to receive and disperse contributions from privately run gambling providers. Typically a government agency or quasi-government agency is created to manage voluntary funds in a way that appears independent of the source.

> The U.K. Responsibility in Gambling Trust (RIGT) was initiated as a mechanism for distributing voluntary contributions by gambling industries for the purpose of reducing gambling-related harm through

investment in problem gambling services and research. The forerunner to the Trust (Gambling Industry Charitable Trust) was originally set up by the British Casino Association as a way of meeting its social responsibility associated with harm from gambling. The Gambling Act in 2005 led to reformation of the trust as a public–private partnership with statutory independence from the industry. In the new RIGT board, half its membership consists of gambling industry representatives and half are selected as "independent" members with relevant backgrounds in areas such as problem gambling services, research, and church welfare organizations. In 2006 the voluntary contribution consisted of around $4.2 million (as against an estimated $15 billion expended on gambling), of which roughly two thirds was distributed (through GamCare) to services and the remainder to operations and research.

The main difficulty with this arrangement is the perception that donor organizations should still retain a significant say in how the money is used. Some gambling providers might even view it as "their" money that they have "given," and therefore they are entitled to have the largest say in how it is managed.[18] The management agencies set up for this purpose tend to establish governance structures that are highly responsive to gambling industry providers. For example, with half the RIGT board comprised of gambling industry representatives, their ability to act in unison and the perception that it is their largesse (and their ability to determine the amount) that creates the fund in the first place, could enable them to achieve a stronger influence on the decisions of the board. This might not matter too much on funding decisions relating to problem gambling services, but it would matter significantly when decisions are relevant to activities that could threaten gambling consumption, particularly regarding health advocacy, social and economic impact research, and public health initiatives. It might also discourage assistance agencies from speaking out about issues associated with gambling expansion (see Chapter 8).

Government-Mandated Contributions

In this arrangement, governments enact legislation that requires gambling providers to allocate a specified portion of their net income to fund projects with a community purpose. Because gambling on EGMs is the major driver for the expansion of gambling, in many jurisdictions funding from this source has quickly become the largest available pool of monies for community sports, educational, cultural, and charitable activities. In the absence of other significant sources, most community organizations find themselves strongly drawn to apply to them for funding.

The majority of EGM providers in New Zealand are required by law to divide their income from gambling into three substantial parts: one portion for provider operational needs, one portion for government taxation, and one portion for community benefit purposes. The community benefit money is administered by trusts that have been specially formed for the purpose of distributing these funds. Because EGMs dominate gambling in New Zealand, this fund has quickly become a very important source of monies for community sports, educational, cultural, and charitable activities. In the absence of other significant sources, most community organizations are faced with an increasing reliance on its beneficence. Governments benefit in two ways: The funding is used to support community initiatives that they would have been pressured to support anyway, and they—particularly local and national politicians—are able to influence distributions in ways that favor their own interests.

The major difficulty with this type of arrangement is the risk to community organizations of increasing reliance on this income source, which in turn leads to a creeping financial dependency that can then result in them becoming major advocates for the provision of gambling. For example, in New Zealand, it is now commonplace for a broad range of community organizations to line up in defense of gambling providers when consumption increases are debated in the media or in government select committees. Their major point is that reductions in consumption will jeopardize their own funding base. In this way, community organizations find themselves being recruited as lobbyists for the industry itself.

No Risk-Free Arrangement

Most national or state gambling policy frameworks allow for a mixture of the preceding arrangements, often varying according to the mode of gambling. For example, the distribution of funds generated by lottery products is usually government administered, whereas EGMs contribute to a government-mandated fund and casinos pursue their own sponsorship programs. However, as can be seen from the preceding discussion, each arrangement brings its own set of problems. From whichever route community benefit funding is derived, for community organizations there are no risk-free arrangements. In some ways the ethical issues have less to do with the way these funds are administered and more to do with the nature of the source itself. By whichever route the funding comes—even filtered through government bodies—the community organization still has to contend with the reality that the funding has been derived from gambling activities. Whatever future arrangements emerge, it will still fall back to people within community organizations themselves to decide how far into an arrangement they are willing to proceed before it leads to intolerable ethical compromise.

DIMENSIONS OF MORAL JEOPARDY

As discussed in Chapter 2, the increasing presence of revenue from gambling, both for taxation purposes and community benefit purposes, creates an environment of increasing moral jeopardy. Although gambling undeniably introduces a range of benefits to communities in the form of enjoyment, social engagement, and funding sources, its consumption also introduces a range of harms. The following sections identify the dimensions of risk that community organizations should consider when deciding to receive funds obtained from gambling industries. These include ethical and reputational risks alongside risks to governance, organizational coherence, and democracy.[19]

Ethical Risks

The essential ethical consideration that follows from accepting gambling monies is that in receiving such funding an organization becomes locked into a challenging ethical inconsistency. How can a community organization that claims to serve the good of a community maintain its credibility when part of its income comes from sources that are known to cause harm to that same community? Some might rationalize such an involvement by claiming the end justifies the means, but to what extent will an organization tolerate this inconsistency? How can an organization set up to reduce poverty and other social ills in all conscience benefit in a real sense, either directly or indirectly, from other people's misery? For example, Charles Dickens contrasted the wealth of the middle and upper classes with the grinding poverty of the working classes. His graphic descriptions challenge the morality of one sector of society building their well-being and comfort on the back of the misery of another sector. Similarly, those who participate and benefit financially from gambling need to think carefully about the source of that wealth. From whom is that source of funding coming and at what cost?

There is another more active possibility that could emerge from a visible relationship with industry sources. Gambling industries that generate the most harm (currently EGMs) are likely to be acutely aware of the negative views that can be formed regarding their operations. Negative public perceptions can have major effects on the sale of their products, particularly with regard to brand image, marketing, site approvals, regulations, and government policies. Visible relationships with community organizations could serve to mitigate potential negative associations and to give the impression either that the activity leads to public good, or that they have at least attempted to rectify potential harm. In this way gambling providers can potentially derive significant benefits from a positive public image. It enables them to interface more easily in community, local authority, and public arenas. It helps support them in venue and licensing processes, in creating new products and venues, and in deemphasizing much of the harm their activities generate. A visibly funded relationship could also provide a respectable platform for industries to negotiate their relationships with government agencies.

A further active ethical concern is that a community organization's acceptance of gambling funds becomes incorporated into the marketing of that gambling product. The positive associations formed in the relationship often provide a base for engaging the spending behavior of punters. For example, it is likely that people will feel more inclined to purchase a ticket in a national lottery when they believe the profits are going to a worthy cause. This perception will be particularly strong when they see their gambling as visibly benefiting their immediate community. This acts to encourage or at least disinhibit the consumer at the point of sale and is thereby likely to increase the amount he or she is likely to purchase. The consequent increase in gambling consumption adds to the extent of gambling-related harm. Thus, from one perspective, the organization's acceptance of gambling funding can be viewed as actively contributing to the negative impacts gambling has on individuals and communities.

Reputational Risks

Putting aside for a moment ethical considerations, organizations contemplating a relationship with gambling monies would benefit from considering how others will see them. *Reputational risk* refers to the perceptions of other relevant stakeholders regarding the decision of an organization to accept gambling funds. Depending on the importance of the stakeholder, these perceptions could have major implications for the viability of such an organization. The perceptions that matter will vary, but they typically include those of funders, consumers, collaborators, and the general public. For example, a theatergoer with strongly negative views of gambling might choose to boycott a theater company that is funded by gambling sources, and for that person the negative association could last long after the company has ceased receiving such funds. At another level, government funding agencies could themselves have concerns about being linked to gambling providers and for that reason prefer relationships with organizations that do not have such associations. The impact of negative perceptions also extends to those working within an organization. For those with ethical concerns, an operational link to gambling providers could challenge their own involvement with that organization. For example, a counselor with strong views about gambling industries working within a problem gambling counseling agency is likely to have serious reservations about his or her organization assisting casinos with their host responsibility programs. The perception of an association could be interpreted as complicity and this would sap the counselor's morale and enthusiasm for the work of the service.

Governance Risks

The primary risk to governance centers on the threats to organizational independence and sovereignty due to an increasing reliance on gambling industry sources for funding. As the proportional level of gambling funding increases, members of a community organization might begin viewing such funding as essential for survival. Often incremental increases in funding creep up on an organization; reliance evolves without those in the organization fully appreciating the extent. In situations where a governance board on balance opposes this source on ethical grounds, on pragmatic grounds they might have little choice but to continue with the funding because they see the organization as simply ceasing to exist without it. A board might consider a small amount of gambling revenue (say 5% of income) as expendable, and consequently they would have no difficulty risking it by criticizing the source. However, for many community organizations, a larger amount (say 10% or more) could lead to perceptions of reliance and they would be reluctant to jeopardize the funding by criticizing or challenging the activities of the source.

In a Canadian survey of NGOs that had received grants from gambling sources, Berdahl and Azmier (1999) found a full 20% received more than half their annual revenues from gambling grants and 50% rated gambling grants as the top funding source. Many of the NGOs receiving funds argued that they would not be able to survive without these grants. The investigators also surveyed and interviewed NGO board members to find that as many as 69% of people in the organization disagreed or strongly disagreed with the statement "Our board members oppose our organization's use of gaming revenues." They noted that opposition was particularly low among sports and recreation organizations. They explored these views further in in-depth interviews with board members and found that although individual board members might object to the funds:

> [T]he greater sentiment is that their commitment to their cause over-rides their ethical concerns about gambling. For these individuals, the acceptance of gambling revenues is seen as a "compromise," or a "necessary evil," that must be accepted to meet their larger goals. As one respondent wrote, "Ethically our staff and board are always debating this issue. Our need for operating money usually wins out however." (p. 15)

Relationship Risks

A further risk to consider is the possibility that receiving gambling funds could jeopardize relationships within an organization. Approaches to achieving community well-being will vary across an organization. Differences in focus and orientation can lead to interpersonal tensions that in turn lead to conflict and dissension, and it is differences in approaches to ethical issues that can generate the most passion and debate. There are two different levels at which this can occur: the suborganizational and the individual.

In larger organizations, such as health services or universities, one section of activity might have considerably less interest in these ethical concerns than other sections. For example in a large health service organization (e.g., a hospital), the less community-oriented sections of the organization (e.g., critical care) might have few qualms about receiving urgently needed funds from gambling sources. They are likely to do so without considering the impact this might have on other sections with more of a community orientation, such as mental health and addiction services. People in these services are then put in a difficult position because their institution's involvement in receiving gambling funds compromises their ability to speak out regarding the negative impacts of gambling. This situation is particularly important to organizations with sections that are likely to champion causes associated with harm from gambling, such as universities and social justice advocacy organizations. Once one part of a university accepts significant gambling funds, other sections of the same institution are less able to comment credibly on gambling issues and, if they do, might find themselves in difficulty with those receiving the funds and perhaps in conflict with central management.

The other situation to consider is the impact on dissenting individuals within a community organization when it decides to receive gambling funds. The following scenario captures some of the dynamics.

Jason was a member of the board of trustees for a golf club. His club decided some years previously to accept major sponsorship from a large EGM provider. Jason initially had no objections to this, but as time went on and he read more in newspapers about the impacts of gambling, he grew increasingly concerned about the club's willingness to accept this funding. He believed strongly that golf was a game that aimed to promote the health, well-being, and moral integrity of citizens. He had increasing difficulty reconciling this with what he heard about gambling. He raised these issues tentatively with the board. They listened, but the ensuing discussion was light and full of quips about betting on the future of the club. He raised the issues again in two subsequent meetings. Other board members began to recognize that he was serious and they engaged more strongly in countering his arguments. Eventually he tabled a motion proposing the club pull out of the funding relationship. The debate then became very personal, with accusations regarding inconsistencies in his own participation in gambling and challenging his credentials to take the moral high ground. Predictably the motion was not carried and from then on Jason sensed that others on the board viewed him as a problem. They joked about him being a moral arbiter and were careful about what they discussed in his presence. He, too, was wondering about his continuing board membership. As time went on his concerns about this funding had not diminished and he was becoming increasingly silent and passive at board meetings.

Persistent dissenting voices are an ongoing problem for an organization. Should they be engaged, challenged, ignored, or marginalized? Their dissent could be corrosive on organizational coherence over time. Consequently colleagues could be sorely tempted to transfer their discomfort onto the individual and treat him or her as the problem; it is the dissenters and not the organization that are choosing to make life difficult. The effect of this response on the dissenters is to silence their voices, but in the long run it could lead to the loss of key and highly committed people within the organization.

MORAL JEOPARDY AND DEMOCRACY

Communities and community organizations are continually in a position of weighing the good and less good aspects of dangerous consumptions such as alcohol and gambling. The way they choose to exercise their judgment on these is critical to determining both the sense of control and sustainability of their relationship to its use. A longer term consequence of gradual losses in an organization's independence and sovereignty is the subtle erosion of its capacity to participate actively in democratic processes. Sports clubs, charities, church and school committees, work social clubs, and hobby groups; from small local groups to large national NGOs; these all comprise the intricate web of interconnections that provide the base for social involvements. It is often through interactions in community groups that people form their views on social issues. Consequently, financial influence at a community level could go a long way in shaping public views on gambling. The charitable contributions of the gambling industry to public good activities quickly translate into community support for their developments and their recognition as responsible community benefactors.[20]

Governments have an opportunity to set out an environment that encourages low-risk involvements with charitable funding and consequently assists in reducing the risk to community organizations of high moral jeopardy. An environment in which large amounts of gambling-generated community benefit funds are circulating will, without any other measures, encourage community organizations to enter into relationships of increasingly higher moral jeopardy. This trend could be moderated by setting up brokerage agencies independent of industry sources or by restricting the visibility or promotional dimensions of the distribution, but, as discussed earlier, these strategies have weaknesses and therefore a limited life. A reliance on them does not in the end protect against progressive threats to perceived influence and control. A nation that values its democracy and the part community organizations play within it will appreciate the link between moral jeopardy and participation in democratic processes. While the next two chapters will shift the focus to examining depictions of gambling in the media, some potential responses to issues raised in this chapter will be examined toward the end of the book. Chapter 9 explores in detail potential safeguards that government agencies could put in place to protect community organizations from high moral jeopardy and Chapter 10 provides some specific strategies for reducing moral jeopardy.

5   Freedom in the Media

Freedom is a core part of any democracy, but as discussed in this book so far, notions of democracy and associated freedoms are multilayered, and this complexity creates opportunities to exploit their various meanings by channeling them in particular directions. In this chapter, I examine ways in which conceptions of freedom are utilized by gambling industry representatives and their allies. I argue that it is, ironically, through manipulations of understandings of freedom that gambling industry representatives seek to disguise the real threats to freedom and democracy that their activities pose. To illustrate this, the chapter draws on comments made through newspapers regarding the expansion of casinos in New Zealand.[1] Although the discussion is specific to a particular time and place, the processes and justifications described are common to other jurisdictions in which commercial gambling has expanded rapidly.[2]

The focus on media depictions is also important because it emphasizes the critical role media outlets play in maintaining the health of a democracy. Media organizations—typically made up of teams of editors and reporters—are doing more than simply reporting on events. They are also engaged in actively framing, positioning, and interpreting their subject matter in line with particular ways of looking at the world. Despite their assumptions, in the process of credentialing their accounts, they also attempt to portray their interpretation of events as nonpartisan and neutral. This is usually achieved by ensuring that strong examples of contrary positions are given equal weight. For instance, a newspaper article on gambling typically seeks to counterpose strong pro-industry views on gambling with strongly critical views. However, the use of contrary positions to foster the impression of neutrality is typically framed in ways that serve to convey less conspicuous underlying understandings.[3] For example, despite the inclusion of views from both camps, the choice to focus only on the rising numbers of problem gamblers leaves out the broader debate on how gambling impacts patterns of social involvement. In this way the constructed neutrality serves more to disguise the nonneutral intent of the key messages of the article. This chapter examines typical statements in print media regarding gambling proliferation and attempts to bring to the surface some of the underlying assumptions that are embedded in the accounts.

BECOMING A "REAL CITY"

Hamilton is a small inland city of New Zealand, located centrally in the heart of the Waikato region, a region identified as the ancestral homeland of the Tainui, a large Maori (indigenous New Zealanders) tribe. Maori currently comprise a significant portion (about one quarter) of the region's total population of approximately 400,000 people. The region consists of fertile farmland that stretches out across a green undulating landscape. Hamilton's central position within the region has enabled it to become a servicing center for its prosperous farming hinterland. Over the last century it has grown steadily from a sleepy small town to become New Zealand's fourth largest city with a population of around 120,000. Its consistent growth has attracted people from both within New Zealand and migrants from overseas countries. Many of these, including a large group of Maori, come from homes at the lower end of the economic ladder, and come mainly to improve the financial base for the future of their families.

Following the opening of New Zealand's first casinos—in Christchurch in 1994 and Auckland in 1996—other cities began vying for their chance for casino licenses, the main contenders being Dunedin, Queenstown, Wellington, Hamilton, and Rotorua. Dunedin and Queenstown were successfully granted licenses (two for Queenstown), but it was the more recent licensing process for the Hamilton casino that attracted national attention. People were interested in the Hamilton proceedings both because it was the last license to be granted before the government imposed a 3-year moratorium on further casinos and because of strongly organized local opposition. Two groups led the charge by presenting class objections to it being licensed: the Hamilton City Council and an interchurch coalition. Both groups presented arguments to the licensing authority on the negative impacts of the proposed casino. They pointed out that Hamilton as a location has little to attract tourists and differs from most other New Zealand cities in being located away from the coast. They noted that casinos in other cities in New Zealand had not led to large increases in outside visitors and that this casino would most likely cater to the local population. They also argued that on balance a casino would have detrimental effects on the quality of life for Hamiltonians by diverting money from other industries with greater development potential and reducing opportunities for those at lower income levels to improve their lot. Surveys indicated that these positions were supported by the majority of the Hamilton public and that social service agencies were concerned about potential increases in crime, family disruption, and mental health problems. The licensing authority, whose terms of reference then did not oblige them to take into account community views, favored granting the license. The objectors promptly sought a judicial review on the grounds that the members of the licensing body had demonstrated a preformed bias in favor of licensing throughout the hearings. The judge ruled in favor of the objectors, but in a subsequent high court review the previous judgment on bias was overturned and the objectors had to face the prospect of large legal bills and court costs.[4]

Media depictions of the Hamilton casino licensing process are interesting because they uncover a variety of ways in which the gambling industry and its allies attempt to advance their interests in the public eye. Embedded within these depictions, various conceptions of "freedom" play a critical role. In the early days of liberalization, depictions tended to emphasize the positive growth potential of having a casino:

> Tourism Waikato has already had an enthusiastic response to the casino from international tour operators: They say "finally Hamilton will be a real city." And the casino may also tip the balance in the conference market. "I've had nothing but positive reaction. The casino will lead the charge in nightlife in Hamilton. I know it will make a difference." (Pepperell, 1997, 14 June; *Waikato Times*)

The irony here is that many New Zealanders outside of Hamilton would still consider it a quiet provincial town, and would question whether a casino should be considered an appropriate symbol of urban sophistication. Nonetheless, a large number of Hamiltonians were keen to see further urban growth and were sympathetic to the increased opportunities associated with a casino. As more voices were heard pointing out the casino's potential for harm, other messages were required to maintain support for the project. In the following portion of a letter to the editor, the casino developer was positioned nobly against unreasonable onslaughts from health advocates.

> This bunch of professional wowsers and state-funded do-gooders has a track record of taking a blue-nosed stance on matters of morality or conscience ... The Sallies [Salvation Army] will appear at a meeting with the Compulsive Gambling Society to speak against Mr Perry's plans. This is like getting a bunch of fat people and drunks to lobby for closure of Hamilton's licensed restaurants. (Murphy, 1997, 7 June; *Waikato Times*)

With these strong words, the writer not only positions anticasino lobbyists as hypocrites, but implies they are advancing minor concerns at the expense of the freedom of the Hamilton public to access an important form of enjoyment. Shortly after the formal opening of the casino, a columnist in the local paper made the following claim:

Hamilton is no longer a boring provincial city. It's a go-ahead place, a metropolitan city which offers its populace a choice in what they can do. Put away your petitions for a while, people, and see what happens. It may not be as bad as you think. (Taylor, 2002, 20 July; *Waikato Times*)

The casino is now a reality; whatever one's views, it is here to stay. It now forms an integral part of the city and its citizens need to adapt to its presence. It has become a legitimate business that has a right like any other business to operate freely.

These excerpts identify ways in which casino advocates make use of common understandings to position their cause as part of a natural progression. Within these understandings concepts of freedom play a vital role. The following discussion concentrates on three ways of speaking about gambling that involve different conceptions of freedom. They are divided into stages to reflect their use in response to rising opposition to gambling expansion. During the first stage, talk is mainly about *freedom to innovate*, which emphasizes the positive opportunities gambling offers those progressive enough to embrace them. As public opposition mounts, the second stage switches to talk of *freedom to gamble*, where the emphasis is on avoiding restrictions to everyone's personal freedoms on the grounds that a few people are experiencing problems. The third stage emerges as the form of gambling finds itself reasonably established. Talk then switches to the language associated with *freedom to trade*, where industry providers are positioned as legitimate businesses alongside other legitimate businesses trading in products that form an integral part of the commerce of that society.

THREE FREEDOMS

In the 50 years prior to 1990, gambling in New Zealand was a highly regulated activity. Betting on horse races had formed a central part of popular culture, particularly for men. Other forms of gambling enjoyed predominantly by women included local church and community-run housie. Many families would purchase their weekly ticket in a national raffle called rather patriotically the Golden Kiwi. Although these forms of gambling were very popular, they were also tightly controlled and confined to a few specific times and locations. The population had become accustomed to the broad array of regulations that restricted the forms, locations, and availability of gambling products. The government was playing its role of protecting the public from harm much as overanxious parents might do in restricting their child's activities. In the mid-1980s a series of radical economic reforms ushered in an extended period of liberalization of marketing and regulatory regimes. For the economy to expand, the marketplace needed to be freed from unnecessary controls by government so that consumers are able to exercise greater influence over their choice of product. In line with this shift, many of the obstacles constraining gambling were removed. This opened the floodgates to a liberalized gambling industry. Motivation for the change was further reinforced by attempts to reduce the size and costs of government departments and to reduce the extent of personal and corporate tax liability. This meant the government was on the lookout for alternative taxation strategies and gambling provided a convenient source to supplement its denuding of the direct taxation base. These two factors—the liberalization of the marketplace and the government need for alternative sources of revenue—led to a series of changes in the regulation of gambling that progressively lifted constraints on the range, availability, and promotion of gambling products. The liberalization in gambling legislation and its consequent increase in the availability of gambling quickly led to unprecedented increases in consumer spending on gambling products. The population was on the whole unprepared for the world of commercialized continuous gambling that emerged in the 1990s. The government had switched in its protective role from an overanxious parent to a neglectful guardian that was abrogating its duty of care.

Freedom to Innovate

In the early phases of these changes, the New Zealand public was generally unaware and unconcerned about the consequences of liberalized gambling. Problems had been minor in the past, so there was little reason to worry about any increases, particularly if gambling provided a financial return to community projects. People who spoke out against more gambling were sometimes seen as somewhat reactionary and viewed almost as opposing change for the sake of it. In the following excerpt, the editor of the country's major Auckland-based daily newspaper took advantage of this perception:

> Gambling, it cannot be denied, has its problems. But are they "major," as that wowser-in-chief, the Minister of Internal Affairs, and his Greek chorus of psychologists and social workers aver, or is New Zealand gambling "modest" by world scales, as the executive director of the Lotteries Commission claims? (*NZ Herald*, December 1992)

The editor contrasted the reasonableness of a liberal approach to gambling against the knee-jerk puritanism of overprotective social guardians. His interpretation reflects the age-old struggle between progressives and conservatives, with progressives depicted as championing social and economic progress and conservatives depicted as "wowsers" and "alarmists." The characterization can be taken further by depicting opponents as backward luddites standing next to the progressiveness of those willing to embrace the new age of urban sophistication. Freedom-to-innovate thus becomes symbolically linked to all that is good about progress and development in modern times. The flavor of this is evident in comments made by Evan Davies, the chief executive of the newly opened SkyCity Casino in Auckland, when he commented regarding the licensing of a casino in New Zealand's capital city, Wellington:

> Thousands of Wellingtonians have already enjoyed casino experiences elsewhere. An appropriately sized gaming facility in the city would provide locals and visitors alike with one more reason to spend their entertainment dollar in the Capital. Wellingtonians are a sophisticated group of citizens who are free to choose how they spend their entertainment and leisure time. (*Wellington Evening Post*, June 1997)

The interpretation of freedom here links the freedom-to-innovate with the freedom of individuals to invest money as they see fit. This was illustrated further when, during debates about the licensing of the Dunedin casino, A. McDonald stated the following in a letter to the editor:

> The opinion expressed by opponents of casinos that they have a negative economic and social impact on a community is pure conjecture with no evidence to substantiate it. What about the negative economic and social impact of not enough business growth and industrial development? A significant proportion of Dunedin's population need more money in their pockets, and if cold water continues to be poured on business and industrial ventures there will be no increase in job opportunities, and we will indeed have a very nice-looking ghost town! (*Otago Daily Times*, October 1997)

As he portrayed, the unreasonable and spoilsport arguments of community advocates stand in the way of reasonable and progressive people who wish to assert their freedom to develop the best environment their city can generate.

Freedom to Gamble

As the consumption of gambling increased, there were discernable increases in the frequency with which people were seeking help for problem gambling. Figures on these increases were trickling out from helping agencies and reporters were drawn to quote them both because they were something new and because they generated controversy and heated debate. As a consequence of this attention, it became increasingly difficult for proliferation advocates to continue asserting that concerns about problem gambling were overexaggerated and alarmist. They required a new vehicle to support their ambitions, and at this stage talk switched from the simpler notion of freedom-to-innovate to the more complex area of individual freedom-to-gamble. The gist of this argument was expressed by a local Wellington politician in the following letter to the editor:

> In an age when how to spend increased leisure time is a significant social issue who are we to say that others should not be able to visit a casino in Wellington if that's their preference, especially when they can visit one in Christchurch and Auckland? The fact that it's Islamic fundamentalist closing down casinos in Turkey and Phillida Bunkle [opposition MP who opposes casinos] trying to stop them here should alert us all that this issue is as much about personal freedom as it is about casinos. (Rainbow, *Wellington Evening Post*, June 1997)

This argument has had a long history of use in promoting the availability of alcohol and tobacco, as indicated in by Bruce Robertson, chief executive of the Hospitality Association, when he stated:

> "It is a bit like smoking, people aren't going to give up until they want to. At the end of the day it comes down to individual responsibility," he says. "The important thing is that information is readily available to problem gamblers when they decide they need help" . . . "It's a matter of how much you restrict the majority for the sake of the minority and how effective those measures are." (*Host Responsibility*, November 2002)

In a similar vein, Malcolm Short, a local entrepreneur supporting the licensing of a casino in Rotorua, stated:

> My advice to George [Hawkins, Minister of Internal Affairs] and Maureen [Waaka, city counselor opposing casinos[5]], and the likes who are opposed to casinos is "don't go in them and stop dictating to other people what they can and can't do". Rotorua is getting left behind and we need to fight for our freedom of choice. (*Rotorua Daily Post*, November 27, 2002)

In each of these extracts, the "freedom of choice" of the majority is contrasted with the needs of a small group of people who are weak and would probably have succumbed to an addiction or another woe anyway. Little is gained by restricting freedoms of the majority and restrictions would only serve to reduce options for fun and enjoyment.

The platform used to justify this shift in focus toward the notion of freedom-to-gamble is supported by three interlocking planks. The first plank involves challenging the right of the state to impose moral values on the behavior of its citizens, particularly when harms associated with the behavior negatively affect very few people. This is captured in the following extract describing a prominent entrepreneur's response to the Wellington mayor changing his position from supporting to opposing the licensing of a new casino:

> While anti-casino opponents welcomed the mayor's turnaround, millionaire property developer Bob Jones told the council to stick to its business. "Who elected a bloke to look after drains and roads to make judgments on morals? Is he going to burn down churches which in my view do more harm than casinos? Casinos mop up idiots. It's none of his goddamn business." (*Wellington Evening Post*, June 1997)

Personal freedom-to-gamble is interpreted here to refer to the autonomy of individuals to make decisions without being controlled by moralistic agencies of the state. The second plank supporting the personal freedom argument involves locating the responsibility of problems associated with gambling as residing squarely on the shoulders of people affected and having little to do with the way gambling is being provided:

> [Christchurch] Casino chief Arthur Pitcher said the casino tended to get blamed for many social evils. "In reality, they see the casino as a focal point. Problem gamblers are problem people who go through drink, drugs or marriage break-ups. The casino becomes a vehicle people can blame." (Auckland's *Sunday Star-Times*, January 1996)

As signaled earlier, the third plank in the argument involves narrowing the responsibility down to a small group of people who cause the problems and the belief that their indiscretions cannot justify restricting the freedom-to-gamble for the public as a whole:

> Supporters, who include the Museum of New Zealand and some city councilors, can see only economic benefits. Some also take the view—not unreasonably, either—that individuals can exercise choice as to whether they darken the establishment's portals. Why, they ask, should those in the community who can't cope with the appeal of gambling penalize the majority who can? It's a question to which no opponent of the concept has yet given a convincing answer. (Editorial, *Wellington Evening Post*, April 1996)

As argued here, the freedoms of the majority of nonproblem, nonaddicted consumers are being sacrificed for a small minority who are weak-willed and ultimately undeserving of these special allowances.

The language of freedom-to-gamble and its advocacy for the rights of individuals to think and behave as they wish as long as it causes minimal harm to others is a strongly embedded resource in the discourses of Western democracies.[6] Taken to an extreme, however, or championed as the only interpretation of freedom, this approach begins to appear as lacking in balance. Even likely supporters started to indicate uneasiness about this lack of balance. In the following excerpt, Jack Elder, then the Minister of Internal Affairs (the ministry that administers gambling), commented after visiting Auckland's SkyCity Casino that he wondered whether the people sitting at their EGMs could afford to do what they are doing.

> I am not a spoilsport. I am a great believer in letting people do what they like. If people want to have a night out that's fine. But I see hundreds and hundreds of people sitting and playing on poker machines and . . . goodness me . . . I just hope the families are being fed this week. (Elder, 1997, January 17: *NZ Truth*)

Cleverly, the Minister paid homage to the importance of personal freedom to gamble, thereby positioning himself outside the circle of spoilsport anti-gambling fanatics. At the same time, however, he was willing to acknowledge uneasiness with the rising visibility of gambling. His uneasiness reflects what were then growing concerns regarding the unprecedented jumps in gambling consumption. In the 1990s, New Zealand was experiencing rapid and sustained increases in consumption that were driven primarily by the introduction of EGMs. Gambling expenditure (money lost[7]) rose from approximately $200 million in 1991 to $800 million by 2002 to $1,100 million in 2005, approximately half of which was attributable to EGMs both inside and outside of casinos.[8] This level of increase was difficult to hide and the rates of people seeking assistance for problem gambling were being reported with increasing concern. During the 2002 year, the total number of new clients using personal counseling was 2,467, up 15.1% from the previous year and up 177% from 6 years earlier. New callers in 2002 to a national telephone helpline numbered 4,715, up 23.6% from the previous year and up 131.9% from 6 years earlier. The primary mode of gambling for those seeking help had also changed in accordance with the increased availability of EGMs. In 1999, 70% of new personal counseling clients and 77% of new telephone helpline clients reported EGMs as their primary mode of gambling, but by 2002 this had risen to 86% for personal counseling and 90% for telephone helpline clients. Added to this were worrying increases in the numbers of problem gamblers seeking help in at-risk populations, particularly Maori, Pacific, and youth.[9]

In the face of growing concerns about reported increases in problem gambling, presentations of gambling in the mainstream media favored an increasingly critical perspective. Comments from community leaders such as the following became more commonplace:

> In sentencing Ian Yee, 34, last month for a $150,000 fraud, Judge Stephen Erber said he had heard the scenario of Yee, a gambling addict, too often.

Erber said Yee's gambling difficulty had started with gambling on horses and then proceeded to the Christchurch Casino.

"On what basis can it have been asserted that casinos are good for this city?" said Erber. "I haven't the slightest idea because manifestly many of the people who come before the court have got caught for gambling, having stolen from their employers or, in the case of professional men, from their clients." (*Christchurch Press*, June 1, 2004)

In the leading news pages of daily newspapers the views of community leaders and health advocates were becoming quoted more frequently and the views of the gambling industry were appearing less often. The main theme was that problem gambling was on the rise and that this was having serious impacts on society. Previous notions of problem gamblers as an insignificant group responsible for constraining individual freedom to gamble was seldom mentioned or implied. Problem gambling was now deemed a serious issue and warranted serious attention. Examples of typical newspaper headlines included statements such as these:

- Problem Gambling Epidemic
- Problem Gambling Spreading Across Classes
- Woman Faked Robbery to Fund Gambling
- Gambling Concern Focuses on Asians
- More Gamblers Ask for Help
- Addiction Blamed for Crimes
- Charities Hooked on Gambling
- Addicted Gamblers Losing Millions
- Youth Gambling Problem Grows
- Pokies Reach 'Excessive' Levels
- Pokie Machines Flooding NZ

Little else appeared to counter the predominantly critical flavor of these headlines. In effect, it was difficult to imagine how within this atmosphere of criticism the advantages of gambling could be advanced. The previous rhetoric concerned with freedom-to-innovate and individual freedom-to-gamble seemed lame in the face of this mounting outcry. The justification for gambling expansion required a new platform.

Freedom to Trade

In response to heavy criticism in the mainstream media of the Christchurch Casino for allowing a man to lose $7.4 million in its facilities, its chief executive, Arthur Pitcher, had the following to say:

We run a business. He used the business and the responsibility must stop with him. We can't be everybody's nanny and minder. It's extremely unfortunate. It does not help the image of casinos and does not help the business and allows all sorts of people to attack us without knowing the conditions we operate under. (*Christchurch Press,* February 28, 2003)

Pitcher's attempt to justify allowing this man to continue his excessive gambling called on support from the previous arguments built on the freedom-to-gamble, but he also brought into his justification a different dimension. He stated emphatically that gambling must be seen as a business, meaning more explicitly that it needs to be seen as a legitimate business alongside other legitimate businesses.

Pitcher's outburst in the mainstream media had become an unusual event. From the early 2000s on, perhaps in recognition of their overwhelming negative coverage in the main body of newspapers, spokespeople for the industry tended to avoid providing explicit justifications for their activities, instead preferring to retreat either into the business columns or into industry-specific publications such as the Hospitality Association's *Hospitality.* For example, in the business columns of New Zealand's largest daily newspaper, Carolyn Hobson, the Host Responsibility Manager for Auckland's SkyCity Casino, was quoted as saying:

"I lobbied to have a host responsibility department established at SkyCity because I believe that responsible hosting is a fundamental element for SkyCity's long-term sustainability as a business." (*NZ Herald,* June 2, 2004)

The shift to the business columns reinforces the impression that gambling is an integral and legitimate part of the commercial life of the nation's economy. Later in the same article when asked what she considered as evidence of success, she responded:

"SkyCity [is] being acknowledged by the community as a responsible business. My role not being [may not be] needed any more because the programs have become an established part of our customer service." (*NZ Herald,* June 2, 2004)

The article does not attempt to discuss or challenge issues associated with the negative impact of the casino on the local community; that discussion belongs to earlier sections of the newspaper, a discussion from which casino spokespeople have withdrawn.

The transfer of industry discussion of itself to the business columns reinforces the central message of freedom-to-trade. Casinos as legitimate businesses have a right to stand alongside other businesses in reporting on their operations and their development in a way that is free from the complications of social debate. Discussion of their activities could now switch to talk of business, markets, shareholders, profits, growth, and so forth. For instance, the chief executive of the Auckland Casino was quoted as seeing

> . . . significant opportunities for domestic growth.
>
> The market was still relatively immature and action undertaken by the company to refurbish and develop its operations "all provide a foundation for some solid growth."
>
> Growth opportunities in Australia and New Zealand would be principally organic.
>
> "The sector has rationalized itself now, to the extent that there is a small number of reasonably large players and I think rationalization or acquisition is going to be limited." (*NZ Herald*, October 28, 2006)

This way of speaking is now liberated from the hampering moral and ethical concerns associated with harm from gambling. Casinos as legitimate businesses join the ranks of other businesses in a world focused on ownership and development.

> SkyCity has moved to full ownership of the Hamilton casino, acquiring the outstanding shares plus retail and office space in the Waikato city for a total of $37 million.
>
> SkyCity said yesterday it had reached an agreement to acquire Riverside Trust's 30 per cent equity in the casino for $33 million, making it the 100 per cent owner.
>
> "This is a sound commercial decision and one we are confident our shareholders will support," SkyCity managing director Evan Davies said.
>
> "SkyCity Hamilton has performed well since opening and, as the majority shareholder and operator of the business, we were naturally interested in acquiring full ownership." (*NZ Herald*, May 11, 2005)

The business orientation inherent to freedom-to-trade also enables shifts in the way responses to problem gambling are interpreted. As with freedom-to-gamble, the seriousness of problem gambling is acknowledged, but it is reconceptualized in business terms as an unfortunate by-product that can be managed using appropriate business strategies. For example, Rod McGeoch, chair of the SkyCity board, stated while reporting to an annual meeting of shareholders:

> We agree that attention must be paid to people in the community who are not able to manage their gaming activity, but we stress that, like all things, an appropriate balance must be maintained between protection mechanisms for at risk persons and freedom of choice for the wider community.

This balance of protection mechanisms versus the right of the wider community to select its entertainment options is a key challenge facing the gaming sector as the various parties confront the issues and consider how best to put in place relevant and sustainable regulatory frameworks and structures. (*NZ Press Association,* October 28, 2005)

These "protection mechanisms" and "regulatory frameworks" convey the impression that these legitimate businesses are supporting appropriate technologies for the effective containment and management of problem gambling.[10]

The delivery of freedom-to-trade is supported by three levels of argument. First, it involves recognizing that high-frequency gambling is here to stay; it is an established part of current lifestyles alongside other legalized products such as alcohol, cinemas, and amusement parks. For example, Paul East, speaking as Chair of the Charity Gaming Association, declared that:

Gambling is part and parcel of life in New Zealand and Australia. Our people are industrious, self-reliant and able to make their own decisions about their lives. The industry provides recreation and enjoyment for many and the substantial sums raised by gaming make an enormous contribution to a large number of worthwhile causes. (*Hospitality,* October 2002, p. 43)

The second aspect of freedom-to-trade is recognition that, as with other businesses in modern economies, success requires an environment in which trade can proceed without the unnecessary impediments of minority interests. For example, the Auckland Casino company responded to new regulations for EGMs in the following way:

SkyCity Entertainment remains critical of "draconian" regulations to curb problem gambling, but views the appointment of new Gaming Minister Rick Barker as positive:
"We're looking forward with rather more encouragement than we would look back," managing director Evan Davies said of the Government. (*NZ Herald,* October 29, 2005)

It is a familiar argument. What would happen to the meat industry, medical science industry, and cosmetics industry if animal rights activists had their way? Businesses, especially well-established and socially accepted businesses, require an optimal level of freedom to trade without undue interference, otherwise they would lose their competitive edge and would languish fatally within a constantly changing marketplace. In the following quote, Bill McLean writing on behalf of the Hospitality Association, captured the flavor of this position:

The Association today continues to represent the [EGM gambling] industry on many of the same issues. On legislative issues, we are faced by a Parliament obsessed with protecting the minority through controlling the majority. It seems that in today's environment, self-responsibility has been replaced with collective mediocrity. (*Hospitality,* November 2002)

"Collective mediocrity" would presumably provide a dampener to the development of a progressive industry.

The third aspect of freedom-to-trade, already signaled in previous quotes, involves recognizing that trade in gambling products not only comprises a legitimate business but also contributes positively to communities and to the overall good of society. This positive contribution is captured—somewhat ambiguously—by the manager of a service providing early childhood care for poorer families who had recently received funding from a casino:

Christine Canty denies the group is compromising itself by accepting the casino generated funds.

But Mrs Canty admits problem gambling is a serious issue facing many West Auckland families.

"By applying for some of their trust money we can start putting bandages on those problems," she says. "There are so many families out there who can't afford full kindergarten sessions for their children. We are seeing families coming out of tragic homes. So by applying this money the children can come along and get some good education in a warm and loving environment." (*Western Leader,* May 13, 2004)

This public good argument is not only a feature of casino advocacy, but is also linked to promotional activities in other gambling sectors. For example, Trevor Hall, chief executive of the New Zealand Lotteries Commission, identified the strong contribution national lottery products make to community development:

I think we have been very remiss in not reminding the New Zealand public about the amount of benefit Lotto provides to the community every single day . . . If you walk into a dairy and you've got a choice of buying a Moro Bar or a $1 Instant Kiwi[11] . . . It's the same discretionary dollar that we're both fighting for. Which is why, like any consumer goods organization, we've got to increase our offering and increase our visibility. (*NZ Herald,* May 29, 2003)

Lotteries, casinos, horse betting, and EGM providers maintain constant reference to their concrete contributions to community projects that spin out from their sales of gambling products. Their efforts position gambling providers in the familiar role of philanthropic industrialists, a role established by major industrialists in the United States—people such as Nelson Rockefeller, Dale Carnegie, and Bill Gates—who made massive contributions to social programs that have formed an important part of the backbone of capitalist society.[12] The ostensive benevolence of gambling providers implies they are not only legitimate businesses but are also good corporate citizens. It thereby reinforces the impression that these legitimate businesses are undeniably worthy of their freedom-to-trade. These sentiments were captured by Peter Dunne, the leader of the government coalition party United Future, when he highlighted the critical importance of their social contributions:

> United Future believes passionately in the importance of the family as the key building block of our society. But we also believe that strong and healthy families live in vibrant communities, which have the facilities like schools, swimming pools, parks and other amenities and the infrastructure through clubs and community activities. And the blunt reality is that much of this is provided through the proceeds of gaming. (*Johnsonville Norwester*, April 30, 2003)

He boldly linked the well-being of families and communities to the "infrastructural" contributions by gambling industries—an interesting position for a member of the New Zealand Government's Cabinet. What his statement also signals is that as a consequence of their contribution to communities, industry representatives no longer need to advocate for expansion because they now have a strong cohort of community groups that willingly advocate on their behalf. The following extract is typical of this advocacy:

> John Davies says gaming trusts are doing a huge amount for the education of New Zealanders. The Blockhouse Bay Primary School principal has used grants from small groups such as the Portage Trust to pay for "luxuries" such as a computer laboratory, sports equipment, televisions, learning resources and property development. He says the Government demands quality education but fails to provide "quality funding" to support that demand.
> Many parents would probably not contemplate the amount of money that came to schools from the pokies. And although Mr Davies, who has been principal at the West Auckland school for 17 years, admits it is a moral dilemma, it is not one he will lose sleep over. "My job is to deliver a high-quality education to the kids and if I have to get pokie money to do that, I will." (*NZ Herald*, September 16, 2004)

The issue of community sector recruitment into legitimizing gambling expansion has already received coverage in Chapters 2 and 4, and is explored further in Chapter 9.

POINTS OF RESISTANCE

Gambling industry constructions of freedom in the media have not occurred uncontested. As identified earlier, casino advocates who used the freedom-to-innovate were eventually challenged by those who contrasted development claims with the costs incurred by rising rates of problem gambling. In the next stage, allegiance to individual freedom-to-gamble was contrasted negatively with the gathering evidence that this choice was coming at the cost of wider and substantial social and economic impacts. During the third stage, the freedom-to-trade as legitimate businesses, a strong counterresponse has yet to fully emerge, but early signs suggest that couching discussion in the language of business does not necessarily insulate it from questions of morality. For example, tobacco products and fatty fast-food outlets are legitimate businesses, but the morality of their proliferation is increasingly contested.

Behind each of these counterresponses lies the belief that although individual freedoms should continue to be protected, understandings of freedom cannot be wholly reduced to the level of the individual. The freedoms of individuals also need to be balanced against the freedoms of the collective. In direct response to a casino executive's argument regarding the positive contribution of casinos, R. Corner, in a letter to the editor stated:

> Mr Davies [CEO for Auckland's Casino] trumpets the millions of dollars paid in taxes, levies and charity . . . Mr Davies makes great play in his letter about freedom of choice. Surely the freedom of choice relevant here is the freedom of choice a whole community should have as to whether it wants an enterprise such as this in its midst. (*Wellington Evening Post*, June 1997)

This quote signals a critical alternative to these and other constructions of freedom. The notion of *collective freedom* moves from reductions of freedom to the ability of individuals (or organizations) to behave as they choose, to freedom in terms of the ability for a society as a whole to achieve where it chooses to go. With fewer problem gamblers, more families can achieve increased and more meaningful participation in their communities and those communities can achieve greater interconnectedness. With less gambling, poorer and more vulnerable people have a better chance of building up their strengths and accordingly that society achieves greater cohesion. Access to EGMs in a bar, at a local casino, or on the Internet is a freedom of sorts, but it is a pallid freedom when contrasted with the collective freedoms that result when a whole community or society achieves something it could not have achieved otherwise.

A second aspect to collective freedom is questioning what is understood as "the collective." In several of the earlier quotes, collective benefit is understood as referring to the benefit of improved business activity, the benefit of people who like to gamble, or even the benefit of particular trading organizations. These groups could be fairly sizable, but are they exactly what is understood when people refer to a benefit to society? As John Beishuizen, a local budget service advisor, commented:

> Pokies are good for business, tourism and entertainment but the fact is we as a society will suffer. Are we living for our society or for the tourists? Where is the compassion? (*Rodney Times,* August 7, 2003)

Talk about a "society" or a "community" does involve reference to an amorphous mass of individuals, but it also refers to something more than the aggregate sum of those individuals. The notion of a collective incorporates the idea that social groupings function as entities in their own right; that they involve structures and processes that are necessary in determining the level of integrity in their own functioning. Consequently, although problem gambling can impact on the freedoms of an individual and surrounding loved ones, what is of more significance is that the loss of a functioning family in the collective has ripple effects that will impact on the freedom and integrity of the social system as a whole. As the scale of the problem grows, so the impacts on the collective infrastructure become more acute.

A further aspect to collective freedom pertains to widening the focus to include notions of collective responsibility. Just as a society is comprised of both the individuals within it and the structures and processes that enable it to function, so reference to the gambling industry refers to the organizations that create and market the product as well as the wider networks that enable those organizations to flourish. In a commentary section of a major daily newspaper, Stevenson wrote:

> "New Zealand is fortunate that charitable trusts operate gaming machines, so all the profits go back to our communities," said the five trusts, which operate a third of the country's non-casino pokie machines . . .
>
> "This is much better than allowing commercial operators to earn millions of dollars of profit from gambling," they advised readers loftily.
>
> But how much better? Does it matter to the hungry family of an out-of-control gambler who is profiting from their food money? Does it matter to the suicidal gambler whose pockets his or her addiction has lined?
>
> Probably not. I doubt very much whether the families know or the gambler cares one whit that some of those hard-earned or stolen dollars poured into pokies will end up providing uniforms for the local touch team or books for the school library.
>
> A key question, which seems rarely addressed, is whether it should matter to all those community groups who line up each year for the largess of gaming trusts that they are profiting from some of the least well-off in their communities. (*NZ Herald,* June 22, 2004)

She was calling on individuals and community organizations that benefit from gambling to consider the part they play in the broader context of gambling expansion. With collective freedoms come collective responsibilities, and those responsibilities apply not only to changes imposed by gambling providers, but also to organizations that assist in this process.

In 2006 the Hamilton casino had been open for 4 years. Since that time, local newspapers have continued to track its development in their business columns, local people have comprised the largest group of customers, and casino and EGM problem gambling has increased considerably.[13] As the scale of organized commercial gambling increases, so does its capacity to influence media depictions of gambling. The threat to democracy of most concern here is the capacity of a strengthening gambling provider sector to engage media outlets and to influence public discourse in ways that advantage their business. Conceptualizations of freedom cut to the core of what it is to be a democracy and, as already illustrated, three variants have been used at different times by industry spokespeople to positively reposition their products within the flow of public opinion. This is to be expected. As with any profit-oriented business, they will of course continue to engage public relations firms and employ their own staff and consultants to facilitate how they communicate in the public arena.[14] The challenge for public health advocacy is to constantly devise and adapt counterresponses that ensure that compromise does not occur in either public understandings of gambling or in the ability to make informed judgments. For this reason, it becomes increasingly important to track the twists and turns in gambling provider rhetoric concerning their own development. Although public health practitioners lack the public communication opportunities of gambling providers, they are still capable of generating opportunities for communicating messages that can assist in developing a critical eye on proexpansion hype.

6   Gambling Advertising

An important part of the industrial complex that drives the expansion of commercial gambling is the expanding business of gambling advertising. As gambling consumption increases, companies invest more in advertising and other promotional activities. For example, in Australia, clubs, pubs, taverns, and bars with gambling facilities increased their expenditure on advertising, marketing, and promotion from an average in 1994–1995 of $16,837 per business to $49,741 per business by 1997–1998, a threefold increase over approximately 3 years.[1] For the same period, total annual expenditure on the advertising, marketing and promotion on Australian casinos rose from $71 million to $102 million (Australian Bureau of Statistics, 2002). Similar proportions are observable in other locations. For example, in the Canadian province of Ontario, with a total net expenditure on gambling of $5.04 billion, the total expenditure in 2004 on marketing, promotions, and "promotional allowances" was $466 million, about 9.3% of expenditure.[2] Despite the scale of increased investment, little is available in the public domain on the role this advertising plays in the behavior of gamblers. Some researchers have commented generally on the important part advertising plays in assisting in the proliferation of gambling (see Becona et al., 1995; Lorenz, 1990). For example, Pugh and Webley (2000) surveyed 256 adolescents in the United Kingdom and found that 56% had participated illegally in National Lottery online gambling and that watching the TV show was one of the best predictors of participation. Nonetheless, the small amount of research specifically into gambling advertising has focused very little attention on the processes by which gambling advertising achieves its effects. Public domain research has yet to explore the nature and function of mechanisms employed in making gambling advertisements a worthy investment.

Advertising, marketing, and other promotional activities can be seen as playing a part in the contribution of gambling to the degradation of democratic systems. Particularly in a population naive to the broader impacts of widespread gambling, advertising can serve to both shape and divert public consciousness in ways that weaken public understanding and reduce support for pockets of resistance. For example, those speaking out in opposition to the licensing of a local casino are unlikely to obtain widespread support when the main message the public is receiving is derived from the high-profile contribution the casino company is making to community charities. The general normalization of gambling might not have been their primary intent, but the use of such promotions inevitably casts gambling in a positive light and, together with other promotions, they cumulatively sway hearts and minds in ways that influence the broader political ecology. This normalization helps isolate the dissident as a temperance-oriented, puritanical spoilsport bent on ruining what the majority enjoy as a part of everyday life. Regardless of whether it is true or false, the promotions accentuate the positive contribution of gambling to societal well-being and gloss over and minimize its negative impacts.

This chapter examines the potential for theories in the social sciences to improve understanding of the role advertising plays in the current global expansion of commercial gambling. It divides these theories into two main explanatory paradigms: The first set comes from the discipline of psychology, the other from the much older study of rhetoric. Before examining how gambling advertising achieves its effects, we first need to consider what it is intended to achieve.

FUNCTIONS OF GAMBLING ADVERTISING

In information presented to the Australian Federal Government Productivity Commission during its comprehensive review of gambling industries, a gambling industry source acknowledged that 80% of its revenue comes from 20% of heavy users (Wunsch, 1998). The Australian Productivity Commission's (1999) own research indicated that the average estimated annual expenditure was $9,558 for problem gamblers compared to $505 for nonproblem gamblers—19 times greater for problem gamblers than nonproblem gamblers. In their national survey of 10,500 Australians, they calculated that 33% of all gambling expenditure (losses) was attributable to problem gamblers, with the share reaching 42% for EGMs. Because higher consumption of gambling is done by a smaller subsection of the population, it makes logical sense for advertisers to focus their energies on grooming and maintaining that subsection. Advertising that shifts a very occasional gambler to a slightly more frequent gambler will have marginal impacts on income, particularly when attracting and retaining a few frequent gamblers will result in far greater income. Consequently, the logical place to focus promotions is on people who are either currently frequent gamblers or likely to become frequent gamblers.

Gambling and other dangerous consumption industries commonly defend their use of advertising by claiming it is not primarily aimed at increasing overall consumption; rather, it serves to increase adherence to one brand over another. The purpose is to convince people that gambling is more fun at this venue than another venue, with this product rather than another product, at this time rather than another time, and so on. This argument has some merit in contexts where overall consumption is stable, but in a context where consumption is rapidly rising, it makes more sense to view company profitability less as a product of carving a share of the current market and more as a product of opening up new markets. Consequently, this chapter assumes that a central goal of current gambling advertising is to increase the consumption of gambling by increasing the likelihood of high-frequency gambling. This position assumes that once a person initiates a session of gambling, the behavior itself has enough intrinsic incentives to turn an intended brief involvement into a lengthier event. With the maintenance of frequent gambling understood as a key goal, and population clusters of frequent gamblers understood as the key focus, gambling advertising can be seen to contribute to consumption increases in the following three ways: (a) *recruitment,* or increasing the chances of becoming a frequent gambler; (b) *retention,* or increasing the probability that frequent gamblers keep gambling frequently; and (c) *normalization,* or increasing the likelihood that the general population will view frequent gambling as acceptable. These three functions are depicted in Figure 6.1 across a variable age continuum. The target window focuses energy on the recruiting and retaining of gamblers into a bulge of probable frequent gambling. This bulge could occur at different ages and for different lengths of time. For instance, it could involve a young man over a 10-year period, a woman in midlife during a brief crisis period, or an older woman coping with long periods of social isolation and loneliness. Through market research, the likely bulges are identified, thereby setting the advertisers' focus on recruitment, retention, and normalization. The following sections examine these functions more closely in turn.

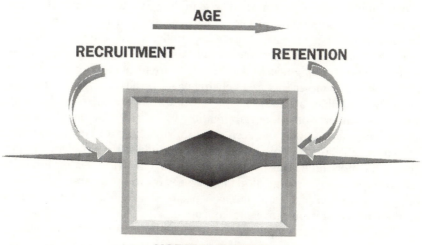

Figure 6.1 Representation of the Three Main Functions of Gambling Advertising

Recruitment

Recruitment strategies aim to encourage people on the edge or approaching a frequent gambling cluster to begin exploring such enjoyment for themselves. For example, in many contexts, a high proportion of young men between the ages of 18 and 24 are frequent gamblers. The key task in recruitment is to ensure that as young men approach the critical age, say between 14 and 17 years old, the factors and influences that promote frequent gambling are sufficient to lead them to begin participating. Once they are participating regularly, the chances increase that they will move on to become frequent gamblers.

Retention

Once people have entered a target demographic zone, and have indeed engaged in frequent gambling, the aim of retention is to ensure their involvement is maintained. For example, in some locations, women with low incomes are frequent visitors to large urban casinos. Their regular gambling is triggered by a range of factors, such as boredom at home, the desire for excitement, being among other people, and obtaining some discretionary income. Retention strategies in advertising aim to reinforce associations with factors that maintain the involvement. For instance, the advertisement might aim to remind women isolated at home that gambling provides a reprieve from home drudgery. The advertisement thereby encourages them to stay in the frequent gambling zone for as long as possible.

Normalization

Advertising strategies that normalize gambling aim to influence the views of the general population in ways that raise the general acceptability of frequent gambling. This increased acceptability serves multiple functions. In the first place, it influences recruitment by decreasing the chances of any potential negative judgments associated with frequent gambling. For example, the young gambler is more likely to engage if the remainder of the family actively gambles and has positive attitudes toward their involvements. Second, normalization supports retention by reducing potential concerns about frequent gambling and decreasing the possibility of being questioned or challenged. For example, it can help camouflage the problem gambler among the more numerous moderate gamblers. Finally, normalization helps improve the positive image of gambling in ways that encourage the whole population to consider gambling as a positive and life-enhancing activity and downplaying its negative consequences.

The next two sections provide overviews of theory that can be usefully applied to gambling advertising. They explore opportunities within two parallel explanatory paradigms and review each theory in terms of their relative contribution to recruitment, retention, and normalization.

PSYCHOLOGICAL EXPLANATIONS

The discipline of psychology provides the first explanatory paradigm within which a range of theories can be used to shed light on the functions of gambling advertising. Three theories have been picked out to illustrate the wealth of explanations available. Explanations are not limited to these theories, but they give a good idea of the future potential of psychology in understanding the role of this form of advertising.

Social Learning

We often learn how to respond in new environments by watching the behavior of those around us and looking carefully at the positive and negative consequences they encounter. Social learning theory, as developed by Bandura (1977), highlights how considerable learning occurs by watching the ways in which others are rewarded or "reinforced" for certain ways of behaving. *Reinforcement* refers simply to an event that increases the probability of an associated behavior. Bandura pointed out that not only is behavior reinforced directly by receiving solid gains, but also by observing how others achieve gains or rewards. This "vicarious reinforcement" relies on the observer identifying in some way with an observed role model and watching the positive association of certain behaviors with certain consequences. In the initial studies, Bandura and Walters (1963) asked children to observe adults expressing moral viewpoints and later observed the children discussing viewpoints that they had changed in the direction of those expressed by the adults. In a related study, Bandura and McDonald (1963) asked children to observe an adult "model" interacting in a variety of ways with large dolls. The modeled behaviors included hitting and saying statements such as "Biff!" and "Take that!" to the doll. When the children were given the chance, they displayed many of the same behaviors towards the dolls that they had observed with the model. The researchers saw the children as having vicariously acquired specific behaviors by watching how somebody else had been rewarded. They went on to show how this aggressive behavior could also be modeled using animated cartoon figures (see Bandura, Ross, & Ross, 1953).

Gambling industry sponsorship of current public heroes, such as prominent sports personalities or famous actors, is the clearest application of social learning theory. Along with many large corporations, gambling providers expend large sums of money to engage sports, arts, and charity events to display their insignias and company identifiers. Common examples include a national lotteries logo being displayed as part of sponsoring a national music competition, a casino logo being displayed on the uniform of prominent sporting teams, and the name of an EGM provider presented as the major sponsor of a local charity. The link between symbols of success and symbols of gambling are progressively strengthened by repeated exposures in billboards, newspaper advertisements, and promotional events. The strength of this link will determine the potency of the learning. The prominent sports team that wears a gambling company logo has the advantage of frequent presentation and wide coverage, but the link to the rewards from gambling behavior is relatively weak. A more potent image would involve an individual sports hero next to or inside a gambling venue, such as the commencement of an international car rally from outside a casino. An even more potent form of modeling would involve the image of a sports hero actually participating in gambling itself and appearing to enjoy it. The viewers identifying with the sports hero would instantly connect with the potential for similar enjoyment for themselves. Some casino promotions will combine all three levels of intensity. For example, a motorsports rally sponsored by a casino would have its logo prominently displayed on most television coverage, the event could start outside the casino, and images of famous rally drivers are likely to be published with them attending dinners in the casino and perhaps playing on casino EGMs. The young person keen on motorsports and identifying strongly with the success of leading drivers will take in all these images, see the enjoyment and endorsement of gambling working for their heroes, and begin to consider the prospects of similar rewards for themselves.

The use of modeling and other forms of vicarious reinforcement do not require strong previous exposures to gambling, and for that reason they are ideal for the purpose of recruiting new gamblers. Their effectiveness relies more on the recipient's ability to identify with an already familiar and positively valued role model. For example, Jamie is an avid follower of the National Football League. He spends considerable amounts of time watching games, reading about them, and discussing their merits with friends. He also spends time thinking about the players, visualizing how he would handle situations, and identifying himself with the struggles and triumphs of his favorite team heroes. Their wins are his wins, their losses are his losses, and their choices are his choices. Although he has not as yet engaged in much gambling, the sight of his favorite player wearing the logo of a local casino sends a variety of compelling signals. If his favorite player is rewarded with an association with gambling, then so can he; if the team's success is linked to gambling, then so might he experience similar success. In this way the linkages within the advertising provide the groundwork for prospective gamblers to see gambling as a desirable activity to pursue.

Classical Conditioning

Classical conditioning is a potent form of learning that relies on multiple exposures to a particular environment. The process starts with a neutral object or "unconditioned stimulus," such as the sound of a buzzer, then is presented repeatedly over time at roughly the same time as an object that has strong rewarding properties, such as food or sex. Eventually the unconditioned stimulus changes to become a conditioned stimulus capable of eliciting the types of reactions normally associated with the rewarding object. In his classic experiment, dating back more than 80 years, Pavlov (1927) repeatedly placed samples of meat powder before a hungry dog while presenting a bright light. It was not long before the dogs salivated to the light alone. The neutral light becomes, over time, a conditioned stimulus capable of eliciting the types of behaviors, in this case salivation, previously associated only with the food. Pavlov argued that the processes of classical conditioning are useful in explaining much behavior associated with potent appetites, particularly those connected with the use of food, sex, wealth, prestige, alcohol, drugs, and achievement. Its power is most pronounced in highly exaggerated appetitive behaviors such as sexual fetishism and intravenous drug user needle fixations.

The rewarding properties associated with a win from gambling provide a potent base for the same conditioning process. Initially the motivation to gamble will be driven by the inherent properties associated with winning. The desire to gamble is cued in simply by thinking about the big win. Indeed, the frequent gambler over time will experience many small wins, some moderate wins, and probably the occasional big win. These wins occur in environments surrounded by sights, sounds, smells, and tactile sensations. The environments might vary, but some features are likely to recur across each winning situation, particularly when the gambler sticks to one mode of gambling. As with Pavlov's dog, the rewarding events become increasingly associated with key recurring features of that environment. The symbols in the reel spin, the sight of the betting page, the chunking of coin delivery from a EGM win, the tactile feel of the betting slips; each of these unconditioned stimuli can over time acquire conditioned properties such that by itself it is capable of triggering the motivation to gamble. Problem gamblers[3] particularly attest to the power of this conditioning process; they describe a wide range of stimuli reminding them and retriggering their interest in gambling. These stimuli—the sight of a betting shop, the sound of horse races on the radio, even the smells emanating from an EGM bar—are enough to activate compelling thoughts and desires capable of triggering bouts of gambling.

Television and radio advertisements frequently combine images or sounds associated with the paraphernalia of gambling. Horse racing advertisements typically overlay speech with the sound of horses' hooves, the cheer of a crowd, or the distinctive sound of a horse-racing commentator. People who have had long or potent exposures to gambling in those environments have learned to link rewarding or positive experiences with key aspects of the environment in which this has occurred. For example, casino television advertisements often combine their messages with familiar sights and sounds from casino environments: the same upbeat music, flashing lights and colors, and the sound of coins entering the slot. These serve both to link the message with the sensations and to engage the attention of those with previous histories with that environment. Their most effective use relies on a prior history of conditioning. The environmental cues would have very little natural influence until a period of multiple exposures alongside strongly rewarding events, which means that low-frequency gamblers are less likely to be responsive to the paraphernalia of gambling. The frequent gambler, with a long history of pairing sights and sounds with gambling and winning, will be far more likely to respond to the images as stand-alone cues. For this reason, the classical conditioning aspects of gambling advertising are arguably focused more on the frequent gambler, that is, those more likely to be problem gamblers. The advertising aims primarily to retain the participation of those who have already experienced a long involvement with gambling. It cues in the desire to gamble and thereby increases the probability of continuing to gamble. What is also interesting is that people other than frequent gamblers are unlikely to be aware of the potency of this process. The sights and sounds in gambling advertisements that appear to the infrequent gambler as relatively neutral, to the frequent gambler are imbued with a wide variety of potent associations. For this reason, gambling advertisers can disguise the true potency of their advertisements on frequent gamblers by referring selectively to the more neutral perceptions of infrequent gamblers.

Social Identity

Social identity theory emerged within social psychology in the 1970s and 1980s as a way of explaining how people behave in groups and how they form and make use of their group memberships in constructing their sense of self (Tajfel, 1982, outlined this theory). A basic assumption is that the way people behave in groups cannot be adequately explained by focusing on the psychology and behavior of individuals.[4] The psychological explanations of group behavior might rely on quite different principles. In the Sherifs' classic studies (see Sherif, 1967), 11- to 12-year-old boys attending a summer camp were arbitrarily assigned into two groups living separately and were gradually introduced to tasks of increasing competitiveness. Part of the study identified how group belongingness was facilitated by creating symbols of identity, such as the use of nicknames, jokes, jargon, and the use of special names for their group with associated symbols such as flags and logos. Even when one group was deprived of sufficient resources, and as a result consistently lost to the other group, the boys responded by strengthening their group identity and intensifying their use of associated symbols. The Sherifs' observations on the power of group identity were further explored by Tajfel,[5] who set out to examine how social categories in themselves are an important influence on social behavior. The material often used in building self-identity is derived from social memberships: being female, being young, being European, living in one part of a city, and so on. What is important here is that a social category and clear membership of that category is critical in itself in building up one's social identity. Furthermore, people will often defend these group affiliations far beyond their merit.[6] The process by which one comes to identify with a particular group might have happened in an arbitrary fashion, but once part of the group, the membership itself has meaning and potency; accordingly, effort is put in to maintaining it.

The tension between being inside a group (the "in-group") relative to belonging outside (the "out-groups") is exploited in advertisements to enhance group-based identifications with the product. For example, beer advertisers targeting adolescent males often link their brand to the positive symbols of particular in-group identities of young men who differentiate themselves from a comparison out-group who prefer another brand. In-group and out-group identifications can occur at several levels simultaneously. All people's identities are composed of multiple layers of these memberships; for example, John is a father, but he is also a baker, a drummer, and enjoys wine tasting. Within each of these strands by which he defines himself lie in-group/out-group differences through which he knows who he is and who he is not: John is not childless, he does not play the piano, and so on. His memberships of social categories are important, and, according to Tajfel, have a currency of their own. Advertisements seek to capitalize on this powerful social process by linking products to potent symbols of in-group/out-group memberships. They often do this by depicting contrasts between attractive in-groups and undesirable out-groups. In gambling advertising, one way of doing this is to contrast the in-group of "winners" with the out-group of "losers." Consider the following slogans from lottery advertisements:

- Win, win, win!
- We dare you to win.
- Play to win!
- $5 Million: It could be yours this week.
- You're a winner!

For most people, day-to-day existence involves a fluctuating course of winning and losing, but the prospect of this turning into consistent losses, in other words to become a loser—or even worse to be seen as a loser—poses a threatening and undesirable group membership. The suggestion in these advertisements that "you are a winner" links the product to highly desirable group affiliation.

Perhaps a more potent way for advertising to exploit these in-group/out-group affiliations is through visual images. Gambling advertisements frequently throw up pictures with symbols of desirable group membership. In casino advertisements the players around the roulette table appear sociable, wealthy, and sexy. In track betting advertisements, the people watching the race appear friendly, successful, and good looking. These are in-groups of people to which one would clearly want to belong; by implication, the out-group of wowsers, spoilsports, and nongamblers is a membership to be avoided. These in-group/out-group identities could be seen to contribute both to the recruitment and retention of frequent gamblers, but their primary function is to present gambling as a normal social activity. The messages and images suggest that going to the racetrack or the casino is something that desirable people do. In this way the processes associated with social identity are applied to normalize gambling as a positive, gregarious, and desirable part of everyday life.

RHETORICAL EXPLANATIONS

The second explanatory paradigm is derived from the ancient and complex discipline of rhetoric. Rhetoric as a study of persuasive communication focuses more on the way something is expressed than what is expressed. However, in so doing, rhetoricians avoid claiming that rhetoric could ever replace having something to say; they contend merely that the manner of delivery plays an important part in determining how a message is received.[7] The study of rhetoric has a long history. In Greco-Roman times rhetoric maintained a prominent position in formal education (Howes, 1961). The ability to communicate ideas in a persuasive manner was seen as indispensable to public careers and the orderly management of the state. Major works such as Aristotle's third book of his *Rhetoric* and Quintilian's *Institutio Oratoria*[8] became basic texts and, as the Sophists had advocated, an understanding of rhetoric, especially in its verbal form of oratory, was viewed as essential to an adequate education (McCall, 1969). In this way thinkers and administrators were not viewed as independent spirits; they were seen to have a responsibility to the state and therefore duty bound to find ways to promote their ideas in the minds of other people. Following the classical period, the teaching of rhetoric figured prominently throughout medieval and renaissance learning right up to the Industrial Revolution (see Corbett, 1971; Vickers, 1988). Rhetoric of the medieval world, although less popularly acclaimed, remained one of the three central disciplines in the repertoire of the medieval scholar (Bolgar, 1954; Murphy, 1974). Then during the European Renaissance, rhetoric was revitalized and a competence in techniques of communication—particularly those relating to elocution or style—regained widespread appeal (for further details, see Baldwin & Clark, 1939; Dixon, 1982). Over the last 200 years rhetoric as an academic study has suffered progressive marginalization (Yeo, 1986). By the 1930s most Anglo-American schools and colleges had ceased formal teaching of rhetoric and by the 1960s its last residue in literary criticism, commonly referred to as "figures of speech," rapidly vanished from most English literature textbooks.[9] To the modern speaker, the term *rhetoric* has lost such credibility that it is frequently used as a derisive term with overtones of empty words, vacuity, persuasive but not reasonable, misleading, and so on. What the ancients saw as a cornerstone to civilization has now become a brutish art concerned with deception and exploitation.

Despite this decline, the last 50 years have witnessed a steadily growing resurgence of academic interest in the field of rhetoric. The revival is paralleled by mounting criticism of the basic assumptions of modernism.[10] Supporters of the revival argue that nonliteral or rhetorical content of a communication does not necessarily oppose or obscure its rational content; instead rhetorical aspects can be understood to bring into view or help highlight the rationality of what is being stated. The modern revival of rhetoric, frequently dubbed the "new rhetoric,"[11] is emerging in a variety of disciplines that include philosophy, psychology, anthropology, education, and literary criticism. For example, although most psychology over the last century has remained firmly committed to modernist presuppositions about knowledge, an increasing number of psychologists are exploring opportunities offered by the range of postmodern approaches to knowledge. *Postmodernism* refers to a cluster of academic approaches that share a shift in emphasis away from objective interpretations of meaning to a closer study of the contextual nature of meaning (see Billig, 1987; Gergen, 1990; Simons, 1989). This shift from universal to contextual truth has revived interest not only in studying the content of communication, but also in studying the manner in which people choose to communicate. It has thereby given impetus to the revival of rhetoric as a study in itself.

Rhetoric has traditionally been seen as a science of tropes. The term *trope* evolved as a means of referring to those elements within a communication that enhance the delivery of the central message. Although in classical rhetoric trope had a more specific meaning, the *Oxford English Dictionary* currently chooses to define trope as a general term for any element in a communication that has "a sense other than which is proper or literal." These elements can be identified at both a micro and a macro level; they might consist of phoneme regularities (e.g., repeated sounds: "the cat is on the mat"), words with special meanings (e.g., metaphor: "a pregnant pause"), changes in structure or grammar (e.g., unfinished sentences), and choices in the style of presentation (e.g., narration or dialogue). Tropes are also referred to variously as figures, devices, or strategies by means of which the communicator enhances the pervasive impact of a message. Advertising aims to convey key messages and impressions, and as such is natural territory for the application of rhetorical tropes. The following discussion explores the use of three common rhetorical strategies in gambling advertising: narrative constructions, metonymy, and binary opposition marking.

Narrative Constructions

Narratives have been used throughout the ages as a trope or device for achieving a range of communicative purposes. For example, most societies adopt narratives in the forms of myths and legends to explain their origins and moral obligations. In conversation, people often use narratives to explain who they are and where they come from. Narratives are also commonly employed in science to explain complex processes such as nerve transmission and the birth of galaxies. Social theorists have for some time taken an interest in the power of narratives to explain and persuade. Burke (1945/1969) was an early advocate for the study of narrative within the social sciences. Since then an interest in narrative has gained momentum in a range of areas of study, in particular critical psychology and sociology, family and systems theory, and postmodern qualitative research.[12] For example, from the field of social psychology, Gergen and Gergen (1987) examined how the uses of classic storytelling genres are embedded in everyday conversation. They illustrated how people will make frequent use of self-explanatory narrative structures in the familiar form of comedy, tragedy, romance, and irony. The ability of these story formats to plug into well-established patterns of chronology and causality enable the teller to exploit it for a range of purposes that include the explanation of origins and depictions of moral purpose.

Narrative structures come in various forms but share some common characteristics. They involve the description of events over time and are usually framed around a constructed endpoint. They also typically focus generally around a limited number of key protagonists, usually one protagonist interacting with a cast of minor players. They often involve depicting scenes of strong adversity and conflict. The manner in which protagonists handle this adversity enables the narrative to convey concepts of ethical and moral conduct. For example, in a job interview, the interviewee will often position himself or herself heroically by describing in detail the struggles it took to obtain key positions in former jobs. A further feature of narrative is the manner in which the familiarity of a particular story structure enables abbreviated versions of what in reality involves a complex intertwining of people, events, and relationships. For example, the long and complicated tale of Shackleton's voyage to the South Pole can be expanded and contracted while retaining the essential focus on his heroism and moral courage. Finally, narratives have the ability to operate conceptually at several levels at once. A surface narrative is often underpinned by identification with more significant events and meanings. For instance, a politician telling a humorous story of failed attempts to market pasta in Italy might have a more serious intent, such as highlighting the importance of marketing strategy or depicting the folly of current marketing policy.

As with all advertising, gambling advertisers make frequent use of narratives to achieve key messages. The following describes a gambling advertisement played on television.

> A cleaner vacuums the floor around the EGMs of a casino. He is blocked in front of one machine by a young man who is totally engrossed with his game. The cleaner sits briefly on the edge of a chair, waiting expectantly. He does not need to wait long before there is a win and he is able to vacuum the floor as the player jumps for joy.

On the surface, the story conveys the predictable regularity with which people win on these EGMs. At other levels, it depicts a young man having fun, that interrupting this enjoyment is inappropriate, and that others will respect and perhaps encourage this type of fun. In this way the receptive viewers, particularly young men, are invited to identify with the opportunity of winning depicted within the narrative. A similar process is employed in the following television advertisement.

> An old woman drives her little old car out of her garage to visit a casino. She returns with a modern car that, because of its larger size, she bangs into the back of the garage.

At one level the story is humorous because of the unexpected outcome. At another level it again conveys the ease with which ordinary people can win. It provides the opportunity for receptive viewers, in this case particularly older people, to identify with the prospect of success.

The use of shorthand narratives is a particularly potent means for advertisers to convey key messages. For example, a daily newspaper publishes a full-page picture of a woman of minority ethnic origin smiling euphorically with a caption below that reads:

> Cindy has just won a $256,542 jackpot to become one of Casino X's Big Winners. You could be next.

The storyline here is highly abbreviated and thereby enables receptive readers to use their imaginations to fill in details of the remainder of the story. The protagonist's position within the central plot is clear: A female member of a minority culture wins a lot of money. The imaginatively receptive reader is likely to add this: She is poor, she has struggled to bring up her children, she has never cheated anyone, she really deserves this break, and so on. Her moral positioning is clearly heroic and thereby receptive readers are invited to identify her as a potential role model within their own personal circumstances. The most potent identifications will be for women from a similar minority culture.

In the three examples just presented, advertisers have cast protagonists belonging to clear demographic target groups: young men, older women, and cultural minorities. The key function of the narratives is to provide opportunities for members of the target demographic to identify with someone else's success. This means narratives are ideally suited for the purpose of recruitment. As explored in the discussion on social learning theory, the use of these narratives presents respondents with a solid role model who is being visibly rewarded for participation in gambling. Receptive readers or listeners observe their success and are thereby invited to consider their own involvement in that particular mode of gambling, in this case casino gambling. The rhetorical use of narratives combines with the psychological processes of social learning to achieve a persuasive device for recruiting new gamblers.

Metonymy

The study of tropes in classical rhetoric has developed a powerful array of concepts to assist in understanding persuasive communication. In particular, three tropes[13] stand out as deserving special scrutiny: metaphor, synecdoche, and metonymy. Each has vital cognitive functions that underlie the operation of many other tropes. Metaphor is the most familiar and exploits the similarities between objects (or complexes of objects) to describe or explain more abstract concepts in terms of more concrete and familiar concepts. The language employed by social scientists makes frequent use of metaphors.[14] For example, psychologists employ simple spatially based metaphors as a means of describing more complicated cognitive and experiential processes (Massaro, 1986; also discussed by Searle, 1984). Spatial concepts are intimated by phrases such as "personal space," "mental distance," and "depth of processing"; and container-based metaphors are signaled in talk of "memory capacity," "perceptual defense," and "inner experience." The list of common examples in any field of discourse is huge and ever expanding.[15]

The other two mastertropes (synecdoche and metonymy) are just as important as metaphor, but less frequently described and therefore more difficult to appreciate.[16] Synecdoche is generally understood as a reference that substitutes either a species for a genus (a part for a whole) or a genus for a species (a whole for a part). For example, consider a busy doctor on a surgical ward asking of his interns:

Have you seen *the appendix* in ward nine?

Meaning perhaps more kindly:

Have you seen *the person about to have his appendix removed* in ward nine?

The appendix is part of the human body—a member of the category of parts of the human body—and in making the synecdochal reference the speaker need only refer to the body part for the listener to understand that the whole body is being referenced. Here are some further examples:

I just bought myself a new set of *wheels* (= car, motorbike)

Watch *those sails* gliding under the bridge (= those yachts)

The ships opened fire (= the ship's guns)

Notice how with synecdoche the link assumes the listener is familiar with the relevant category and the conditions of membership for that category. The listener needs to know that guns belong to a ship and sails are a part of a yacht. So, in linking parts to whole and vice versa, the conceptual links exploited by synecdoche can be considered as essentially categorical links.

With metonymy the communicator makes a reference by substituting something that has come to be associated with the intended object. Unlike synecdoche, the essential conceptual link is not categorical; rather it relies on the presented reference having past associations or a history of standing next to the intended reference. For example, a waitress whispers discretely to the restaurant manager:

The filet mignon wishes to complain about his meal.

She intends by this to mean:

The person who ordered the filet mignon wishes to complain about his meal.

Between waitress and manager, an understanding has been built up that one particular person is associated with one particular meal. By means of this shared association, the waitress need only refer to the meal for the manager to understand she means the person. Here are some further examples:

You're always reading *Carl Jung* (= the writings of Jung)

The White House has refused to comment (= the U.S. President's office)

We need *a stronger boot* on the team (= a better kicker)

Metonymy usually occurs in the form of more than one association, and over the course of a text, these associations interlink into a complex tapestry of nonliteral references. The rhetorical function of metonymy is often likened to constructing boxes within boxes, all with the ability to cross-link with each other. Their application is also not only confined to verbal communication. Nonverbal communications, signals, symbols, and even artistic expression all regularly exploit metonymic linkages. For example, in David Lean's film version of Boris Pasternak's *Doctor Zhivago,* the death of Lara's brother is metonymically represented by showing his little round glasses lying on the blood-stained snow. Instead of showing the brother dying, the film shows an object that has come to be associated with his appearance. The effect is very powerful, and leaves it to the viewer's imagination to fill in what horrific other things might have happened to him.

Gambling advertising regularly employs all three of these mastertropes. For example, metaphors of flight, such as the image of a person flying in clouds, are used to represent the soaring ecstasy of winning.[17] The power of synecdoche is operating when gambling providers refer to their product as 'gaming'. Gambling is a subcategory of gaming, a broader category encompassing a wide range of entertainments. By referencing the broader category (i.e., by referring to the whole rather than the part) the speaker sidesteps the more specific negative connotations unique to gambling. However, although these devices play a role, it is metonymy that is most commonly and most persuasively used in gambling advertising. Consider the metonymic references in the following example:

> Hollywood Gaming, where the stars come out to play

Besides the reference to the way celestial stars come out at night, the more important association signaled here involves linking the product with the desirable qualities of well-known Hollywood movie stars. They are famous and beautiful and they play these games, so by association anyone else playing them links themselves to these qualities. Some further examples are given here:

> You *call the shots* (= initiate the action)

> Have a bit of a *flutter* (= gamble in ways that raise your heart rate)

> Come along for *a laugh* (= fun from gambling)

> For a slice of *action* (= involvement in winning)

In each of these, the power of the reference is derived through associations with other objects. 'Shots', 'flutters', 'laughs', and 'action' have over time acquired positive associations with fun and enjoyment. With repeated and varied use, they can then be used to link the products in with these positive associations.

Similarly, the symbols and icons associated with gambling can be seen to have essentially metonymic roots. The picture of a dice, signs from packs of cards, the image of horses, lemons, roulette wheels, certain sounds and types of music, and so forth each have acquired a relatedness that has built up over time and is used and reused in ways that play on associations with fun, winning, and conviviality. Similar to the processes discussed earlier with classical conditioning, the associations enable a previously neutral term or symbol to stand in for another term. The advertiser will take a well-established symbol, such as dice, and place it in the foreground or in the background, perhaps animate it, draw it with human qualities, and so on. The key function of the symbol is to plug into its accumulated positive linkages, thereby ensuring its survival and further enabling its capacity to form other future potent associations. It acts like a shorthand code that opens up a world of interconnected meanings and images that cloak related objects with an aura of positivity.

The potency of metonymic word and imagery associations will vary according to the recipient's level of exposure to gambling. A person who has had few exposures to positive experiences of gambling is less likely to be responsive than someone with frequent involvements. The infrequent gambler lacks the exposures that give these words and images their vitality and potency. With a prior history of enjoying gambling, frequent gamblers are far more responsive to the associations. They are likely to interpret words like *win* and *fun* and images like cards and dice as cues to thinking about their positive gambling experiences. For this reason, the use of metonymy can be seen as functioning similarly and often in conjunction with classical conditioning processes, in that they both assist in the retention of experienced gamblers in choosing to continue their participation in frequent gambling.

Binary Opposition Marking

Studies on the language of advertising (Macarte, 1970; McLuhan, 1965) have explored how advertisers frequently adopt strategies that emphasize or mark out the trade name of the product they are trying to promote. Consider the forms of emphasis employed in the following examples:

CORFU
The Fabulous Jean
Pure fashion jeans. With a
Fabulous fit.

Brooks Original Wine Cooler is made with only
NATURAL fruitjuice.
Taste the difference

Two forms of marking are evident in the preceding examples: First, emphasis has been superimposed onto the trade names by strategies such as capital letters (NATURAL), leaving spaces above and below labels, and by changing typefaces (**Pure**). Other superimposed changes in the original advertisements but not shown here were changes in color, size, orientation, and background shading. This type of superimposed emphasis is referred to as *analogue marking*. The second form of emphasis involves surrounding trade names with an array of qualifying terms that serve to accentuate them in a positive light: Corfu Jeans are "fabulous" and "pure fashion," Brooks Wine Cooler is "original" and "natural." This form of emphasis uses verbal markers and is referred to as *binary opposition marking*.

An array of different ways is available for singling out specific words and phrases within spoken discourse. One might choose to raise or lower the tone, pitch, or volume of delivery; hand gestures and facial expressions might mark out the importance of certain phrases; and competent speakers also learn to exploit changes in the pace of delivery and cleverly timed pauses. Binary oppositions are a subspecies of this type of semantic marking. They consist in pairs of linked terms, usually attributes in the form of adjectives for which, when one pole is used in association with a term, by implication the other pole can be read as indirectly marking other terms with the opposite attribute. The language of advertising is rich with examples of this strategy:

> Sentence: Come and hear our *new* and *fantastic* offer
> Binaries: new/old, fantastic/not so fantastic
> Implication: other offers are old and not so fantastic

> Sentence: Anchor butter, *smooth* and *natural*
> Binaries: smooth/rough, natural/unnatural
> Implication: other butter is rough and unnatural

As with the other types of marking, binary oppositions do not add much to the informational content of a sentence; words like 'new', 'tremendous', 'dependable', 'simple', and 'affordable' have become so overused that they convey little about the product, yet the use of these binaries still persists. Their function in advertising extends beyond informing the consumer, and serves to both cloak the product in an aura of positivity and by implication link competing products with their negative polar opposites.[18]

Binary oppositions have attracted recurring interest in the discipline of semiotics. It started with de Sassure's (1916/1959) contention that language could be treated as a system of differences and oppositions (see also Holenstein, 1976). Jakobson (1974) extended this view in a phenomenological analysis of the presence of binary oppositions, and argued that by specifying one pole of a binary, the speaker automatically implies its opposite. For example, if someone were to say, "It's a good day," that person also means, "It's not a bad day," and by implication that "Other days are bad days." By looking closer at such binaries, Jakobson was able to examine a range of meanings and implied meanings in the way people speak. Levi-Strauss (1966) began to apply this analysis of binaries in his anthropological study of communication patterns within cultures and social structures. Benveniste (1985) studied binary oppositions in traffic lights, music, and the plastic arts. Leymore (1975) researched their prevalence in the language of advertising.

Binary opposition marking can be used to mark a particular brand of gambling product and signal its superiority over other brands. For example, advertising signs hanging outside a bar might refer to the EGMs inside as:

> Totally *new*, *state-of-the-art* gaming machines

The object here, 'gaming machines', is qualified by several binary opposition markers ('totally', 'new', and 'state-of-the-art'), the presence of which provide little informational content for the reader. Taking a closer look at just one, the assertion that, "these machines are new" carries with it the meaning that "these machines are not old" and by implication "machines in other locations are old." Using the binary opposition, reference to one pole of this continuum intimates a connection (albeit negative) with the opposite pole. Other examples the bar owner might use on the signs could include these:

A *warm*, *friendly* gaming environment (other venues are less warm and friendly)

A *fantastic* place to be (other places are not so fantastic)

Super jackpots (jackpots in other locations are less impressive)

Free games!! *Free* money!! *Free* Fun!! (other games, money, and fun cost money)

The connections across one end of the continuum point towards other unspecified objects with attributes from the opposite end of the continuum. In this way the bar owner is able to indirectly signal the superiority of his or her gambling machines over his or her competitors.

Binary opposition marking is more commonly used in gambling advertising to positively mark a consumer group and to imply negative marking of a nonconsumer group. In this way it links with the earlier discussion of ingroup–outgroup processes that serve to increase the normalization of gambling in target populations. Consider the following promotional slogan placed on all materials for a major track gambling provider:

[X venue], where everyone is a winner.

Along with the suggestion that winning is a regular event, the use of the binary term *winner* serves to positively mark anyone who turns up in the venue and by implication negatively mark those who stay away. This binary opposition is linked to a familiar binary with a history of application in the marketing of both alcohol and gambling. The binary depicts those who regularly gamble or drink as free, open, sociable, successful, and fun-loving, contrasting them by implication with people at the other end who are wowsers, spoilsports, and antigambling. Consider some further examples:

Betting for the *serious* gambler (other modes are not so serious)

Your *best* chance in ages (gambling at other times involves less luck)

Where the *fun* people gather (nongamblers are not so much fun)

In each example, the binary terms directly reference the fun-loving ingroup and indirectly the wowser outgroup. The potency of the verbal binary marking is often further reinforced with analog binary opposition marking, with images of people who are clearly attractive, well-socialized, amusing, and affluent. Words and images combine to positively mark the fun-loving ingroup and to imply negative marking of the spoilsport outgroup. They indicate to the receptive reader or viewer that membership in the fun-loving ingroup is normal and to be desired. It serves to allay any negative public perceptions of the frequent gambler and to promote frequent gambling as normative.

CONCLUSION

The function of gambling advertising has attracted very little academic attention, and yet the disciplines of psychology and rhetoric provide a wealth of explanatory theories that can assist in understanding how gambling advertising achieves its effects. These theories help in understanding how gambling advertising contributes to the recruitment, retention, and normalization of people engaging in frequent gambling. The array of theories that were explored is presented in grid form in Table 6.1.

In terms of recruitment, the use of social learning processes and the presentation of abbreviated narratives illustrate how potent sporting and acting role models together with the repetitive use of embedded success narratives present receptive individuals with compelling images of the attractions of gambling. For those who have already engaged in frequent gambling, the use of strongly paired sensory stimuli or the repetitive use of paired meanings (metonymy) through the processes of classical conditioning provide a reference base to cue-in continued participation. For the general population, the power of social identification with a non-anti-gambling, fun-loving ingroup is established and encouraged by frequent reference to ingroup or outgroups and through indirect references using binary oppositions. These identifications serve to normalize and perhaps glamourize frequent gambling and thereby decrease the chances that the behavior is identified, discussed, or even challenged.

Table 6.1 Theories on Advertising Divided by Function and Discipline

	Psychology	*Rhetoric*
Recruitment	Social learning	Narrative constructions
Retention	Classical conditioning	Metonymy
Normalization	Social identity	Binary opposition marking

7   Researchers

Research and other academic activities play a special role in the long-term evolution of a democracy. It is the activity of enquiry that generates the knowledge base that informs other end users of research—media, policy-makers, and the public—on what is actually going on. For example, the quality of a magazine article on problem gambling will be only as good as the quality of the sources of information that are used to support its main points. Without solid research, discussion and debate remains at the level of conjecture and guesswork, and thereby opens the topic up for capture by lobbyists with vested interests in one particular persuasion. A pressing illustration of this is occurring currently over whether or not the consumption of fossil fuels is leading to significant global warming. Those with financial interests in fossil fuel consumption (e.g., car manufacturers, fuel producers, and some governments) have a strong interest in denying or playing down any negative effects from global warming. Despite the power behind these interests, researchers have managed to play a critical role in measuring the extent and effects of global warming and repeatedly presenting the evidence in the public domain. Industry advocates and politicians have tried their hardest to discredit the figures and bamboozle observers, but their efforts have not managed to stem the ongoing flow of worrying information.

Many of these same dynamics occur with gambling. As the burning of fossil fuels is heating up our natural ecologies, so the global expansion of commercial gambling is leading to global warming of another kind: a global warming of gambling consumption that is also stimulating the appetites of interested parties in the profits it generates. Also, those with vested interests (entrepreneurs, gambling providers, and governments) have similarly actively sought to distort information in ways that suggest the expansion is having minimal impacts on economies and social ecologies. However, the difference here between this and fossil fuels is that quality gambling research has not been generated in sufficient quantities to correct any misrepresentations. Quality information on the wider impacts of gambling is simply not being generated at the same rate it has for global warming. We have been let down by research at two levels: The quantity of solid research on the effects of global expansion is, by and large, missing, and the research that has been produced is questionable because researchers often maintain ambiguous relationships with interested parties that leave their results in doubt.

In 1997 I attended the Tenth Conference on Gambling and Risk Taking in Montreal, Canada, hosted by the University of Nevada, which was my first international conference on gambling. Little could have prepared me for what I observed. Prior to involvements with gambling research, I had attended a variety of international conferences in other areas such as psychology, mental health, and alcohol and drugs. These events were typically organized by university departments or service organizations within these fields and much emphasis was placed on ensuring academic quality and independence of focus. This, my first gambling conference, turned out to be a different kettle of fish. It had all the hallmarks of an academic conference—eminent keynote speakers, a program with several streams of paper presentations, registrants from all around the world, and ample breaks for discussion and networking—but the forum differed in important ways from others I had encountered. The first clue came in an early plenary address in which the speaker began to outline, in all seriousness, the weight of evidence pointing overwhelmingly to the positive social and economic impacts of gambling. I then became aware that many attendees, perhaps as many as half, were employees from various gambling industries. I noted that subsequent whole-conference addresses tended to either focus on the social and economic benefits of commercialized gambling or on highly medical perspectives on problem gambling that reinforced the impression that it was an unfortunate condition that afflicted relatively few people who would have acquired this or other addictive disorders anyway. These orientations were backed up by plenary addresses by industry spokespeople and industry-friendly government officials. So, on the main stage at least, a critical voice on the expansion of gambling was strangely silent. In the many smaller presentations in breakout streams, presenters were openly challenging gambling expansion; for example, competent researchers were presenting evidence on gambling-related harms and what to do about them. However, their audiences were small and tended to be made up of that subgroup of attendees with an already well-formed commitment to addressing harms. When it came finally to my contribution, at 5:30 in the evening shortly before the conference dinner, I copresented on the idea of an international charter on gambling to a very small and tired audience who no doubt were distracted by thoughts on how fast they might get dressed up for dinner. In the adjacent room an industry fun club—from memory called something akin to the "Knights of the Round Table"—could be heard loudly chanting strange songs and verses. A fashionably attired Australian woman chairing our session began her introduction by referring to us as "health nazis,"[1] a comment that seemed congruent with how we experienced our position at the conference. As we launched into our presentation to the accompaniment of strange noises and chants in the room next door, I could not help wondering why we had traveled around the world for this presentation.

The conference dinner that followed was naturally a lavish affair in the local casino.

I have since attended other similar conferences with many of the same features: an absence of open criticism of gambling expansion in favor of a safer emphasis on host responsibility and treatment; plenary presentations dominated by industry-funded research with negative social and economic assessments relegated to minor breakout sessions, and obligatory visits to casinos for dinner and speeches from industry executives regarding the contributions they make to communities and advances in developing their responsible gambling policies. The conferences are clearly underwritten by industry funding and consequently conference organizers are understandably careful about avoiding situations where their donors could be embarrassed. When asked about their willingness to accept funding from this source, organizers typically identified gambling industries as an important part of the sector and indicated that people are more likely to achieve changes working alongside them than taking up antagonistic positions. They also pointed out the difficulties and dilemmas that result from trying to host international conferences and in finding adequate resources. On the one hand, large conferences, like major research projects, are complex and expensive to run. Significant amounts of money are required to ensure their success and gambling industry partners often provide a willing source of support. On the other hand, researchers and academics play a critical role in modern democracies in providing clear, accurate, and unbiased windows for the public to view the way gambling plays out in their societies. This democratic function relies heavily on their perceived integrity and independence, and a forum with strongly visible support from the gambling industry will cast doubt on this independence. When organizers choose to accept industry funding, although they take on board the need to minimize criticism of the industry, they usually counterbalance this by ensuring all the trappings of independent research are visibly present and that the main authorities play a prominent role.

In the frontier society formed during the initial proliferation of commercial gambling, researchers are also seeking a place to lay a stake in the ground and find space to make a contribution on which to build their reputations. The broader population, new to the presence of commercial gambling, slumbers in sentimental memories of noncommercial forms of gambling. Levels of concern have not as yet reached a threshold sufficient enough to fire up significant research endeavors. In the absence of public interest, the infrastructure for independent gambling research has yet to evolve (Adams & Hodges, 2005). Researchers in this space are forced to scavenge for resources where they are able. Small projects are attempted in their own time, and gambling as an issue is attached as a minor part of other health research projects.[2] Despite these attempts, researchers recognize that the most likely way to fund the type of research they desire is via funding from the gambling providers. However, this creates a difficult dilemma. Reliance on funding from industry sources could in the long term channel research into areas that are unlikely to threaten the business of gambling; not taking the money could mean no research gets done. The dialogue in the next section has been put together to highlight this central dilemma for researchers regarding the availability of industry funding.[3]

THE RESEARCHER'S DILEMMA

The Beach Cottage

Three university colleagues are taking a well-earned weekend break at a beach cottage. It is late summer, they have been busy completing a major research report on gambling, and, as a result, they are keen to have some time in the sun before autumn. As they unpack the car, they chat and joke excitedly about finally escaping work.

Their destination, a small dark-green cottage, is nestled on the side of a hill overlooking a beach. They clamber out of the car, stretch and groan, and then begin to struggle up the rough, pebbly path carrying bags and boxes filled with clothing and provisions. Flustered and puffing, they reach the cottage door, unbolt it, then enter the dark, musty-smelling interior and deposit their boxes on a central table. On drawing back the curtains they can see that the cottage consists of one main room that functions as a kitchen, dining room, and lounge, and attached are two smaller rooms that serve as cramped bedrooms. Turning around and looking out the main window they are confronted by a dramatic outlook onto a wide expanse of beach, cliffs, rocks, and ocean.

They unpack their gear and begin to discuss how best to spend their time. James is short and slightly overweight. He speaks in an energetic and engaging manner. He is clearly excited because it was his idea to stay at the beach. His original training was as a clinical psychologist with a specialist focus on addictions. He then moved gradually into clinical research, which led to his appointment as a university teacher. He has maintained a small client load at a local addiction services center and it was his clients who first introduced him to problem gambling. Margie stands at the door looking out to sea. She is tall and thin, with a sensitive and mobile face that can switch quickly from a warm smile to a frown. She was originally trained in public health medicine, which led her later to a career in population research. She has only recently begun to focus on risk factors for problem gambling. Patrick, the youngest of the three, is carefully unpacking food into the cupboards. His passion for sports has kept him looking fit and strong. He tends to speak at a slow, measured pace. He has devoted his entire career to teaching and research in the field of social psychology and his interest in gambling emerged from lively staff-room discussions with James.

The three colleagues spend the remainder of the day relaxing, walking along the beach, swimming in the surf, and fishing off a nearby wharf. Toward the end of the afternoon they walk back to the cottage planning their evening meal. It is late summer and the sun hangs brightly above the horizon, its rays glinting and sparkling off the waves. The evening will be long and sunset is still 2 hours off.

Around the Stove

James is leaning over the stove stirring onions in a pan. Margie is carefully cutting up tomatoes at the table and Patrick is leaning up against the bench. They speak generally about the day, about the sea, the sun, and the fishing. As energy for this line of discussion wanes, Margie shifts the conversation by commenting: "We desperately need more funding so we can keep researching together."

"I agree," responds Patrick thoughtfully. "I think we've only just begun to ask the right questions about gambling." He pauses and stares at the bubbling tomato mix. "By the way, I've really enjoyed working with you two, and I would like it to continue."

"Me too," chip in the other two.

"Up 'til now," Patrick continues, "most of my research has involved giving students questionnaires and I've never had a chance to apply my work more to the real world. I can see this gambling stuff is full of all sorts of unexpected applications."

"Pity you haven't worked out how to predict roulette spins," quips Margie.

"Yeah. A pity. That reminds me," says Patrick, "The other day I received a phone call from some guy at the casino. He said he was impressed with our presentation at the conference last month and wondered if we would be interested in helping evaluate a new host responsibility program."

"Hmmm . . . and what did you say?" asks James.

"I said I needed to talk with you two first, and that I'd get back to him."

"That's incredible. We've been chasing research money for ages and they just ring up and offer it to you!" exclaims Margie.

"Hold on . . . um, I'm . . . I'm not so sure we should get involved with that lot," James comments hesitantly, not wishing to sour the mellow mood of the afternoon.

"Don't be so silly! What do you mean 'that lot'?"

"Well they are a 'lot.' A lot of crooks."

"You're not going to get on your moral high horse again, Jim, are you?" Margie queries in a taunting but friendly manner.

"At least I have a horse. You wouldn't know a moral horse if it ran over you. You don't . . ."

"Break it up you two," interrupts Patrick in a mock judicial tone. "Seriously, Jim, why are you worried about casino funding?"

"Why? Well, in a nutshell, if we receive money directly from something like the casino, we will quickly become beholden to them. They will call the shots on what we do and what we say."

"Oh come on!" retorts Margie.

"Excuse me, hold on Margie ... what do you mean exactly, Jim?" enquires Patrick.

"Well, I mean if a place like the casino funds our research then technically they own it. They paid for it, so they decide whether or not it's published. If they don't like it, they will just bury it. They can also decide whether or not we get more money for future projects. We would just end up jumping up and down to suit them. Up and down. And we would jump a little higher each time. 'How high this time, sir?' "

"Jim, I think you're being oversensitive," Margie responds. "Gambling providers are not that stupid. For one thing, they are all getting increasingly concerned about the rise of problem gambling—it's a scourge for them, as it is for us—they don't want to be viewed as ripping off the weak ... and for another, they simply can't afford to be seen as manipulating the facts. The media and the public would be outraged; it wouldn't be worth their while."

"Yeah, I agree with Margie," says Patrick, giving tentative support. "They aren't going to be able to control us that much, Jim. All we need to make sure of is that any contract has a clause in it that states clearly we can publish whatever the outcome. It happens with pharmaceutical research all the time. If we find their new program is useless, that's what we'll report. Tough luck. If they are not willing for us to publish, we walk away, we simply refuse to participate."

"Yes, that's it, Patrick," Margie adds. "Should they agree to this clause, what's the difference? It's the same relationship we have with any government funders."

"I reckon it's more complex than that," James states, as he begins to lay the knives and forks on the table. "This approach is okay for single projects, but think about the situation where we might be wanting to work on a series of research projects. Let's say ... hmm ... let's say results for the first industry project are inconclusive and they fund a follow-up study. Then the results for the second study are negative for the casinos. We publish the report and as a result they make it clear to us they don't intend to fund further research. All they need to say is that the research question is no longer important to them. In order to protect future projects we might then think twice about publishing the negative results of the second study. We might have been tempted to sit on the report or even water down the conclusions by criticizing our own methods."

"I would never stand for that," Patrick retorts.

"C'mon you lot," interrupts Margie. "Dinner's cooked. Let's sit down and eat."

The onions, herbs, and tomatoes simmering in the pan have filled the cottage with rich smells. Outside the multipaned windows the sun has lowered and its rays are reflecting in bright glints off a regularly ruffled sea. The three colleagues bring the cooked dishes to the table, find their seats, pour some wine, and begin serving food onto their plates.

Spaghetti Bolognese

They are hungry from the day's activities so they eat quietly with the occasional slurp and clink of cutlery. Waves can be heard gently crashing in the distance and nearby birds announcing the approaching sunset. Patrick breaks their silence.

"Jim, do you really think we are capable of twisting or hiding the truth for money?"

"No . . ." James pauses. "Well, at least, not initially. I think it would be something that creeps up gradually."

"How would it work?"

"Um . . ." He pauses again, finishing a mouthful. "You know how much our university is keen to bring in research dollars?"

"Yes, they make that fairly plain; quote: 'Research-Led University of International Standing.'" All three laugh and repeat the phrase in various mimicked voices.

"Much of what we each want to achieve in the future," continues James, "comes down to us meeting their expectations regarding increased research dollars. Patrick, you've been trying for years to get promoted to associate professor. What do they keep saying knocks you back?"

"They always praise my teaching, which is nice, but then say my research productivity isn't good enough. I've tried—oh, how I've tried—but it's really difficult to balance a large teaching load with the time required to conduct research."

"The trick is to find sources of funding to pay others to cover part of the work. What you do is set out to obtain money for research assistants, research students, and perhaps something for teaching assistance so you are freed up for project management and writing. This will really boost your productivity."

"Yeah, I know that, but research money isn't so easy to come by these days."

"Exactly! That is why the availability of money from the gambling industry is so enticing. They have such a lot of money and are falling over themselves to engage compliant researchers who boost their do-good public profile."

"Yes, I must admit, it has occurred to me as attractive."

"So, why not do a research project with them? Only one small study? It won't do any harm. Why not? So you do. You've taken the bait, they've got you hooked. You continue with their funded research, but only if it suits their interests."

"That's a bit mean!" interrupts Margie, who up until then had been quietly listening as she ate her meal. "The larger gambling providers are in the game for the long term. They want to know how best to manage problems because in the end they know that problems brushed under the carpet have a nasty habit of jumping up again and biting them. Their interest is in how to ensure the environment can sustain their business. Sure, some cowboys will want to make the best of the short term and rip people off then get out, but they don't last. The larger providers mostly aim for long-term sustainability. They are serious about the research, because, just like the fishing industry, it will help in the long-term management of a sustainable gambling industry. They are not out to control the researchers."

"Yes they are!" retorts James. "You suggest I'm naive. Look what happened with the tobacco industry. They definitely managed the broader environment. They managed it really well . . . they managed it by employing their own researchers and funding others such that any public good research on harms was countered by positive findings . . . they managed it so well. They dominated the literature with selective publication of favorable results. This way they were able to slow down, and, at times, even stall policy changes for 30 years. In the meantime millions died from smoking-related illnesses."

"Let's not overdramatize the issue," Maggie replies. "The situation with tobacco is very different from that of gambling. Tobacco definitely kills millions. While gambling may contribute to a few suicides, it does not carry the same risk to life. The risks from gambling just don't compare with those of tobacco."

"How can you be sure, Margie?" Patrick queries. "The proliferation of gambling is *so* new worldwide, so new we know little of its true long-term effects. Sure, gambling doesn't kill like smoking but it does cause a whole range of other problems, including crime, mental health issues, and family strife . . . you know. Besides this, high-intensity gambling has only hit most countries in the last decade—we have little knowledge of its broader impact on economies and quality of life."

By this stage all three are sitting back in their chairs gazing out the window. They all sensed that the conversation had become a little too heated and they wanted a return to their earlier happy mood. A large golden sun hangs over the horizon, surrounded colorfully by distant clouds. The sky has deepened to a turquoise blue and the smooth swell on the ocean rolls gracefully into iridescent white breakers. Together they clear the table and then prepare for a walk along the beach.

The Evening Stroll

They walk quietly along the cool sand, listening to the hissing and cracking of the surf. The beach arches into the distance, finishing with the dark outline of rocks and cliffs. Margie resumes their discussion.

"I'm not worried about receiving research money from the industry."

"Do we need to get into this again?" queries Patrick. She ignores his comment

"I'm not worried, in fact I welcome it. Their products are causing the problems; they are personally prospering from people's vulnerabilities. Why should the taxpayer dish out to clean up the mess they've created? The gambling provider should pay for cleaning it up, and research will be an important part to us working out how to conduct the clean up."

"Yes, good point," admits James.

"It would be nice," adds Patrick, "if they were required to pay for the full costs of the damage."

"The other thing is," continues Margie, "if we really want to make a difference to gambling, we are not going to get very far by putting all our energy into fighting the industry. Keeping separate won't be productive for anyone. You just end up wearing yourself out in exhausting conflict. The providers determine the product and its manner of delivery; they are constantly interacting with the gamblers themselves, and they create the gambling environment. If we have any chance of changing gambling behavior, it is really only via the industry that we will have access to the minds and hearts of gamblers."

"Yeah," chips in Patrick. "You have to admit it would be hard to get strategies like host responsibility codes and consumer education off the ground if you haven't got the gambling providers themselves on your side. There are so many ideas we could explore with gambling machines. We could work with manufacturers to design information screens, warning messages, forced breaks . . . we could even research patterns of betting by problem gamblers and then use that research to identify those at risk and provide some form of brief intervention such as feedback on a screen or cue in a staff member to enquire, or . . ."

"Hold on," James interrupts. "I'm not arguing against us having a relationship with the industry. On the contrary, I agree entirely that we should be seeking to build as strong an involvement as possible for the very reasons you've mentioned. My main concern isn't about having a direct financial relationship; it's about our level of independence within the relationship. Once in a financial relationship with the industry, how do we keep ourselves adequately free from their influence?"

All three pause for a moment and look out at the darkening sand. Patrick breaks the silence. "Easy. It's easy. We are part of the University and government legislation protects the rights of universities to research and report independently. We work through them to ensure our independence."

"I dunno about that," responds James. "The moment a researcher accepts funding from the industry, their research from then on is tainted by that connection. I've seen it happen elsewhere. People find out that a researcher has received funding support from a gambling provider and we all start talking about them as being in the pocket of the industry. No matter how carefully you conduct the study, other people will look at you and accuse you of appeasing the industry. It may have been only a little amount, but the question mark regarding industry influence spreads to past, present, and future efforts."

"That's true, Margie, remember last year?" observes Patrick. "Remember that person—that person who will remain nameless—who undertook a large social impact study for the casinos? He put in considerable work, but because he was funded directly by the industry, we rubbished his report. You did, too. What's worse, we've continued to rubbish any work he produced since."

"I agree there is a risk," responds Margie hesitantly. "How other people see you is important, and reputations are easily damaged, but . . . but it's simply a matter of perception. Most medical faculties nowadays are involved in drug research funded directly by pharmaceutical companies. There was resistance at first, but now such research is mainstream. It is simply a matter of universities working out adequate protocols around information owner-ship and reporting. We just need to develop and monitor the right proce-dures and people will soon come to trust and accept it."

They cut across the dunes toward an estuary behind the beach. A foot-bridge spans the central stream of the estuary. The water is very still and reflects the flecks of blue, pink, and gold in the postsunset sky. They stop in the middle of the bridge and lean on the rail looking down over the stream. The glassy surface is disturbed occasionally by feeding fish.

"Margie," James resumes, "it really does worry me that if we accept industry money, it's not only our reputation that will be affected, but the perceived independence of our university itself. If we were to pursue ongo-ing research funded directly from the industry, our university will begin to be seen as supporting their interests. This could affect its reputation as a whole."

"Mmmm, I understand the risk, but it is fairly unlikely."

"Once we accept industry money, even if it's only a small amount, we buy into an association . . . an association that other people will continue to connect us with. Another thing. How can we as academics, once we have received some money from the industry, stand up in all honesty and criti-cize what's going on? I know I would lose all confidence, and even if I felt strongly about something, I wouldn't speak out because I would feel a hypo-crite. I would know deep inside myself that other people will be looking at me side on and thinking 'He doesn't really mean it.'"

"Other people?"

"Yes, I mean colleagues, researchers here and overseas, government offi-cials, reporters, students, public health advocates . . . our credibility will drop and we will eventually lose our ability to say things about gambling."

"I can understand your concerns." Margie is speaking slowly and care-fully. "But this risk needs to be balanced with other objectives, in particular, the objective of getting things done. There is simply no significant source of research funding other than the industry. Even government sources come from contributions from the industry. The way I see it, either you receive money from the most likely source or you end up out in the cold, achiev-ing nothing at all. You may as well pack up. I've seen it all before in other areas. The leading university researchers decide not to receive money from an industry source; other less able researchers seize the opportunity to pursue specific interests; they end up completing pieces of work, publishing them, and getting recognized as the main authorities in the area; this, of course, leads to more opportunity and further strengthens their position. What annoys me is thinking what could have been achieved if the leading and more academically competent researchers had gotten involved in the first place."

The colors of the sky have faded to black with a spreading array of stars. They walk in the dark along the short path back to the road, then up to the cottage.

Coffee and Banana Cake

After putting on some warmer clothes, the three colleagues take their cups of coffee and some cake outside to sit on a rough bench. They look out over the vast dark expanse. There is no wind and crickets can be heard up and down the hill beginning their nightly chorus. Patrick resumes the discussion.

"I have listened carefully to you both. I've found myself pulled one way then the other. I would really like to find some way through this disagreement, but I also accept that maybe it won't be completely resolved."

"Maybe," grunts James.

Patrick continues, "I can see from your point of view, James, that receiving industry funding can provide industry barons with access in a number of ways of influencing the research agenda. But I also take Margie's point that not receiving funds will achieve very little and allow the research dollar to be wasted on low-priority projects."

"Exactly right," mutters Margie.

"Once everyone recognizes the dangers, what I think we need is some form of honest broker who, acting on behalf of the public, receives industry funding then manages its dispersal according to a carefully worked out strategy."

"And who do you think can be an honest broker?" enquires James.

"That's an interesting question . . ." Patrick pauses. "I guess the most likely candidate is some adequately empowered branch of government—a section in a department, an independent council, a government commission . . . I don't really understand such things, but some agency with clearly delegated authority and protected independence."

"Yes, that's a possibility," states Margie. "Industry contributions to research could be managed by a central agency. The industry people could have their say along with everyone else during the process of devising the research strategy, so some of their research questions would get included. But they will not be in a direct relationship with individual researchers, thereby guaranteeing independence in the research and protecting both parties from perceptions of undue influence. What more could you want?"

"There's one small problem," responds James. "The idea is good, but you have forgotten something about the role of government in all this. Our

government, like many elsewhere, is actually a player in the gambling industry. They run the national lottery and they are shareholders in the racing
industry. On top of this, an expanding and not insignificant portion of tax
revenue comes from gambling. There is no way they are going to allow anything including research to jeopardize this income stream. Treasury simply
wouldn't allow it."

"Here we go again, conspiracy theories," interrupts Margie.

"No, no, it's just common sense. Imagine their response if the main thrust
of our research identifies that the best way to reduce gambling problems
is to reduce gambling consumption. Reduced consumption means reduced
revenue. Government departments benefiting from this revenue are not
going to welcome such a conclusion. They will seek to protect their interests
by influencing the research agenda and the best way to do this is to focus
researchers on short-term solutions, leaving the bigger solutions unexam-
ined. You forget just how powerful research evidence can be within government. So how could a government agency ever achieve independence in this
environment?"

"Government officials are simply not that calculating," retorts Margie.

"They are, particularly when we are talking about large amounts of
money."

"Oh, as I said earlier about responsible gambling providers, governments
are in the business for the long haul. It is a liability for them to allow gambling to keep expanding to unmanageable proportions. They will want to
know as much as possible about problems and how to manage them. It is
really the only way they will sustain a long-term gambling industry."

"But industry sustainability surely cannot be the only driver for the
sector."

"No, but . . ."

"Okay, let's look more closely at this," intervenes Patrick. "What if the
research funding agency is set up with every effort to protect its independence, including independence from other parts of government? Law could
be enacted that requires the agency to comply with a range of independence
checks. The measures might include annual reports received by all elected
politicians, regular reviews by multiparty select committees, active judicial
monitoring of conflicts of interest, an independently managed complaints
process . . . I don't understand the mechanics, but surely processes like these
can be set up."

"C'mon James" Margie adds. "We are not in an ideal world, and if we
are aware of these dangers, we can at least try to make something like this
work."

"Yes, I can see it could work . . ." James ponders. A gentle breeze is blow-
ing in from the sea. All three are beginning to feel cold and tired. "But, how
on earth could we get government to recognize the need for these measures?
That would be a real challenge."

"Perhaps we can talk more about that tomorrow," suggests Patrick.

The three colleagues turn their backs on the ocean, return to the cottage, shut the door, and busy themselves with preparing for bed.

Comment

This dialogue was devised to highlight the ongoing dilemmas researchers face regarding industry funds.[4] The debates generated are real and I have participated in them on more than one occasion in my university contexts. I have also found that differences in viewpoints can lead to troubled relationships and professional fragmentation throughout the field. Personally I believe the role of researchers and other academics in a democratic society is vital to its functioning and that any risk of association should ideally be avoided or only entered into following a thorough assessment of the risks involved and that strategies are devised to reduce them to acceptable levels (see Chapter 10). As consumption of commercialized gambling products rises, I find myself agreeing more closely with James's position that any relationship of researchers to the gambling industry involves risk. It simply becomes increasingly difficult to conceive of ways that researchers can protect their activities from ethical and reputational risks.[5] The fundamentals of independence and academic freedom are immediately compromised by association with this source of funding. Nonetheless, I also have sympathies with some of the points raised by Margie and believe the debates are what all researchers in this sector need to consider.

RESEARCHER–INDUSTRY RELATIONSHIPS

As the widespread proliferation of commercialized gambling has only occurred relatively recently, open and informed discussion of the ethics of researcher–industry relationships has yet to emerge.[6] Other legalized and commercialized dangerous consumptions—particularly alcohol and tobacco—share a similarly variable and often fraught relationship between those who manufacture the product and those involved in responding to associated harms. The longer history of open commercialization for tobacco and alcohol could provide some useful clues as to how this issue might unfold for gambling. The following section explores ways in which their experience might shed light on the dynamics between researchers and gambling providers (see Doll, Peto, Wheatley, Gray, & Sutherland, 1994).

Tobacco and Alcohol Funding

The most lively and lengthy debate on the morality of industry funding has occurred regarding tobacco. The debate has been assisted by two sources of information: first, the increasing evidence that tobacco has contributed significantly to cancer and other fatal illnesses, and, second, increasing revelations of how the tobacco industry managed to manipulate scientific evidence to stall restrictive legislation. In a study of tobacco industry internal documents Drope and Chapman (2001) identified ways in which the tobacco industry had built up networks of scientists sympathetic who supported its position that environmental tobacco smoke is an insignificant health risk. They concluded that "Industry documents illustrate a deliberate strategy to use scientific consultants to discredit the science on ETS [environmental tobacco smoke]" (p. 588). In a similar study, Fields and Chapman (2003) reviewed internal industry documents concerning a large cigarette firm, Philip Morris, and its grooming over a 40-year period of a leading tobacco scientist, Ernst Wynder. They provided detailed evidence from documents that revealed the thinking of the firms at the time. For example, in considering the rising antitobacco health lobby, Philip Morris executives commented:

> Get scientists who are against us on the primary issue to speak up in our favor on the ETS [environmental tobacco smoke] issue. There are probably quite a number of scientists who would be ready to do this— Wynder is one example. These people should address scientific meetings, conduct interviews with the media, appear on talk shows, etc. We should attempt to arrange debates between these scientists and the more rabid or silly antis. (p. 574)

They were subsequently amply supported by scientists eager to embrace what appeared to be an important source of research funding. In the conclusion of their analysis, they stated:

> In austere funding environments, today's scientists face ongoing funding challenges. The tobacco industry can provide comparatively easy access to allegedly no strings research funds, but there is growing momentum among universities to refuse to permit such funding because of its track record in corrupting the integrity of science. (p. 576)

These concerns have stimulated considerable debate in several of the world's most prestigious medical journals, particularly the *British Medical Journal, Tobacco Control,* and the *Journal of Epidemiology and Community Health.* For example, Richard Smith, the chief editor of the *British Medical Journal,* has published several editorials challenging the willingness of scientists, institutions, and publications to engage in activities associated with tobacco funding. A similarly strong position has been adopted by Simon Chapman at the University of Sydney and editor of the prestigious journal *Tobacco Control.* In considering these issues Turcotte (2003) concluded, "Universities should not enter into any kind of co-operation with the tobacco industry on the grounds that are related to their responsibility, the nature of tobacco problem and the behavior of the tobacco industry" (p. 107). Smith took this position one step further; he resigned from his position as professor of medical journalism at the University of Nottingham after the university accepted $7 million from British American Tobacco to fund an international center for the study of corporate responsibility.

This willingness to move beyond debate to taking action or instituting policy is becoming increasingly common regarding tobacco funding. More organizations are declaring publicly that they will not engage in funding relationships with tobacco manufacturers. To name but a few, these include the American Public Health Association, University of Toronto's School of Social Work, Brigham and Women's and Massachusetts General Hospitals, the M. D. Anderson Cancer Center in Houston, the Roswell Park Cancer Institute, and the University of Sydney (Cohen, 2001; Cohen, Ashley, Ferrence, & Brewster, 1999). All these prestigious establishments have had involvements with tobacco control research. In a discussion of this trend, Cohen et al. (1999) concluded, "We urge colleagues in these settings to demand that the issue of dependence on the tobacco industry in all its forms be explicitly put on policy agendas of their institutions and organizations" (p. 76).

At another level, some health funding institutions are also moving from debate to action by announcing they will not fund research institutions that accept tobacco money. These include the U.K. Cancer Research Campaign, the Norwegian Cancer League, and some members of the Union Internationaele Contre le Cancer (European Cancer League; see Cohen, 2001). At yet another level, some organizations are beginning to explore cross-institutional understandings regarding such funding. In 2004, U.K. universities and the charity Cancer Research U.K. signed a joint protocol on good practice on industry funding that acknowledged that individual universities can decide what research funds to accept or reject, but agreed that they would "consider carefully" whether to accept from any source "if to do so would be potentially detrimental to their reputation" (Mayor, 2004, p. 9). Admittedly, the signing of cross-jurisdictional agreements is a relatively new and controversial development and is contested on a number of grounds, including its threat to academic freedoms.[7]

Alcohol research funding, like gambling, does not share the clear-cut association of tobacco with widespread mortality. Although alcohol has wider impacts in terms of psychological and social harms, the precise nature of these effects is more diffuse and difficult to quantify. Furthermore, alcohol (like gambling) occupies a more ambiguous position in people's minds because of the perception that it contributes positively to most people's quality of life. Nonetheless the question over whether or not alcohol researchers should receive funding from liquor industries has led to many of the same debates that have occurred with regard to tobacco. In an article debating the merits of alcohol funding, Edwards (1998), a leading alcohol and public health researcher, stated:

So should researchers take research money from a tainted industry which exploits vulnerable populations, mounts attacks on valid research and independent researchers, and which, through its front organizations, tries to distort the truth? Those considerations suggest perhaps an answer tilting towards a "no" in a more obvious way than some scientists might on first inspection have thought. (p. 336)

Indeed, as with tobacco, global advocacy for expanding alcohol consumption has enlisted the support of research establishments.[8] However because the ubiquitous nature of alcohol generates more widespread acceptance than tobacco, criticism of their activities is less developed.

The World Health Organization (WHO), through its involvements with both tobacco and alcohol, has maintained an ongoing interest in the link between dangerous consumption manufacturers and public good organizations. These organizations include the WHO itself and its various branches, academic bodies, and civil society or nongovernmental organizations (CSOs or NGOs). In a report as part of its Civil Society Initiative, WHO (2002) examined the principles that could be used to protect such organizations from unmanageable moral jeopardy. For example, WHO (2002) pointed out that NGOs often provide insufficient information regarding governance boards and their funding sources:

> There is also a lack of information regarding those who govern NGOs or sit on NGO boards. This information can be important when board members have connections to certain industries whose goals are considered contrary to WHO's basic public health goals, such as tobacco or arms industry. (p. 16)

From its deliberations, the report recommends that WHO adopt a new policy based on two fundamental principles:

Basic agreement of aims and purposes:

> For both accreditation and collaboration, the basic interest of NGOs shall be consistent with the WHO Constitution and not in conflict with its public health mandate.

Clarity about the nature of Interests:

> Whether for accreditation or for collaboration, the interests of each party shall be clear and transparent. This would include NGOs readily disclosing information on structure, membership, activities and source of financing. (p. 18)

This was further emphasized in WHO's most recent world assembly, which confirmed a policy regarding links to NGOs and in which "collaboration shall not compromise the independence and objectivity of WHO and shall be designed to avoid any conflicts of interest" (as described in WHO, 2004). Again no specific reference is made to gambling, but WHO's understanding of the dynamics of funding from dangerous consumption industries suggests that if it were willing to recognize gambling as a global health issue, it would provide an excellent platform for influencing ethical practice.

General concern about the ethical behavior of researchers in the areas of alcohol, tobacco, and gambling also contributed to the formation of the International Society of Addiction Journal Editors (ISAJE, 2005). At a meeting in Farmington, Connecticut, in July 1997, participating addiction journal editors agreed that members were required to support what they dubbed the Farmington Consensus. This agreement specified ethical standards for journals in the conduct of authors, referees, and editors. The key clauses in the consensus are with regard to "maintaining editorial independence" and include the following:

4.1 We are committed to independence in the editorial process. To the extent that the owner or another body may influence the editorial process, this should be declared, and in that case sources of support from the alcohol, tobacco, pharmaceutical or other relevant interests should be published in the journal.

4.2 We will publish declarations on sources received by a journal, and will maintain openness in regard to connections which a journal or its editorial staff may have established which could reasonably be construed as conflict of interest.

The spirit of the consensus is aimed at reducing industry influence and most addiction journals have agreed to its terms. However, some also contest these clauses on the grounds of academic freedom, arguing that restrictions on industry support could prevent important studies from being published (Davies et al., 2002).

Gambling Funding

An equivalent literature on the ethics of researchers accepting gambling funds has yet to emerge.[9] A literature search we conducted revealed little published discussion and no formal protocols or policies that purport to address this issue.[10] The absence of formal discussion is presumably a function of the relatively recent nature of the global expansion of commercial gambling. However, many examples of the way gambling providers establish relationships with researchers can be observed. These include funding professorial chairs, contributing to university staff development funds, direct funding of research projects, sponsoring academic conferences, sponsoring overseas travel, engaging academic consultants, recruiting academics onto advisory boards, and so forth. With each opportunity, the ethically aware researcher is placed in a quandary as to whether to or how far to engage in any such arrangement. An example that captures this quandary happened to Tim Costello in Melbourne, where he provided prominent opposition to the rapid expansion of gambling in the state of Victoria and throughout Australia. He had summarized the reasons for his opposition in a provocative book published in 2000 (Costello & Milar, 2000). In 2003 he also occupied a senior position in World Vision and was instrumental in that organization refusing to accept $390,000 from a gambling industry source for tsunami relief for nations bordering the Indian Ocean (Pountney, 2005). However, in January 2004 he declared that World Vision had subsequently reversed this decision and had accepted the funding, pointing out that the need for funding was too urgent for them to refuse. The switch highlights the tensions and issues that can accompany financial associations with the profits from gambling.

INCONVENIENT RESEARCH

Parallel to the "inconvenient truths" that Al Gore identified in his campaign for recognition of global warming (Guggenheim & Gore, 2006), inconvenient gambling research has the potential to disrupt and divert the interests of governments and gambling industries in their ongoing pursuit of proliferating gambling consumption. Accordingly, the most convenient position would be to ensure that no research into the harmful effects of gambling take place whatsoever. However, in the public eye, the very newness of high-intensity commercialized gambling appears to demand some form of investigation and the various signals of trouble that percolate episodically into the media (fraud, crime, suicide, etc.) appear to require some form of monitoring. As when any commercial product is introduced on a large scale, research is needed to reassure the public that the product is safe and its use is unlikely to impact negatively on everyday living. In recognition of this expectation, gambling providers and governments accept—or are forced to accept—that some form of research will be a condition of further development. However, if research is going to occur, it is important that its efforts are channeled in directions that are unlikely to throw a questionable light on current activities.

The disruptive potential of well-conducted research cannot afford to be underestimated. Inconvenient health research has included the alarming findings on the negative effects of hormone replacement therapy, research on the fat content in fast foods, and ongoing evidence on environmental tobacco smoke. This type of research has severely disrupted the businesses associated with each of these consumptions. It highlights how well-funded, high-quality research provides a critical source on which media build their descriptions, governments make their decisions, and the public forms its views of the product. If research has the potential to throw a questionable light on rising gambling consumption (and associated profits), it needs to be managed in ways that divert attention away from questions about the product itself. Table 7.1 provides two lists of gambling research activities: one that focuses on research that could be classified as involving low inconvenience to government and industry, and the other that focuses on topics that are highly inconvenient.

What characterizes differences between the two sides of Table 7.1 is how common research on the left is funded compared to that on the right. For example, over the last 15 years state and national governments have regularly invested in large-population telephone surveys of gambling behavior and, with the price tag for a moderate survey costing upward of $1 million, this type of study has soaked up by far the lion's share of investment in gambling research.[11] Relative to other research endeavors, however, the question remains regarding whether this type of research truly advances our understanding of harms from gambling, especially when the outcomes vary little among countries of relatively similar gambling consumption. The main preoccupation in most of these studies has been on establishing the prevalence rates for problem gambling, perhaps suggesting that the 1% to 2% of problem gamblers can somehow summarize the full negative impact of gambling consumption. However, problem gambling, as discussed elsewhere in

Table 7.1 Examples of Low and High Inconvenience Research Topics

Research of Low Inconvenience to Gambling Industry and Government Bodies	Research of High Inconvenience to Gambling Industry and Government Bodies
• Large-population telephone surveys of patterns of gambling and problem gambling prevalence	• Well-conducted social and economic impact studies of harm from gambling
• Surveys of the needs and access issues for problem gamblers	• Research into relative contributions of gambling to other alternatives in a local economy
• Population surveys of current attitudes and beliefs about gambling	• Behavioral research into modifications to gambling technologies that could reduce their harmfulness
• Development of instruments for measuring problem gambling	
• Clinical research on treatment development, treatment services, and treatment effectiveness	• Social research on gambling's contribution to determinants of health such as poverty, crime, poor housing, and so on
• Development and evaluation of public education packages on the risks of problem gambling (brochures, videos, manuals, Internet sites, etc.)	• Investigation of government–industry relationships
	• Design and evaluation of effective community capacity building and health promotion initiatives
• Development and evaluation of youth intervention and education programs	• Research on the effects of gambling advertising

this book, accounts for only one part of the wider socio-ecological impacts of gambling expansion. Further, the method of answering preset questions over a telephone has difficulty capturing the true impacts on families and communities. A second area of high investment—although considerably less than the telephone surveys—is on evaluating treatment strategies for problem gambling. Again the focus on treatment has little potential to challenge or disrupt the business of gambling because, as explored in Chapter 5, the notion of freedom to gamble carries with it the sense that problem gamblers are troubled individuals who would have succumbed to some form of addictive behavior anyway.[12]

The pattern of differential investment into research of low inconvenience calls into question the processes that determine research funding and prompts an interest in those people who are in positions that decide how monies will be allocated. Perhaps sensitive to the criticism of bias, many governments have chosen to establish a range of committees and boards to "advise" them on how they allocate research funding. For example, in Ontario, Canada, where gambling is state-owned, the Ontario Problem Gambling Research Center is funded at "arm's length" by the province's Ministry of Health and Long Term Care. The Center's governance board has members who reflect a combination of community, government, and academic stakeholders, but, despite this apparent independence, with their funding coming from one source—a branch of the same source that manages their gambling industry—it would be foolhardy for the Center to venture into highly inconvenient research. Another common arrangement is the formation of a committee made up of key stakeholders, usually a combination of gambling industry, government agency, and "community" representatives. For example, in Queensland, Australia the Responsible Gambling Advisory Committee is just such a tripartite model, where the three parties together play a central role in defining (through the Queensland Treasurer) priorities for research. Similarly, the directions for research in the United Kingdom are determined by the RIGT, whose board is comprised of industry and community representation; in Ontario, the Responsible Gambling Council has a board of directors with a similar composition. The problem with such arrangements is that both industry and government representatives have a vested interest in ensuring that low-inconvenience research is more likely to occur than high-inconvenience research. The "community" representation (which often consists of church and assistance agency representation) is comprised of representatives from disparate organizations, bringing with them their own ambitions within the gambling sector (many also have gambling services to sustain; see Chapter 8) and often lacking experience and understanding of the business of producing research. Consequently, the equal balance of power is typically an illusion.[13] The more organized and committee-savvy government and industry representatives have far greater influence and can easily ensure that low-convenience research is all that is finally commissioned. In a sense, these committees often provide the impression that community needs are being taken into account when in reality they function in ways that protect government and industry interests.

Linda Hancock Rides the Panel

The State Government of Victoria in Australia embarked on an experiment in research funding that provides an interesting case example of these processes. In November 2000, as a result of the Gaming Machine Control Act 1991 and after exploring a range of other alternatives, the Labor Government led by Steve Bracks established the Victorian Gambling Research Panel for the purpose of directing the funding of research into the impacts of their rapid proliferation of gambling. Linda Hancock was chosen to chair the Panel because of her established university background as associate professor in politics and policy at Deakin University, her role there as the Director of the Public Policy and Governance Program, and her appointment as President of the Victorian Council of Social Services. She was joined on the panel by two other leading figures in business and employment who also lacked ties with or interests in the gambling sector. In reflecting back on the early days, Dr. Hancock commented:

> I think the Bracks Government tried a very brave experiment, if you like. We are the only State to have had an independent research panel, all the other States have their research capacity from within government and quite honestly I think we need an independent panel for research.[14]

Over the next 3 years the Panel commissioned a broad range of research projects, much of them innovative and all of them shedding new light on the impacts of gambling. As late as 2 years into the Panel's operation, the Labor Government praised its activities as

> conducting the most extensive gambling research ever undertaken in Victoria into the social and economic impact of gambling, the causes of problem gambling and strategies to minimize harm from gambling. (Baker & Hannan, 2005)

However, this positive assessment was soon to change. In the ensuing year, members of government were showing signs of increasing discomfort with the content of research reports commissioned by the Panel. Inconvenient outcomes included an in-depth study of the social and economic impacts of gambling a report that indicated that 90% of Victorians wanted a cut in EGMs, and research into the contribution of gambling to poverty. The focus for funding was clearly shifting from research on low-inconvenience topics toward high-inconvenience topics. Perhaps unsurprisingly, government members conveyed increasing discomfort with the activities of the Panel, culminating with the decision in early 2003 to sack Hancock and to disband the Panel altogether.

Explanations for the demise of the Panel after only 3 years of operation are varied. In an article in the Melbourne's main daily newspaper, *The Age*, Hancock indicated she had

> no doubt why her team was dumped by the Bracks Government. "The research findings were not only politically embarrassing for the Government, they showed what little they had done since they came into office." (Baker & Hannan, 2005)

Later in the same article she commented that the Government appeared to be scared of research influencing its gambling revenue:

> "The Government would appear to have two major concerns: to maintain the impression that they are doing something and to keep the industry on side in such a way that it maintains the revenue flow" . . .
>
> Hancock says the industry has been lobbying hard to have research moved from "risky to safe" topics. Now, she says, the future of research planned by the panel into topics such as crime and gambling, suicide and gambling and depression is uncertain . . .
>
> "Our brief under legislation was to look at the social and economic impact of gambling . . . The industry want their industry to be seen as recreational. They want a nice little industry development model when it is actually an industry that's incredibly damaging to the community."[15]

The Minister responsible for disbanding the Panel, John Pandazopoulos, understandably described his dismantling of the Panel as a necessary step. He criticized the Panel for providing insufficient peer review of its reports, inadequate community input, and that its processes had "really become redundant." In December 2003 he signaled the government's intention for gambling research to be managed more "in house" through formation of the Responsible Gambling Ministerial Advisory Council.[16] This new body would be comprised of nine representatives of the gambling industry and nine "community" representatives from diverse contexts such as church organizations, social services, and universities. In a radio interview he explained the new arrangement in these terms:

> There isn't a link between our round table, the community, industry and Government working together to continually reduce the impacts of gambling and research. They have been two separate pieces. Like it or not, World's best practice, Ontario Gaming Council, is what we have modeled this new approach on. Canada has the best models about problem gambling strategies and that means having to work with industry and community.[17]

There are undoubtedly many perspectives regarding the 3-year rise and fall of the Victorian Gambling Research Panel. The many events and processes that happened behind the scenes are likely to be more complex than portrayed here. Notwithstanding these complexities, the overall sequence of events does illustrate the issues discussed earlier in the chapter: An independent process was established to guide research funding; the commissioned research shifted toward high-inconvenience topics; the government is then forced to field embarrassing research outcomes; the independent process is replaced by a process that is directed primarily by government and industry interests; and subsequently, the research commissioned shifts in favor of low-inconvenience projects.

The content in Chapters 2 and 4 explored the concept of moral jeopardy with regard to community organizations accepting funds from gambling industries. The notion of moral jeopardy applies equally, if not more so, to academic and research organizations. As depicted in the dialogue earlier, the moral jeopardy that researchers face involves the same four dimensions, namely ethical risks (e.g., trying to do good from proceeds from doing harm), reputational risks (e.g., judgment by others for having associations with a source of harm), governance risks (e.g., increasing dependence on this source), and relationship risks (e.g., relationship conflict between colleagues). Later Chapter 10 will explore ways for community and research organizations to assess these risks and to make informed decisions on their level of involvement.

8 Helping Professionals on the Frontier

A natural by-product of the expansion of commercialized gambling is the steady rise in the numbers of those troubled enough by gambling to seek professional help. This demand has propelled the emergence of many small organizations that seek to assist people with gambling problems. The majority of these consist of organizations that provide individuals with short-term counseling, but other variants include telephone helplines, family counseling, budgeting services, longer term residential programs, and cultural programs. Helping professionals dealing with problem gamblers have a special role in the interface between gambling and democratic societies. They are interacting daily with the tough realities faced by problem gamblers and their families. During these interactions they hear detailed accounts of how gambling losses have impoverished families and led to crime, violence, and separations, and how these effects have sliced deep and permanent wounds into the minds and hearts of those most affected. Through these exposures they are placed in a unique position during the initial expansion of commercial gambling because few others have access to the range and depth of accounts of the full extent of the suffering and chaos that enters the homes of those affected. Consequently, this exposure carries with it a strong obligation for helping professionals to bear witness to what they have heard and to carry this out into the public domain. This is a critical democratic role. They are presented with the challenge of acting as a mouthpiece for the lived experience of problem gambling. In the absence of other voices, they also face the moral imperative to extend their mouthpiece role to the more active role as advocates for change. In the context of the broad expansion of extractive gambling industries, this chapter examines features of the early years of problem gambling helping organizations and how people working within them encounter pressures to compromise these democratic responsibilities.

PROBLEM GAMBLING HELPING ORGANIZATIONS

Parallel to the rapid rises in gambling consumption, the small frontier helping organizations that first respond to problem gambling can grow at surprising rates, particularly as cries for help rise in intensity.

Responding to Need

The costs associated with problem gambling have escalated as the proliferation of commercial gambling has spread through Western-style democracies. In an attempt in 1999 by the National Opinion Research Center at the University of Chicago to estimate these costs across the United States, based on estimates of 2.5% of adults being pathological problem gamblers they settled on a figure $5 billion per year and an additional $40 billion in lifetime costs for productivity reductions, social services, and creditor losses (Gernstein et al., 1999).[1] At around the same time, a similar exercise by the Australian Productivity Commission (1999) estimated the costs of problem gambling in their country as falling between $1.4 billion and $4.3 billion.[2] Another indicator of rising levels of problem gambling is the amount countries are choosing to spend on services. For example, expenditure on problem gambling services across the provinces of Canada rose from $12.8 million in 1997 to $38.8 million 5 years later (Azmier, 2001). Although most problem gamblers choose not to seek help, and the rates of those who do are subject to the availability of suitable services, increases in presentation rates can also give some idea of increases in problem gambling. Unfortunately problem gambling services are dispersed across different agencies and often incorporated as a part of broader services, such as addiction and mental health services.[3] Consequently it is difficult to track changes in the numbers of people presenting for help. For example, in the United Kingdom, the major provider of gambling services, GamCare, reported an increase from 792 face-to-face client counseling sessions in 2001 to 3,268 in 2005,[4] but this information misses presentations to other services (e.g., their BreakEven partners) and presentations to other addiction and mental health services. One exception is the way data on problem gambling services have been collected in New Zealand. Their system was advantaged in having close to all of its problem gambling services developed from one funding agency, which chose to develop a uniform data collection process more than 8 years ago.[5] They were able to track in New Zealand, parallel to rising gambling consumption (driven particularly by increased EGM use), the rates of problem gamblers seeking help has increased markedly. During 2002, the total number of new clients using personal counseling was 2,467, up 15.1% from the previous year and up 177% from 6 years earlier. New callers in 2002 to a national telephone helpline were 4,715, up 23.6% from the previous year and up 131.9% from 6 years earlier.[6] The primary mode of gambling for those seeking help had also changed in accordance with the increased availability of EGMs. Whereas in 1999, 70% of new personal counseling clients and 77% of new telephone helpline clients reported EGMs as their primary mode of gambling, by 2002 these proportions had risen to 86% for personal counseling and 90% for telephone helpline clients.

Emergent Responses

Across these flagship democracies, the picture that emerges is one of commercialized gambling plowing ever onward into communities. In the process these communities accumulate significant numbers of problem gamblers requiring help. The assertive citizenry within grows increasingly aware of the issues and begins to demand that if there are serious problems then some attempt should be made to address them. In response to demand, problem gambling organizations establish themselves in different shapes and sizes throughout these communities, and then proceed to spread their operations in a wide variety of forms. The first organizations often consist of small NGOs that have either sprung from the energy of affected people or form as a revenue-generating diversification of an established helping service, such as a relationship counseling service or a generic telephone helpline service. These pioneer organizations typically lack clear reference points or precedents that could be used to guide their development. They are first on the spot and either forge their own pathways or attempt to imitate other related services such as addiction or counseling services. As with the birth of any new service sector, the initial environment is volatile and opportunism is rife; funding structures change with little warning, broader infrastructural supports (e.g., workforce development, research, and ethical standards) are unformed and gambling industries tend to play influential roles in key events. In response to this volatility, the life cycle of individual helping organizations tends to follow a boom and bust pattern. They form quickly, rapidly expand, and then disappear just as quickly; sometimes they mutate or are absorbed into other organizations; sometimes they split into smaller units with specialist functions. Again, the volatility tends to reflect the broader changeability of the gambling sector as a whole.

One way to approach this early period of helping services is to view them as ancillary industries to the broader expansion of the gambling industries themselves. Consequently, in accordance with what was portrayed in Chapter 1, if the expansion of commercial gambling can be likened to the early days of primary extractive industries (e.g., mining and native forestry), then helping organizations can be viewed as resembling small frontier towns that have been established to service an aspect of this expansion. As with new industries, the growth of these helping organizations reflects what occurs in frontier societies.

Much of what is popularly understood by the character of frontier towns is derived from the large number of novels and movies that depict life in the pioneer towns of the American "Wild West."[7] These towns provide the ideal settings for stories that emerge from contexts of rapid development on new terrain. They are stories involving high drama, outrageous adventures, lawlessness, and morality plays of tragedy and loss, triumph and success, violation and reconciliation. They tend to involve larger-than-life characters driven as much by optimism and hope as by ambition and greed. The interplay among these characters underpins set pieces for encountering and resolving raw ethical dilemmas. For example, a farmer on cramped marginal lands in the East moves to the West in search of new opportunities. He enters a small Wild West town and soon finds many of the controls that limited his previous life no longer apply; he is free to pursue interests and develop his potential in ways he sees fit. However, he finds the lack of societal constraints places greater reliance on his individual capacity for ethical decision making. The town lacks adequate systems to respond to fraud, corruption, violence, and other predatory activities. On a daily basis as an individual in a general environment of lawlessness, he faces ongoing and difficult decisions on the morality of his involvements. Similarly, in other societies pioneered by Europeans (e.g., those early communities in Latin America, Canada, and Australasia) these pioneering towns formed a critical network in the breaking in of the land for agriculture and in servicing the exploitation of native forests and the mining of precious metals.

INHABITANTS OF FRONTIER TOWNS

The last 14 years of my involvement in remedial responses to problem gambling has enabled me to observe the evolution of specialist problem gambling professionals and the organizations in which they practice. I have participated extensively in the development of these frontier organizations[8] and what has struck me on many occasions is how the process of moving into new and unexplored territory carries with it features that are unique in themselves. In particular, people drawn into these volatile and unpredictable environments tend to resemble particular character types that are shaped by certain key motivations. As is often the case in frontier towns, the characters are larger than life, almost exaggerations of personalities encountered in established societies. As is required for people who break new ground, they tend to be bold, ambitious, and purposeful. They are driven first by the limitations they have experienced from where they came from and then by the prospects for change, success, and adventure in the new environment. The following sections describe four common character types that capture what I have observed within these organizations: these consist of missionaries, glory seekers, traders, and medicine men.

Missionaries

Missionaries are driven primarily by their commitment to working for what they understand to be the greater good. This greater good could refer to the divine or an altruistic desire to improve the lot of society, it could refer to a belief and a willingness to transfer advantages from one culture to another, or it could stem from a strong inner commitment to social justice. These qualities can be seen in the Jesuit missionaries in the jungles of South America, the clergy from the London Missionary Society who opened up the Pacific, and to some extent the in modern equivalents of Mother Teresa in Calcutta and Bob Geldof's campaigns for Africa. The causes vary but their zeal for what they believe to be right fuel almost superhuman capacities to overcome enormous obstacles and to endure extreme peril in pursuit of their worthy causes. Their commitment to God, humanity, and justice takes them into zones that few others would dare to tread. They are often the first to enter a new territory, and they set up their mission stations, which later provide the base that attracts adventurers and traders and around which the first frontier towns are established.

Missionaries on the frontier of gambling expansion tend to be larger-than-life personalities with an ardent zeal for gambling as a social justice issue. Like other missionaries, they are usually early entrants into the field and whereas most others are slow to appreciate the broader implications, the missionary is highly sensitized to the socially distorting dimensions of wide-spread commercial gambling—particularly its potential to support uneven and unjust discrepancies in power. They often arrive before any funding mechanisms have been created, well before the prospects for money and glory have emerged. Consequently their activities are often poorly remuner-ated and they are motivated more by a deep concern about the impacts of problem gambling and are attracted by the opportunity to make a differ-ence for the future. For some, their commitment has emerged from their own experiences of problem gambling. Often they themselves are recovering problem gamblers or they have loved ones who have been severely affected. For others, the motive springs from a lifelong interest in and commitment to issues of social justice. They might have participated in broader movements concerned about poverty and discrimination. They might also belong to reli-gious organizations that have a social justice agenda. From whatever back-ground, missionaries tend to have managed early on to identify the potential for gambling to further affect the poor and disadvantaged, and accordingly they feel compelled to fight further expansion before commercial gambling establishes a permanent power base.

The commitment of missionaries on the frontier of gambling expansion will often lead them to expend sustained amounts of effort for little personal gain. Their efforts often create a rallying point for the formation of fledgling helping organizations. Missionaries are prepared to work long hours for little pay; they are willing to put up with uncertain income, poor wages, and cramped housing, and to become linked with what on the whole is seen as an unpopular cause. Their willingness to put up with unpredictable and adverse conditions and to persist with an enterprise that at times seems hopeless draws other people toward them and inspires them to make a simi-lar commitment. In time a rudimentary mission house is established that soon functions as a meeting point for like-minded crusaders and thereby becomes a place for conceiving, planning, and implementing activities aimed at constraining gambling expansion. These small, vulnerable locations provide the seed for forming helping organizations both within and attached to these locations.

Glory Seekers

A second group of entrants into the frontier towns of gambling services are those attracted by the prospect of obtaining positions of power and influence. Although making money is typically a part of what initially motivates their interest, the primary goal of glory seekers is to establish their reputations and make a name for themselves. The frontier calls to them with promises of new opportunities; it holds out to them the tantalizing prospect of new adventures with the hope of gaining fame and fortune. The range of new entrants responding to this call can include people in the roles of soldiers, social innovators, lawmakers, local politicians, newspaper owners, and so on. The frontier town established by missionaries is soon peopled by those hungry for a chance to prove their worth and willing to invest in risky ventures. Accordingly, such people often see their future prospects constrained in the slow-moving structures of established and settled societies, and view the fluid and arbitrary processes of the frontier as ideally suited to their talents.

In a similar way, the helping professionals that seek glory by venturing into gambling services often perceive themselves as trapped and constrained within their previous contexts. They have worked hard to obtain the appropriate tertiary qualifications only to find themselves caught in poorly funded and inadequately supported addiction and mental health services with little prospect of change or advancement. They watch the new field opening up; they talk with colleagues who have packed up to explore the new frontier; they begin to see their own prospects unfolding in the quickly changing frontier environment. They are drawn by the prospect of developing a reputation, creating new positions of influence and power, setting up new enterprises, and so forth. To delay involvement could mean missing out and risk arriving when all the opportunities have consolidated into organizational structures. Indeed, the first glory seekers who venture into this new world soon encounter a line of people seeking their advice. They find their opinions regularly solicited by news media and when a controversial story breaks, they could be interviewed by reporters as many as 10 times in one afternoon.[9] For example, when figures on increases in the rates of people seeking help are released, news media outlets will seek out helping professionals to provide more solid accounts of what these increases mean. From virtual obscurity, counselors are thrust into the limelight of regular newspaper, radio, and television interviews. The public wants to know directly from them details on the effects this new phenomenon of problem gambling is having on individuals and families.

Glory seekers play an important role in the early development of frontier helping organizations. They not only enhance their own profile, but more importantly, they play a central role in raising public awareness of the negative impacts of gambling. This is critically important, particularly during early gambling expansion when a naive public lacks a sense of the dangers associated with high-frequency gambling. The glory seeker's regular media presence provides an identifiable focus for the key issues. However, for glory seekers themselves, this constant media attention and their membership on high-level administrative committees can have a distorting and sometimes tragically disorienting effect. What was perhaps initially a vague interest in profile has been sharpened through constant attention into a driving interest. The exposure magnifies this one aspect of their character to levels that later prove difficult to manage. Furthermore, some glory seekers are thrust way beyond what their qualifications and experience have equipped them for. Their appetite for profile now outstrips their ability, a recipe that can result in either public humiliations or extreme disappointment when their contribution is no longer sought.

Traders

Traders are primarily interested in the capacity of the frontier to turn a profit. In some ways they resemble the gold miners and lumberjacks of the primary extractive industries in that they are driven by the prospect of either personal fortune or of setting up money-making enterprises from which they will eventually derive personal fortunes. However, in other ways they differ from people in the extractive industries. They have a less direct relationship to the primary product. They come into the new towns to set up their business entities; these include food stores, clothing shops, hotels, and bars, as well as businesses that service needs or equipment peculiar to the industry itself, such as chainsaw repair, digging equipment, and the need for special chemicals and medications. They rely essentially on interaction and exchange within the frontier environment, and for that reason it is their businesses and not the products themselves that provide the base for building their future prosperity. The traders' success relies entirely on the volume of trade and the premium placed on their product or service. They remain derivative and dependent on the level of commercial activity in the broader region, but besides the extractive industry leaders, they are often second in line to turning a profit.

Addiction, mental health, social service, and other professionals are often acutely aware of the limited opportunities available in the strongly structured and hierarchical systems of their settled services. They sit feeling trapped and constrained in their current jobs, with a burning desire to demonstrate their capacity to lead developments in new directions. They look out at the wealth created by the gambling industries and they notice the public pressure being applied to these industries to respond to the increasingly visible line of problem gamblers. They anticipate that at least part of this wealth will inevitably be channeled into new services for problem gambling. They then recognize that providing services will require the development of organizational structures that support service delivery and that within these structures a variety of skills and abilities will be required. They also have a sense that the opportunity to build such structures is exactly what they have been denied in their current circumstances. Some begin their trading by applying directly for leadership and managerial roles. Some respond to job advertisements for clinical supervisors or project coordinators and work up from there. The more adventurous lead consortiums in securing direct bids for funding and from this success consolidate the activity into a new organizational base. By whichever route, the trader has moved from being a minor player in a stable and constrained environment to being a major player at the center of a volatile and unstable structure imbued with risks and opportunities.

Traders contribute strongly to the formation of frontier helping organizations. It is their energy that helps secure ongoing funding, it is they who work tirelessly at enticing and retaining suitable staff, and it is their efforts that build up the organizational systems and procedures that enable services to operate. Furthermore, they are often called on to initiate these systems all at the same time. Perhaps cobbling together funding from one source, they are engaging staff on limited terms from another source and recruiting semiwilling acquaintances into governance and advisory roles. In a fickle funding environment, it appears to them that they are playing a fine balancing act involving considerable guesswork and risk-taking, where one mistake could trigger a chain reaction that could entail the collapse of the organization as a whole. To reduce these risks, traders put enormous energy into diversifying activities and sources of funding and fostering relationships with power brokers.[10] Although their efforts are often rewarded with rapid organizational growth, it still remains a very risky business. For example, the frontier trader typically lacks qualifications or experience in management and as the organization grows they feel progressively more out of their depth and typically respond by trying to directly manage all aspects of the business. They might employ qualified managers, accountants, and business consultants, but because of the perceived risk, they are often unwilling to relinquish hands-on control. Others involved can become disenchanted with this level of control, and as the organization grows, deficiencies in management emerge, which can lead to crises and even outside investigations.

Medicine Men

Medicine men (and women[11]) are attracted to frontier society by the prospect of trading in treatments that meet the growing demand for remedial services. People on the frontier typically lack access to the level of health care enjoyed by people in settled societies. Consequently those who encounter health problems, lacking other opportunities, will enthusiastically embrace whatever remedies happen to pass their way. In response to this demand, medicine men move across the frontier pedaling their various potions and pills or offering forms of therapy that vaguely make sense based on the nature of the affliction. Pills are pedaled claiming to relieve a wide range of symptoms, bad-tasting concoctions are explained to poison out an illness, or a massage contraption is claimed to knead out muscle injuries. The early cures tend to combine folk logic with some active therapeutic ingredients that in some cases might provide genuine relief, but in others provide more the perception rather than the reality of remediation. As the remedies become more recognized, they establish stable markets, and the medicine man is able to settle in one place and concentrate specifically on developing cures on an ongoing basis.

On the frontier of gambling expansion, the emerging group of problem gamblers reaches out in increasing numbers and with rising levels of desperation for cures to the miseries associated with their relapsing disorder. Frontier helping organizations, working alongside the primary extractive industries, seek to address this need by offering some forms of credible remedy. Gambling providers themselves are concerned about ways of reducing at least the appearance of harm caused by their products and are therefore also interested in supporting what medicine men can achieve. However, in a new territory it is unclear what remedies are appropriate, let alone knowing which approach actually works. Along with their clients, the new organizations reach out strongly and grasp at any strategy that appears to offer the hope of cure. The range and diversity of what is soon being offered can be staggering. With regard to psychotherapeutic methods, variations include psychoanalytic and psychodynamic therapies, psychodrama, natural process therapies, and hypnotic induction. The range of systemic approaches includes couples, structural, strategic, cybernetic, and narrative therapies. Psychotherapists were the very early pioneering medicine men for problem gambling, and some were operating well before the current global expansion of gambling got underway.[12] With regard to counseling methods, many medicine men have drifted across from other areas of addiction and mental health, perhaps attracted into the new territory because of its undefined nature. The application of counseling approaches has been diverse and include methods such as Rogerian client-centered approaches, problem-solving approaches, motivational interviewing, rational emotive therapy, and group therapies that include applications of therapeutic communities and 12-step approaches developed by Alcoholics Anonymous and adapted for Gamblers Anonymous (for discussion of these approaches, see reviews by Ledgerwood & Petry, 2005; Orford et al., 2003; Pallesen et al., 2005; Raylu & Oei, 2002). With regard to behavioral methods, strategies that have been applied include aversion therapy, systematic or imaginal desensitization, and cognitive therapies that range from traditional cognitive behavioral approaches to more recent hybrids that incorporate dialectical and stress-coping methods (see, e.g., Blaszczynski & Silove, 1995; Jackson et al., 2000; Ladouceur & Walker, 1996; McConaghy, Armstrong, Blaszczynski, & Allcock, 1983; Petry et al., 2006). Other medical practitioners also join the list in interventions such as the use of antidepressants, opioid antagonists, or combinations of both (see, e.g., Grant & Kim, 2002; Lim & Sellman, 2004). Also of interest is the migration of medicine men from practice domains other than casework. These include those transposing approaches from public health, health promotion, and social marketing, plus an array of cultural approaches, all developed in other contexts.[13]

The presence of medicine men in the frontier town can generate considerable energy and innovation with what they have to offer. They typically participate actively in the formation of new services and provide a focus for treatment activity. The contribution of medicine men can also lead to pointless quackery, with exaggerated claims of effectiveness and the emergence of approaches better suited to other contexts.

Operating in the Frontier Town

The characters just outlined combine to form an interesting mix of people working together and forming relationships in the frontier town. For many, it is not always clear-cut as to their primary motive for migrating into the area; this tends to emerge over time. Many more have bits of each motive and might change their orientation as time goes on.[14] What is surprising is that in the early days of the frontier town, these people driven by very different motives can, perhaps out of necessity, function together quite well. In other circumstances, the diversity of motives could form the basis for conflict, but as in any frontier town, the imperative for development overrides interpersonal differences and the most unlikely characters find effective ways of forming close working relationships. I have observed clusters of all four character types working amicably and effectively in developing their services: Glory seekers present the experience of problem gamblers to the public; missionaries challenge the gambling industry; traders initiate and build up the platform for delivering help; and medicine men assist in the formulation of initial cures.

In this flexible and at times volatile environment, when these various characters pull together, services can take shape quickly. Unimpeded by formal structures and years of tradition, the frontier team can change strategies quickly to suit the circumstances. For example, in a frontier team I participated in 1996 and 1997, the funding organization suddenly cut support for the central part of the service, a national telephone helpline. Such a blow to funding in more established environments would have been fatal, but the frontier team rose immediately to the challenge. In a matter of weeks counselors were engaged in various locations throughout the country, offices were opened in the main centers, we quickly reinvented the organization as a national face-to-face counseling service, and then successfully negotiated funding on that basis. In this way the frontier team, perhaps out of necessity, operates in a flexible and innovative fashion, with, missionaries providing the direction, medicine men providing ideas, glory seekers providing the profile, and traders providing the operational base.

INDUSTRIAL RELATIONS

The significantly larger extractive gambling industry stands as a formidable structure next to these fledgling helping towns. Small clusters of helping professionals often persevere with few resources, uncertain funding, and transient membership. The frailty of their survival leads them to take a critical interest in the status of their relationship with the gambling industries that dwarf them. What's more, their funding is often derived either directly from industrial activities or indirectly from that source but mediated through government agencies. Their existence is so small and vulnerable that gambling industries could collectively choose to ignore them; that is, they could ignore them except for one thing: Those working in helping organizations have direct access to the suffering caused by problem gambling, and speaking out about this pain could form the basis for community disquiet. This is of concern because although helping organizations operate in the shadow of the gambling industries, they also possess this challenging capacity to unveil the human reality of harm from gambling. For helping organizations, this combination of dependence and antipathy unfolds in a series of tense and often testy interactions with gambling industries. Both parties have some level of reliance on each other, but both also maintain disdain for the overall intent of their operations. Government ambivalence toward this extractive industry further complicates the scene. During the phases of liberalization and normalization, government agencies and their officials recognize the imperatives to provide some assistance to those who have fallen prey to gambling, but they, too, are wary of the capacity of assertive helping organizations that could openly question their policies.[15]

Professional helpers tend to view speaking out independently about harms from gambling as an important role. They view themselves as having a democratic duty to act as a mouthpiece for the accounts of misery they hear every day from problem gamblers and their families. They recognize that few other people are in a position to attain their level of understanding on the human impacts of addictive gambling. However, the pursuit of this duty will, of course, create challenges for their relationship with their larger and parallel communities, the gambling industries. Gambling providers with an eye on expanding operations and governments with an eye on increased tax revenue will not wish their voices to become loud enough to unsettle their plans for development. These voices need to be contained, limited, and perhaps even neutralized in ways that do not appear conspicuously as though a stronger body is silencing a weaker one. One way extractive industries neutralize these potential threats is by exploiting the diversity of characters that reside in the frontier helping towns. As the newly commercialized extractive industries bed in, they are able to invest in risk management activities that allow them to develop the intelligence and strategies to influence the behavior of helping professionals.[16] As larger and more powerful organizations, they can mobilize resources to manage this risk. Often casinos with larger centralized operations are better equipped to lead these activities, but their initiatives often involve links with other gambling providers.[17] They also have varying levels of support from government agencies, particularly in early expansion and liberalization, so they can expect little interference in actively managing the sector. The following explores some the strategies they might deploy to minimize these threats and that involve exploiting the vulnerabilities of each of the frontier characters discussed earlier.

Radicalizing the Missionary

As discussed in Chapter 5, during the early stages of gambling expansion, public interest is low and gambling industries can afford to ignore the lonely voices of their detractors. As the impacts of gambling become more visible, the uncompromising objections of missionaries can prove very effective in mobilizing public outrage. For the sake of business growth, gambling providers can no longer afford to simply ignore missionary protestations because as the suffering becomes more obvious their credibility with the public increases. A different approach is required, ideally one that involves silencing or discrediting their criticisms. However, the task of finding an effective response to missionaries can prove very problematic. In the first place, missionaries are not easy to engage in frank dialogue and when gambling providers attempt to communicate, missionaries tend to exploit it as a basis for further criticism. In the second place, missionaries tend to build up a strong support base within their home institutions (e.g., a church, service, or academic organization) and any deviations from their strongly stated principles would pose issues for them with their support base. For example, if such a person in a church organization were to engage in cordial relationships with a local casino, others in that church might feel strong discomfort and perhaps confusion at the involvement.[18] Finally, missionaries are also unlikely to respond to strategies based on offers of money and glory. On the contrary, they are more likely to balk at such offers and end up protesting even more vigorously and proclaiming very loudly that they are being bribed to compromise their principles. Missionaries need to be managed in a different way that bypasses the strengths and exploits the weaknesses in their character. It is in their allegiance to issues of principle that provide gambling industries with their main opportunity.

Missionaries will be in the forefront of protesting against gambling expansion and will typically speak out openly and forcefully about the negative impacts of increases in consumption. In this way they become publicly identified with the position of opposing gambling expansion. This public and intensely principled opposition is undoubtedly their main strength, but it also underlines their main weakness. Their typically poor financial base means they have limited capacity to manage how the public perceives this principled position. In contrast, gambling providers are not so restricted and with their stronger financial base they are typically capable of exerting influence on public understandings of gambling through their direct investment in public communication. For example, as discussed in Chapter 6, one of the primary goals of gambling advertising is to normalize the consumption of commercial gambling. The increased accessibility to gambling is depicted as modern, sophisticated, enhancing "our" way of life, good for the economy, and, through charitable contributions, good for communities. With repeated exposure to these marketing messages, what is deemed "normal" shifts progressively from low-frequency gambling to acceptance of moderate and responsible consumption as an acceptable part of everyday lifestyles. Opposition to this change is positioned as abnormal—or at least counter-normal or radical—and thereby the onus of justification is transferred from the shoulders of those who are introducing new forms of consumption to those who are opposing it. What right do these few self-appointed moral guardians have to deny a mature public access to some relatively harmless fun? It is fun that everyone can enjoy, and although a small number might be negatively affected, it on balance benefits most communities. This message sustained over time positions missionaries as countering common and acceptable views and so it becomes their responsibility to find evidence that justifies the restrictions they are advancing. Furthermore, the repositioning links them with the fun-spoiling conservatism reminiscent of the protestant puritanism that characterized the temperance and antipornography movements of the last century.

Representation of missionaries as radical puritans places them in an awkward position. The more loudly they speak in opposition to expansion, the more they appear to be adopting positions that seem radical and unreasonable. They might try to tone it down with claims such as "I am not opposed to gambling" and "We are not against people having fun." Yet, no matter how toned down they describe their position, once they get into criticizing expanded consumption, they immediately appear to be opposing public enjoyment. Because missionaries are committed to a position of principle they can be relied on not to conceal the strength of their position for long, it might only take a little prompting for their core views to emerge, thereby giving their opponents further opportunity to cast them in the role of radical puritans. The dilemma this creates is excruciating: Do they speak out openly and risk ridicule and ostracism or do they tone their views down to a more publicly palatable form and risk not delivering their primary message? Some missionaries choose to ignore this repositioning and embark openly in a "No Pokies" or "casiNO" campaign.[19] Their openly radical position can alienate them from public opinion and sometimes put them in conflict with colleagues and organizations that are adopting a more conciliatory course. Other missionaries work more strategically by speaking out on issues (e.g., youth gambling, suicide, and consumer protection) where public support is likely to be more sympathetic. In doing so, they run the risk of being perceived as too compliant with expansion trends and perhaps also as weak and inconsistent. Whichever of the two directions they choose, missionaries are likely to experience this environment as increasingly unsatisfactory. They are repeatedly disappointed with their own achievements and discouraged by the lack of moral integrity and commitment in the frontier town. As the town transforms from frontier to settled society, they become increasingly tempted to move on to new frontiers where issues of principle can be more clearly championed.

Partnering With Glory Seekers

In the early days of the frontier, glory-seeking helping professionals find it easy to acquire the profile they seek. Media outlets are hungry for stories of woe and they have few people they can call on for informed comment, so counselors and other practitioners new to the field can find themselves quoted on the front pages of local newspapers, thrust into interviews on national television, and courted for their expertise by a variety of organizations that include regulatory committees and government agencies. For many professionals the attention is alien and disconcerting; but for those motivated by glory, the attention is highly engaging and a recognizable public profile is soon formed. The glory seeker is then in a position to contribute positively to providing a public voice to the suffering associated with public gambling and accordingly they are valued and often celebrated members of the frontier helping organization. However, as more people with similar motives move into the territory, the opportunity for profile and reputation building is contested and the early entrants can soon find themselves crowded by others vying for the same attention. To make matters worse, the newcomers are perhaps better qualified and hungrier for expert profiling. Instead of being actively sought by the media, seasoned campaigners can find themselves joining a queue of experts brandishing press releases with equally sad stories and shocking statistics. The media are now in the driver's seat and can pick and choose with whom they speak according to the angle of the story they have resolved to pursue. The task of maintaining either a public profile or a recognized reputation then depends on either finding some way of maintaining an advantage over other contenders or finding a specialized niche that others would have difficulty providing.

This emerging competitive situation presents a prime opportunity for gambling industries to play an active part in the interaction. When profile for helping professionals becomes a scarce resource, glory seekers are vulnerable to being enticed into a range of new territories that involve partnerships with industry providers. Associations with gambling providers allow them to access a platform on which they can continue to profile their activities and abilities. This can happen in a variety of ways. In some circumstances the gambling provider engages key people through their helping organization. For example, a local EGM provider might engage a problem gambling service in providing staff training as part of developing a credible host responsibility program. Through their involvement, helping professionals enhance not only their own reputation, but also the profile of their organization. In other circumstances helping professionals are contracted on a limited basis for specific tasks such as advising on the development of systems for staff to screen problem gamblers. In yet other circumstances the helping professional is recruited out of the helping organization (frontier town) and employed directly by the gambling provider. For example, a casino might offer full employment to a helping professional in managing their harm minimization and risk assessment programs.[20] The professionals who accept this role will find themselves accessing opportunities and resources that they had never thought possible in the frontier helping organizations. They are now able to mount high-profile harm minimization initiatives that enhance the credibility of the gambling provider and further boost their own profile.

As already mentioned, glory seekers are often a positive force within helping organizations. They bring energy, innovation, and high profile to their activities. The loss of their contribution and their move to supporting the extractive activities of gambling providers is likely to be experienced as a double blow. Not only do helping organizations lose a source of positive energy, but that energy is now focused on enhancing the credibility of activities associated with the further expansion of gambling consumption.

Splitting the Traders

The main interest of traders is in continuing to trade, for it is the activity of trading itself that determines the size and stability of their working platform. For this reason they devote the majority of their energy to fostering increased activity. They put energy into designing new projects, securing contracts, accessing clients, attracting credible staff, and so forth. With each success their trading base expands and the strength and security of their organization grows. This effort is critical to survival on the frontier, where circumstances can change very quickly and organizations need to be prepared to adapt. Accordingly, traders play an important role in the vitality of frontier societies. They have built up their careers by creating thriving helping organizations that hire people, fill buildings, service clients, enhance reputations, and so forth. Their main interest is in keeping the volume of exchange going. Any interruption to the volume of activity will place their organization at risk.

Gambling providers in many situations share a common interest with governments in keeping threats to increased consumption to a minimum. Large, assertive, and outspoken helping organizations are undoubtedly a threat because they are capable of speaking out about negative impacts in all sorts of ways. A safer environment for them is where these frontier helping organizations never reach sufficient critical mass or independence that they are capable of advocacy without risking their future funding base. This can be achieved by engineering a funding environment in which small trader-led organizations are constantly vying with each other for funding opportunities.[21] Keep the agencies small, fund activities on a limited term, and make sure several agencies are providing similar services. The perception of insecurity will naturally escalate and traders can then be relied on to keep other helping professionals in line. When one organization grows too outspoken, they receive reduced funding, which jeopardizes their future and acts as a reminder to other traders that their business is vulnerable.

I have on a variety of occasions and in several different countries had the opportunity to speak with helping agency staff and their managers about how industrial relationships affect their capacity to speak openly about gambling expansion. In each situation they have described reluctance and sometimes fear about the consequences of speaking out explicitly about the impact of gambling on their communities. For example, a counselor working in a small gambling counseling organization in Australia disclosed how, after he was quoted in his local newspaper commenting on the impacts of problem gambling in his community, he received a phone call from a government official reminding him of the source of his funding and that further advocacy could jeopardize its flow. However, direct threats from government officials such as this are uncommon. In an environment where helping organizations are kept intentionally small, what is more common is control that is maintained by traders concerned about threats to income. The threat of missing out in the next funding round, whether real or perceived, is enough to motivate traders into maintaining some restrictive control over their staff. For example, staff members from several agencies have spoken to me about how it is their own managers who take active and often punitive measures to restrict their speaking out about harm from gambling. From the traders' perspective, several managers in Australian agencies have described how after taking an active stand on expansion issues, their agencies subsequently missed out on major funding opportunities. For traders the decision is simple: Why burn out resources in standing up valiantly on one issue when the survival of your organization and the people it helps are more important in the long term? The cost of advocacy for small helping agencies is simply too great. This position can lead naturally to generating self-fulfilling suspicions. For example, a senior member from a Canadian helping agency indicated that people were reluctant to speak out not because of any specific threats, but because there was a general, almost unspoken awareness that staff should avoid particular issues in case it embarrassed funding bodies.[22]

Hiring Medicine Men

In the early phases of gambling expansion, medicine men, like glory seekers, find what they have to offer in hot demand and have little difficulty engaging the interest of clients and helping organizations. Psychological methods developed in other related fields (e.g., addiction and mental health) are shipped in and, with some minor changes, are administered with enthusiasm to those in need. As the frontier matures, more medicine men crowd into the territory, adding progressively to a lengthening list of treatment options. Helping organizations and their funding agencies can find themselves bewildered by the range of possibilities with little in the way of solid research to help in distinguishing effective from ineffective interventions. In a sense, anything goes. Each approach to intervention shares an equally undeveloped research base. To contain costs, funders attempt to limit the extent of what they are prepared to finance. One containment strategy involves the release of best practice guidelines with only one or two approaches identified as acceptable.[23] However, at this stage the guidelines can only justify choices on a limited and questionable research base, and these are easily discredited. Another containment strategy involves limiting the number of organizations that are funded to provide interventions with the expectation that fewer agencies mean fewer types of intervention.[24] Although this strategy risks the formation of strong and assertive agencies, as long as competition for funding continues between these agencies their ability to challenge the expansion is contained.

The motives that propel medicine men differ from those of glory seekers in that medicine men are less focused on increasing their profile per se and more interested in advancing a particular approach or methodology. The frontier offers them promising new opportunities to further develop what for them has been a long-term commitment to their preferred approach. Whereas in more established sectors the development of methods has proceeded down well-trodden paths, with gambling they now find themselves in a new and unexplored territory with people around who appear eager for adventure. Their main challenge now is finding the resources to develop their application. A few medicine men are able to find a place within frontier helping services that allow them to explore the application of their methods, but these opportunities are limited and are swallowed up early in service development. As explored with research funding in Chapter 7, the more promising prospect is to engage in direct funding from those with a vested interest in gambling expansion, namely gambling providers, governments, and local entrepreneurs. These opportunities have been set up in a variety of forms in places where gambling expansion is occurring fast. For example in Queensland, Australia, their Responsible Gambling Advisory Committee (RGAC) is set up to guide the state treasury in funding research and development projects on harm from gambling and consists of a tripartite representation from state government, gambling providers, and "communities." Similarly, in the United

Kingdom the RIGT is governed by a mix of gambling industry and helping sector representation, and it funds both research and service initiatives. In each of these contexts gambling industry and government representation are visibly present and consequently any funding arrangement will involve accountability to the interests they have in gambling expansion.

A more worrying and hazardous trend is the direct employment of medicine men by gambling providers. Indeed, with each major change in gambling regulations, it is common to see medicine men contracted by providers to apply their methods in demonstrating how little harm these changes will incur, and how if harm does eventuate, what approaches could be used to keep them to a minimum. Medicine men, perhaps naive to the power dynamics of their engagement, willingly compile reports based on social impact surveys, environmental scans, public surveys, economic modeling, product testing, and so forth. The reports tend to share a common format. They typically scan the positive and negative aspects of increased gambling in a particular environment, they take a close look at the potential problems and at ways of reducing them, they then widen the gaze and conclude that, although some harm will occur, on balance these harms are minor compared to the overall advantages to that community. In their own eyes they have applied their methods with integrity and they leave it to their funders to make use of the report as they choose. Conveniently, their relatively neutral conclusions ensure that in all likelihood they will be asked to provide similar work in the future.

For medicine men who are hired either indirectly through quasi-government development funds or directly by gambling providers, their links to interests associated with gambling expansion have a disruptive effect on those working with helping organizations. First it creates further rifts for residents in helping towns between those who are willing and those who are not willing to engage in servicing industry needs. Second, the reports tend to focus on issues that draw attention away from the broader issues associated with gambling expansion. For example, large-scale problem gambling prevalence studies are repeatedly funded, whereas the development of effective public health intervention strategies has received scant support. Third, although parts of the work provided by medicine men can have merit, it is difficult for frontier helping professionals to recognize this merit when the general orientation of the material is focused on justification of industry perspectives. Finally, the hiring of medicine men provides a credible profile for the extractive activities of the gambling industry and thereby assists in camouflaging the level of harm and confusing observers.

FROM FRONTIER TO SETTLEMENT

Over the course of time, commercialized gambling will establish and normalize its operations and high-frequency gambling will be incorporated as a part of everyday life. As explored in Chapter 5, gambling operations become increasingly identified as legitimate businesses, a part of the fabric of the economy where relationships between government agencies are well ordered and the sharp and blatantly exploitive practices of early expansion have been replaced by corporate organizations with more interest in the long-term future of gambling. The days of the Wild West are over. The frontier towns begin turning into provincial towns. For the frontier characters that inhabit them, this means either moving on to new frontiers or transforming their characters and how they operate.

The Demise of Frontier Helping Towns

As high-frequency commercial gambling merges into forming a part of everyday life, frontier helping towns enter a new environment and are either forced to mature into new forms or collapse and disappear. Postfrontier societies are often littered with ghost towns, and similarly many of the early gambling helping organizations fail to survive beyond the initial period. For some their financial and governance systems are too flimsy to cope in a more managed environment.[25] For others their wild and erratic ways of operating tend to not suit tighter contractual processes. However, in most contexts it is the disorienting effects of these changes on the frontier characters that cause the most disruption. In a frontier organization I worked in, as the scene changed the service came close on several occasions to collapsing entirely. Looking back, the main factors appeared to be that the glory-seeking ambitions of different members of the team created rifts, the missionaries were marginalized, the traders sought more and more control, and the glory seekers became disillusioned with shrinking prospects. Whereas in the frontier town people with radically different motives seemed to work well together, as they moved into the provincial town the divergence of motives appeared to pull people apart. From within the organization tensions grew among the missionaries, glory seekers, and traders. The goals of the organization could not cater to all interests. Outside the organization, other frontier towns were vying for a piece of the action, and, as the gambling industry became more organized, they improved their capacity to pursue their interests and to influence splits between the main players. Through a period of crisis and reorganization, the frontier organization I worked in was able to make sufficient changes to adapt to the more closely managed environment.

However, when compared with the frontier town, the provincial town is a far less colorful place. The larger-than-life characters sketched earlier have either settled down or chosen to move on in search of new frontiers. The new, more regulated environment is settled, with clear structures and processes. A new breed of professional is moving in with an eye to long-term sustainable employment and a dislike for the excesses and lawlessness of the previous period. The contracting of problem gambling services has moved from special arrangements positioned outside mainstream health and welfare funding to being incorporated as valid part of mainstream structures.

Provincial Towns and Beyond

It is with some sadness that I reflect on the gradual demise of the frontier helping town. This pioneering environment involved an energy, a rawness, and an honest directness that is stimulating and refreshing compared to the staid protocols of established services. Perhaps it is because frontier organizations stand outside mainstream purchasing regimes that they are able to attain high levels of innovation and creativity. For example, in the services in which I was involved, we worked at integrating public health understandings into work with clients and we managed to initiate a broad range of culturally based approaches to gambling issues. These innovations would have been very difficult to achieve in mainstream mental health or addiction services. Nonetheless, although brilliant and innovative at times, they were also locations that could involve the most arbitrary and wasteful practices; practices that entailed large anomalies and distortions that were difficult to defend. For example, a public education project might invest more resources in boosting the organization's public profile than in conveying key messages about gambling, or large amounts from clinical budgets are spent in bringing staff together for workshops, symposia, and entertainment. In a more settled and regulated environment, these practices would not be tolerated, so as helping towns move from the frontier into mainstream systems, these rough edges—the creative and the corrupt—are smoothed away, thereby generating more consistent and manicured arrangements.

The challenges to democratic structures and processes for the provincial town remain strong but take on new shapes and guises than on the frontier. Whereas on the frontier, moral jeopardy emerged from direct relationships with the interests of the gambling industry, in a more settled environment these connections are less visible, more diffuse, and relate more to structural linkages than individual relationships. Most importantly, there is a risk that helping organizations will grow increasingly comfortable with the ongoing growth of commercial gambling and will cease to challenge its expansion. In a sense they become a settled part of the machinery of extraction, equally reliant on increasing levels of frequent gambling. Here is how this might happen. Helping services are contracted specifically by a government agency that has little involvement with the regulation, enforcement, and policy associated with gambling (e.g., a health or mental health department). These services are then delivered by either specialist gambling services or as part of a broader addiction service. The services now have tightly defined objectives focused on delivering remedial services for problem gambling and have few legitimate linkages to the broader mechanisms associated with gambling expansion. The helping professionals employed in these services can now devote their energies to their clients' needs without having to be distracted by the broader issues. They do their job as required, and begin feeling that even if they could raise issues with the broader expansion, they are merely one isolated voice and unlikely to make any difference in the broader context.

Because most countries that are liberalizing their commercial gambling are still involved in frontier extraction, the patterns associated with a more settled and regulated environment have yet to take form. Nonetheless, it is predictable that settlement will entail more rigid and multitiered management of the gambling sector. The challenge for helping organizations is to keep maintaining an active involvement in public discourses on gambling, and to avoid the perception—or the reality—of benefiting from expanding gambling consumption. Unless they challenge the key drivers, they can easily be accused of surviving symbiotically on the unfettered rising consumption of gambling. In a settled environment where relationships between organizations have consolidated into stable arrangements and where the real drivers for policy and regulation are occurring at high levels in trade-off deals and background alliances, it is understandable that helping professionals within these organizations will feel that they have little influence and that their organizations should shy away from advocacy. The onus therefore falls even more strongly on responsible governments to set up systems and processes that reduce the level of potential moral jeopardy associated with gambling. This will be the focus for the following chapter.

9 Protecting Independence

As an aside, it is curious that the major growth of gambling has occurred in societies that pride themselves on democratic freedoms. This could be explained by noting that those nations with well-established democracies also tend to be those that are most affluent and therefore their citizens are more likely to have the capacity to afford regular gambling. However, other explanations are possible. It could be that in an ostensibly freer society, when given the choice, its members actually want more gambling and accordingly seek to increase its availability. This explanation is at variance with discussions in Chapter 3 that explored how in most democracies opponents to gambling expansion tend to outnumber those who support it, and the primary impetus for expansion usually emerges from within alliances between government and gambling industries. In its place, this book proposes that something more fundamental is operating here; something associated with the nature of democracy itself.

At a root level, both gambling and democracy share a common preoccupation with interpretations of freedom. Just as democracy provides systems that enable individual citizens to choose their leaders, commercial gambling provides systems that enable individuals further choice in how they invest their money. However, as explored in Chapter 5, notions of freedom are complex, and constructions that reduce freedom down to the capacity of individuals to choose to behave in certain ways leave out the perhaps more important multidimensional nature of freedom that involves the ongoing interplay between individual and collective interests. Placing a bet is both an individual and a collective act. The capacity to gamble is both created by social systems and in turn impacts upon these systems. Similarly, the capacity to determine who is in power is generated through social systems and this in turn impacts the structures that enable powerfulness. Gambling and democracy shadow each other in their interplay between the individual and the collective, between freedoms and constraints and between social and political ecologies. Consequently, if it is the case that fundamental linkages exist between the nature of gambling and the nature of democracy, then in an environment of commercial expansion it becomes increasingly important to embed within these systems measures that conserve and protect the integrity of that political ecology. This chapter examines some of the principles and strategies that could be employed to protect the independent base required to set up these safeguards.

MINIMIZING HARM TO DEMOCRATIC SYSTEMS

Earlier chapters have argued that in an environment of rapid gambling expansion, harms to democratic processes and institutions are not only a possibility but also, over time, highly probable. They further point out that many of the risks to democracy involve distortions that are subtle, diffuse, and likely to continue unchecked. These distortions are generated by a broad scatter of individuals working in isolation whose roles are incrementally compromised, thereby contributing cumulatively to a collective degradation of democratic systems.[1] This chapter points out how part of a preventative or harm minimization strategy[2] targeting gambling should include explicit measures to protect people from pressure to participate in potentially distorting practices. Such measures are likely to require the introduction of forms of checking or monitoring and responding to potential risks. Similar to the commercial logging of primeval forests, it would be unrealistic to expect gambling industries to monitor their own behavior.[3] It is in the nature of competitive commerce to push the boundaries and for the more immediate impulses to maximize profits to override the need for care regarding the longer term and subtler impacts on democratic functions. Faced with ongoing competition, logging companies and the gambling providers are continually urged to make the most of their opportunities; not doing so would hand over advantages to competitors and thereby jeopardize survival. Governments, in their role as protectors and promoters of public good, have a primary duty to establish processes that safeguard against unwarranted and harmful exploitation.

In line with a public health approach to gambling that places an emphasis on minimizing harm and promoting well-being,[4] a longer term vision would incorporate ways of preventing and minimizing circumstances that lead to high levels of moral jeopardy and associated impacts on democratic systems. A major challenge to governments in establishing these initiatives will be the complications created by their own interests and involvements in commercial gambling. Similar to logging and other extractive industries, a government with a keen interest in the revenue potential of gambling will find itself establishing a range of links with industries and thereby find it progressively more difficult to institute credible processes to protect its natural and social ecologies. The more connected governments become to gambling the less credible they will be perceived in protecting the public from gambling-related harm. To counterbalance their gambling interests, extra effort is required to establish credibility in their protection role. The key ingredient in reducing the risk of degradation will inevitably involve identifying an independent focal point within government that can be seen as providing credible monitoring of roles and responsibilities and their links with power. This perceived independence is critical; the stronger the revenue income from gambling, the stronger the need for ensuring those responding to harms are working independently from revenue interests[5]. As yet, a literature that looks into prevention approaches on this topic remains undeveloped. The following discussion provides a preliminary exploration of some of the issues and opportunities in developing a preventative approach.

Principles in Minimizing Moral Jeopardy

Discussions throughout this book on the risks gambling poses to democracy and freedom have returned repeatedly to four critical ingredients that when compromised are likely to promote environments of high moral jeopardy. These ingredients can be conceptualized as: awareness, transparency, independence, and responsibility. In the following discussion and for the purpose of developing a preventative approach to moral jeopardy, these concepts have been converted into positive guiding principles that will be applied later as a basis for planning future action.

Principle 1: Ethical Consciousness

A community organization's or government agency's capacity to identify and respond to the risks associated with gambling industry funding will be a function of the degree to which people belonging to that community develop a level of ethical awareness regarding the relationships they pursue with gambling. A considered response to these issues is unlikely to occur if the majority of people are unaware of or have only a peripheral understanding of the issues. As discussed in earlier chapters, during liberalization phases, such awareness is low for most of these organizations at all levels of their operation. Consequently, a key task is to promote widespread appreciation of moral jeopardy issues associated with gambling industry funding and its potential to compromise participation in democracy.

Principle 2: Informed Participation

Another issue that emerges repeatedly from the literature on this topic is the importance for people to have readily accessible information regarding sources of funding and the expectations attached. This principle calls on the need for transparency regarding sources of funding and the means by which this funding has been obtained. In particular, the absence of information denies potential consumers the opportunity to weigh whether they wish to engage with this organization. For example, a problem gambler might have strong views on the impact gambling has had on her and her family and have a strong reluctance to engage in services that were directly funded by gambling industries. Increases in transparency would have two effects: First, it would inform people on the extent and reliance of community and government organizations on gambling funds and, second, it would enable those who do have ethical concerns to exercise their judgment on whether to maintain an involvement.

Principle 3: Independence of Function

The major long-term threat from receiving gambling industry funds is the likelihood that over time dependency on this funding builds and an organization finds it is unable to function independently. All major decisions begin to be influenced by considerations regarding how to avoid jeopardizing this funding source. Moral jeopardy prevention strategies need to identify threats to organizational independence and devise ways to protect systems and processes from undue influence. Strategies are required to preserve the independent decision making of community and other public good organizations. Their independence is not only important for maintaining their own purposes, but it also enables them to speak out as required about the gambling environment and thereby actively participate in the democratic vitality of wider society. In situations where direct funding could compromise an organization's independence, mechanisms would be required to ensure organizational independence is preserved. For example, the academic independence of a university to conduct gambling research is likely to be compromised if the research is purchased directly by a casino. This independence might be better protected if the funding came through another agency with government-supported independence of function.

Principle 4: Government Duty of Care

Government and its various associated agencies (departments, ministries, and quasi-government agencies) have a key role in determining the environment in which gambling occurs. For example, they have a primary role in setting the parameters determining those who benefit from gambling profits, for monitoring the effects on the population and for protecting public good organizations from exposures that compromise their function. In many jurisdictions, particularly those where governments benefit directly from gambling revenue (e.g., Canada, New Zealand, and the United Kingdom), the environment looks set to generate high levels of moral jeopardy for a considerable time to come. In creating this high-dependency environment, government also has a primary duty to ensure that the range of risks identified in this book do not lead to compromises in the purpose of community and other public good organizations. Putting aside the government's own interest in the revenue generated from gambling, it is hard to see from where else an adequate level of protection is likely to come.

PROTECTIVE MEASURES

The prevention of moral jeopardy and the related preservation of democratic systems could involve people at a variety of levels. The following sections explore the prevention opportunities for people and organizations with differing roles within the broader environment. These roles include those people working in government agencies, community organizations, media organizations, academic institutions, and problem gambling helping services.

The Role of Government

Chapter 3 identified a range of complexities and dilemmas posed to government by the expansion of large-scale commercialized gambling. The significant revenue governments derive from gambling will flow through a variety of government agencies both in terms of its collection and its disbursement. Commentators have raised concerns that during the phases of liberalization and normalization, gambling industries might develop favored relationship status with governments.[6] The sheer scale of money being exchanged and the associated taxation revenue is capable of attracting more official interest than concerns about possible harms. For example, the state revenue from gambling in Victoria in is trending above 15% of all its revenues (Banks, 2003). With this level of income, politicians are unlikely to risk their political futures by jeopardizing either losses in programs that depend on this fund or replacing it with funding from higher personal taxation.[7] In such a situation, significant issues of public policy emerge, with reduced likelihood of appropriate measures to prevent ethical distortions in key relationships. Furthermore, it is easy to see how funding could become overtly politicized where agencies delivering treatment and support for problem gamblers and their families are placed in subservient roles to the extent where many feel muzzled, public advocacy is scorned, and independent research is difficult to establish.

The key individuals in the government sector with relevant roles include politicians (and their staff), government agencies (departments, ministries, and quasi-governmental agencies), and individual government officials. Possible protective measures for each of these will be considered in turn. First, as explored in Chapter 3, politicians can find their roles progressively compromised through the benefits that accrue from gambling funding in terms of increases in their party income, their influence within constituencies, and their capacity to form high-level networks involving power and influence. These associations have important consequences for the structures and processes by which their democracies operate, and concerned governments could consider setting up protections in the following ways:

Protective Measures: Politicians

1.1 *Declaration of gambling funding*

That politicians and their political parties are required by law to declare all sources of income (both direct and indirect) for political purposes. This should also include declaration of all gifts and benefits received from gambling sources.[8]

1.2 *Management of conflicts of interest*

That in situations of real or potential conflicts of interest, these are identified and declared, then managed in such a way that the overlap between roles is no longer an issue. For strong conflicts of interest, the politician would be obliged to step down from one of the roles or accept a high degree of ongoing independent scrutiny.

1.3 *Independent monitoring body*

That an independent government agency with no (or minimal) interest in the revenue from gambling is empowered to monitor whether the manner in which income from gambling is applied has any direct or indirect influence on the interests of politicians. Ideally this body should report directly to parliament and not through ministers or government agencies, thereby further protecting its independence.

The relationship is between governments and gambling monies is further complicated by governments participating directly in the provision of gambling. For example, governments in Canada and the Netherlands which either wholly own or are the main shareholders in several of their industries—including casinos, lotteries, and racetrack betting. As discussed in Chapter 3, government agencies that participate in the money trail will from this involvement derive increases in influence, status, and opportunities to move money around to expand their programs. Chapter 3 also explored how, whichever revenue framework is adopted (e.g., state-provided gambling vs. private commercial provision), more gambling will translate into more government revenue and thereby increase the difficulties in establishing a credible and workable level of independence. Government ownership has the advantage of toning down the competitive excesses of private ownership and of ensuring maximal revenue benefits for the state, but it also embeds the interests of gambling provision into their structures. The best compromise here involves ensuring there are clear and credible boundaries between those managing the money and those parts with other roles (policy, regulation, etc.). However, as revenue interests intensify, the integrity and credibility of these boundaries diminish. The independence of one government department marketing a product while another department manages responses to the harm is questionable, particularly as gambling revenue rises to a significant percentage of government income. In some countries, such as in New Zealand and the United Kingdom, the same agencies have supervised both the government gambling interests and aspects of the government's response to harm. The agencies in these situations will naturally lean toward balancing respective interests, and such balancing is likely to involve selectivity in the choice of remedial strategies. For example, support for the treatment of severe problem gambling is likely to be favored over public education or prevention strategies that are likely to reduce overall consumption. It is difficult to imagine adequate containment here, but the following measures could be considered in further reducing influences on government agencies:

Protective Measures: Government Agencies

1.4 *Separation of gambling-related agency functions*

That key roles and functions (e.g., policy development, government-provided gambling, regulation, enforcement, and remediation) are separated (ideally across different agencies) to avoid role confusion and undue stakeholder influence.

1.5 *Separation of agency functions*

That government proactively separate government agencies that manage or directly benefit from gambling tax revenue from those that regulate or manage associated harm. The separation and independence of function would require regular scrutiny (subject to management and ethical audits).

1.6 *Independent monitoring body*

That those governments approve the formation of an independent monitoring body reporting directly to government (not through ministries, departments, or other government agencies). This agency would need to have high-level powers to run its own investigations and report independently on the outcome of inquiries.

The politicians who form a government and the smaller group who comprise its executive (i.e., its executive or cabinet committee) will ultimately determine the government response to the risks of democratic degradation. Earlier chapters explored how increases in government revenue from commercial gambling (including direct revenue and community benefit distributions) pose an increasingly difficult dilemma for governments. The revenue allows them to achieve many of their social objectives, but the revenue comes at a social cost. As the revenue increases, it becomes progressively more difficult to contemplate a reversal. Reductions in gambling revenue would mean either significant increases in taxation or intolerable reductions in social or community programs. Despite ethical concerns, governments can reach a point where thoughts of constraining gambling expansion have too many negative consequences and consequently they feel they have no alternative but to enable continued expansion. In such circumstances their democratic function would become progressively compromised. Accordingly, governments need to look ahead and ask what might protect the moral integrity of the political ecology they inhabit and, in the long term, what will enable them to continue functioning on behalf of the public? In response to these questions, the following measures are worth considering:

Protective Measures: Government

1.7 *Restrictions on direct industry contributions*

That laws are enacted whereby gambling providers are prohibited from contributing directly to political or government organizations. This is a strong measure. Depending on levels of concern, measures could vary across a continuum ranging from increasingly tighter regulation and monitoring to a complete ban.

1.8 *Independent disbursement*

That the proceeds from gambling for community benefit purposes are managed independently of government. This is likely to require formation of an independent agency to receive and manage the disbursement. This agency should ideally also function independently of local or regional government to protect their roles and avoid direct involvement with gambling providers.

1.9 *Independent monitoring*

That an independent agency is established for ongoing monitoring of government–industry relationships. This agency would need to report directly to government (not through ministries, departments, or other government agencies) and its reporting would be required to provide clear recommendations on ways to improve the level of independence within government structures.

The Role of Community Organizations

In high-frequency gambling environments where significant amounts of funding are being directed for community purposes, it is sensible to anticipate that community and other public good organizations will end up in relationships of high moral jeopardy with gambling providers (see Chapter 4). It follows, therefore, that government agencies have a responsibility to assist community organizations in either avoiding or managing these relationships. Naturally, arrangements will need to vary according to time and place. However, community organizations themselves also have an essential role in preventing their organizations from entering uncritically into risky funding arrangements with gambling providers. In current circumstances, with people in most organizations having low levels of awareness of the risks, the first and most critical step is to develop an appreciation of the ethical issues across all organizational levels of community organizations. This includes those people functioning at the level of governance, those involved with management and administration, as well as employees within the organization. The following are some prevention possibilities:

Protective Measures: Community Organizations

2.1 *Restrictions on receiving funds directly from industry sources*

That community organizations include within their charters or constitutions a declaration as part of their public good function a clause that restricts receiving funds directly from gambling providers. This could vary according to the nature of their activity and the nature of the source, but it would need to be explicit regarding the circumstances in which the organization is and is not willing to accept funds.

2.2 *Consciousness raising*

That all community organizations receive assistance in recognizing the risks of direct association and are equipped in assessing and deciding to what extent they are willing to engage in receiving gambling funding.

2.3 *Governance training*

That the governance boards of community and other public good organizations are assisted in their deliberations on gambling industry involvements by presentations or workshops aimed at raising their awareness of the issues and helping them reach an informed position on the extent of gambling industry involvement

2.4 *Financial transparency*

That community organizations are required to declare in their annual reports the extent and nature of funding from gambling industry sources. This should also include a declaration by key office-holders (board members, executives) of interests or associations with gambling industry companies. Ideally this information should be available to other stakeholders, including consumers.

Community professionals and support workers, including social workers, community professionals, general practitioners and other health professionals, counselors, lawyers, court workers, budgeters, council officers, hospital workers, health promoters, cultural professionals, and so forth, have a special role in helping to prevent risky relationships with commercial gambling providers. These professionals often operate at the interface between community organizations and their consumers, as well as between their organizations and the regulatory environment. The following measures could enhance their preventive role:

Protective Measures: Community Professionals and Support Workers

2.5 *Professional training*

That basic health and social professional education and continuing professional education programs include content that sensitizes trainees to the ethical dimensions of gambling industry funding.

2.6 *Position within professional organizations*

That professional organizations (e.g., practitioner bodies, guilds, health promotion associations) are engaged in stating their position on the ethics of receiving gambling funds. Their position could be incorporated into codes of ethics and act as a guide for members on how they perform in employing organizations.

2.7 *Ethical scrutiny*

That professional organizations provide mechanisms whereby people both inside and outside their organizations can express concerns or complaints regarding ethical individual or collective conduct in relation to the proceeds from gambling.

The clients, consumers, and members of community and other public good organizations have a critical role in determining gambling industry involvements because it is they who are often at the receiving end of such arrangements. As explored in Chapter 4, they are also at risk of having their ethical concerns silenced by the compliance of the organization that they access or to which they belong. For example, a person who is concerned about the level to which a bowling club is receiving funds from gambling is likely to experience social pressure not to speak out, particularly when trips and new equipment are at stake. As with the government sector, community organizations require structures and processes to protect the democratic roles of those who choose to question organizations on ethical grounds. In the background, government still plays a critical role in determining the broader environment and the level to which people are able to challenge community–industry affiliations. However, the duty of care also extends to the community organization. Collectively they—and for that matter the general public—can play an influential role in assisting these organizations in deciding how far to proceed with gambling industry connections. The following outlines ways in which their role could be enhanced.

Protective Measures: Clients, Consumers, and Members

2.8 *Consumer sovereignty*[9]

That clients, consumers or members of health, charity, leisure, and other public good community organizations have access by right to clear information regarding any sources of gambling industry funding. This measure would enable them to both challenge industry involvements and, if needed, shift their involvements to other services that have not engaged in receiving industry funds.

2.9 *Consumer advocacy*

That consumer advocacy groups identify moral jeopardy as an issue and seek to engage a broad range of stakeholders in improving standards of ethical practice.

2.10 *Promotion of ethical awareness*

That resources are devised to assist consumers in both appreciating the ethical issues and in recognizing the influence they could exert on community and other public good organizations. These resources could take the form of posters, pamphlets, and other materials that prompt consumers to enquire into organizational and funding affiliations.

The Role of Media Organizations

Chapters 5 and 6 examined the relationships between the media and commercial gambling and raised concerns regarding the capacity of media depictions to minimize concerns about gambling expansion and justify unethical gambling associations. Chapter 5 focused on how industry depictions of themselves in the print media exploit and distort fundamental understandings of freedom in ways that normalize commercial gambling. Chapter 6 examined the various marketing strategies that are used to normalize gambling and to engage new consumers and maintain ongoing heavy consumption. Although government will continue to play a critical role in the monitoring and management of these practices, media organizations themselves can contribute in a variety of ways to protective strategies. For example, media provider organizations—newspapers and magazines, radio and television companies, Web site providers, advertising companies, and so on—play a significant role in providing the public with access to information, ideas, and opinions on the expansion of high-frequency commercial gambling. The presentation of diverse views on this expansion is important in assisting the public to develop a critical understanding of the ethical balance between harms and benefits from gambling. However, similar to government, media organizations are also likely to be conflicted by their various relationships to gambling industry providers. In contexts where commercial gambling is expanding, media outlets are likely to derive a significant portion of their revenue from advertising and promotions. Media organizations might also be pursuing strong business associations with the main gambling providers and might even invest directly in their businesses. As key players in the vitality of any democracy, protection of the independence of media organizations is a grave matter, and the organizations themselves can participate in this protection by considering the following protective measures.

Protective Measures: Media Provider Organizations

3.1 *Declaration of vigilance*

That media provider companies include within their objects or charters a declaration of vigilance regarding their independence from gambling industries. This statement of intent commits the organization to recognizing and protecting themselves from threats to their democratic role.

3.2 *Declaration of income from industry sources*

That media provider companies report regularly and publicly (ideally in their annual reports) the income they derive from gambling industry sources. This would include any direct contributions, funding for advertising and related promotions, and indirect benefits through associations (e.g., joint charitable sponsorship, etc.).

3.3 *Systems for scrutiny*

That media provider companies develop structures and processes that enable independent responses to complaints and expressions of concern by people both within and outside the organization. These measures would need to put in place mechanisms that protect the safety of those who raise concerns.

Chapter 2 explored how gambling subtly degrades democratic systems by incrementally compromising the roles of individuals at key points within political ecologies. By way of example, it explored how individual media professionals (reporters, columnists, and editors) can find themselves caught in a dilemma of wanting to report accurately on gambling developments but at the same time not wanting to jeopardize the commercial interests of their employers. It also discussed how industry-compliant responses occur quietly and in ways that often silence and isolate media professionals. The following measures could be adopted in strengthening their democratic role with respect to gambling.

Protective Measures: Media Professionals

3.4 *Ethical consciousness-raising*

That media training programs and ongoing professional development include content that sensitizes media professionals to the ethical dimensions of gambling industry funding. Discussions in these training sessions would also encourage open talk on these matters within the workplace.

3.5 *Declaration of sources of income*

That with articles or items on gambling, the reporting media professional state all actual or perceived interests that they or their organization might have with respect to gambling industries.

3.6 *Ethical scrutiny*

That media professionals actively seek to talk over with colleagues their ethical concerns regarding associations with funding from the proceeds of gambling. This might involve systems of confidential advice and mentoring.

Professional organizations (professional associations, bodies, guilds, and academies) have a special role in monitoring ethical standards within a profession. For example, real estate professional bodies aim to reduce exploitative practices that might bring the profession into disrepute. Their definition of standards and their procedures for responding to complaints have led over time to improvements in how they are viewed by the public and consequently an increase in the demand for their services. Media organizations and their employers can play some role in reducing the likelihood of unethical influence from gambling interests, but media professional organizations (along with government support) are best positioned to promote standards of independence from gambling industry sources. The following lists some of the initiatives they could undertake.

Protective Measures: Media Professional Organizations

3.7 *Ethical position with respect to gambling*

That national and international media professional organizations clearly state their position on the ethics of receiving gambling funds. Their position could be incorporated into their codes of ethics or practice and act as a guide for members on how they perform in employing organizations. They might also set up systems and processes to monitor membership adherence to standards of independence from gambling providers.

3.8 *Advertising codes of practice*[10]

That media professional organizations adopt an advertising (and other promotions) code of practice that sets limits on the use of exploitative marketing practices, particularly those that take advantage of vulnerable populations. These codes are more likely to be adopted when they are endorsed by government, and ideally managed through legislation.

3.9 *Independent ethical review*

That media professional organizations set up an independent committee that is empowered to investigate complaints of undue influence on the media, and the use of exploitative media and marketing practices.

The Role of Academic and Research Bodies

Chapter 7 examined the various ways in which the roles of academics as critics and the conscience of society and knowledge generators can be compromised by accepting funds from gambling providers. It pointed out various ways that acceptance could impact ethical standards as well as the reputation and the independence of an academic institution. As with the media, the independence of universities is vital to maintaining a point of critical scrutiny regarding the relationship between gambling and society. Chapter 7 also examined how academic and research bodies are typically large organizations and because of their size have difficulty holding a consistent position on gambling funding. For example, once one part of a university accepts gambling funding, it is difficult for another part to take a strong stance on such funding. It is therefore important for governance structures to provide policy positions that can help direct the behavior of employees. The following measures focus on the role of academic governance and management.

Protective Measures: Academic and Research Organizations

4.1 *Ethical awareness*

That people in key governance and management positions are assisted in their deliberations on gambling industry involvements by activities (depending on interest; see examples in Chapter 10) aimed at raising their awareness of the issues and helping them reach an informed position on the extent of gambling industry involvement.

4.2 *Policy restricting direct funding*

That university councils (or other governance bodies) consider devising policies that restrict all parts of the organization from accepting funding directly from gambling providers. This could be linked to their policy positions relating to funding from other dangerous consumptions industries such as alcohol, tobacco, and pharmaceuticals.

4.3 *Processes for monitoring and reporting on funding sources*

That central committees monitor and report annually on all sources of funding from potential gambling sources. These include funding for research, teaching, scholarships, travel, staff positions, and so on. The nature and extent of funding from gambling sources should also be disclosed to staff members and other stakeholders.

With the independence of academic institutions as public good organizations assured, they are then in a position of providing high-quality independent sources of knowledge and providing critical feedback on directions and trends of gambling within society. However, their progress depends to some extent on the availability of resources to develop this role. In other words, they are dependent on the level to which governments choose to invest in gambling research. In many jurisdictions to date, gambling research has either been meager or narrowly focused. For example, research on public health and host responsibility interventions have attracted less support so far than treatment research and population surveys. This has led to a paucity of significant research into interventions that could contribute to moderating or reducing gambling consumption.[11] This lack of product and consumption research is, coincidentally, consistent with government interest in capitalizing on increases in gambling consumption. The challenge for research funders is to protect their independence in allocating research money from the revenue interests of other parts of government as well as from the influence of gambling industries. The following measures are likely to assist.

Protective Measures: Research Funders

4.4 *Functional independence*

That the processes for allocating gambling research funds are established separately from other parts of government with interests in the revenue from gambling. This would need to involve active and independent scrutiny of any of these potential influences.

4.5 *Brokerage of research funding*

That independent intermediary bodies are set up by government to receive, disburse, and manage gambling research funding. The independence of their funding mechanisms could be monitored by mandatory requirements of full disclosure of funding sources and potential conflicts of interest.

4.6 *Full disclosure of funding intentions*

That research funders are required to publish a research strategy in which their goals, values, and priorities are clearly articulated and against which their funding decisions can be examined.

Researchers are often unaware of the subtle and diffuse impacts receiving gambling funding can have on their democratic roles. The dialogue in Chapter 7 highlighted the pressures and dilemmas that individual researchers encounter when faced with the prospect of significant gambling funding, particularly when other prospects remain uncertain. Researchers can also find themselves slipping progressively into dependency relationships with industry-associated funding sources. The counterbalance among researchers to such processes is the system of peer review. Peer review of research outputs not only focuses on the quality of scientific methods, but also on the quality of ethical procedures. The procedures researchers use to protect their research from conflicts of interest has become increasingly part of the peer review process. With this in mind, the following measures can assist in protecting researchers from moral jeopardy.

Protective Measures: Researchers

4.7 *Full disclosure of funding sources*

That for all research outputs (proposals, reports, publications) researchers are required to disclose all direct and indirect sources of funding associated with gambling consumption (ISAJE, 2005).

4.8 *Independent peer review*

That for all gambling research outputs, independent gambling researchers (i.e., those who do not currently have or have not previously received funding from gambling industry sources) are engaged by sponsoring bodies (e.g., government agencies and journal editors) to provide independent feedback on both the quality and absence of proexpansion bias in the way the research is reported.

4.9 *Ethical awareness*

That all researchers are provided access to presentations or workshops (depending on interest) aimed at raising their awareness of the issues and helping them reach an informed position on the extent of gambling industry involvement.

The Role of Gambling Helping Agencies

Problem gambling services have in most jurisdictions been dominated by the development of counseling and support services. More recently many service agencies have broadened their activities into providing a range of public health services that include public education, social marketing, health promotion, community advocacy, and harm minimization interventions.[12] In many places the development of helping services has been directly linked to the proliferation of gambling, with indirect and sometimes direct links to gambling industries.[13] Chapter 8 examined how in the pioneering phases of gambling intervention services, high mobility both in terms of movement in and out of the sector and in terms of relationships with the industry, create an environment of change and unpredictability. The people attracted into the sector are often larger-than-life characters willing to play hard and fast with and around sector processes. As the sector has matured, the democratic role of gambling helping agencies has emerged. They play a vital role in informing the public of gambling harm and advocating for change. For example, in their sessions with clients, problem gambling counselors become intimately acquainted with the negative impacts of gambling and they can subsequently give voice to these experiences and help raise general public awareness of the complex impacts of gambling expansion. The following measures would assist service professionals and their employing agencies in protecting their contribution.

Protective Measures: Problem Gambling Provider Organizations

5.1 *Awareness of moral jeopardy*

That professionals working within organizations that provide remedial services for problem gamblers are assisted in recognizing the special duty they have regarding the ethical and moral issues outlined in this book. In many circumstances they will have opportunities to assist their clients, colleagues, and community organizations in serious consideration of these ethical issues.

5.2 *Declared governance position*

That governance boards for provider organizations formulate policies that clearly state their position on whether or under what circumstances they are willing to accept funding from gambling industry sources.

5.3 *Declaration of industry funding sources*

That at the point of accessing a service, clients are informed as to the extent to which that service derives its funding from gambling industry sources. Service users, counseling clients, family members, communities, and so on might have understandable feelings about the way they and the people around them have been affected by gambling. For many, they will at least partially associate this suffering with the practices of gambling providers. Consequently many consumers will have a critical interest in knowing the source of funding for the services they are receiving.

Gambling service funding agencies are small in number but can play an influential role in the responses of the gambling helping sector. In some jurisdictions service funding and purchasing is managed within government agencies, whereas in other contexts, funding and purchasing occurs in independent organizations. Either way, the funding agency has opportunities to strongly influence the ethical conduct of the agencies that they fund. In other sectors (e.g., hospital and mental health services) they might choose to employ strategies that monitor the integrity of services such as insisting on a particular level of training by staff; performing financial, cultural, and ethical audits on organizational processes; and responding to consumer complaints and expressions of concern. Similarly, the democratic and ethical functions of service organizations can be promoted by the following measures.

Protective Measures: Service Funding Agencies

5.4 *Policy declarations*

That agencies that fund gambling service organizations clearly state their position on receiving gambling funding within their strategic and purchasing plans.

5.5 *Disclosure of gambling funding sources*

That service funding agencies insist in funding agreements that full and accurate disclosure by service organizations is provided on whether they receive gambling industry funding. This disclosure should be available to both the funders and service consumers.

5.6 *Ethical awareness*

That all staff working for service funding agencies undergo training aimed at raising their awareness of the ethical issues and at helping them reach an informed position on the impacts of gambling industry involvement.

THE WILLINGNESS TO PROTECT

The degree to which the protective measures outlined in this chapter achieve their purpose will be a function of the seriousness with which relevant people and organizations embrace their role in reducing the moral jeopardy. The measures are unlikely to be utilized in contexts where the threats are poorly understood. I suspect that in the short-to-medium term the subtle degradation of democratic roles will for many countries continue unchecked. This in turn will feed the culture of permissiveness described at the end of Chapter 3. In the longer term, the threats commercialized gambling poses to democracy will continue to gather momentum to a point that crises will compel people to confront the processes of degradation. Unfortunately, by this stage, the capacity of democratic systems to respond to pressure points of degradation has been seriously compromised. The nodes of independence and ethical integrity required to drive the necessary changes are no longer available, and the system would have difficulties correcting itself.

By way of illustration, consider a democracy in which commercialized gambling has been allowed to proliferate. Imagine it 20 years into the future. Gambling consumption has continued to grow and government reliance on gambling revenue has steadily increased to a point that it comprises a significant percentage of revenue—significant enough for such a government to recognize that reductions could jeopardize its chances of reelection. In such a context the relationship between gambling providers and government would have consolidated on several levels: Politicians respect the way charitable distributions influence communities; health advocacy groups find themselves increasingly battling with their own communities; government officials respect the prestige and influence the revenue provides their agencies; the media have clearly learned which gambling topics they need to keep quiet on to avoid jeopardizing what by now has become a highly significant income from gambling advertising; and the academic careers of researchers who receive gambling funds have enabled them to rise into prominent positions, whereas those who refuse funds are unable to continue and move into other fields. For the public, frequent gambling has become progressively more normalized to such an extent that gambling merges with other forms of entertainment and people find it hard to think of it as involving risk. People who challenge public enjoyment of gambling are increasingly marginalized and open criticism of gambling is dismissed as spoilsport, overprotective, moralistic, and even unpatriotic. However, behind the veneer of acceptability, something else is happening; a storm is gathering. At a community level, commercialized EGM gambling has eclipsed other forms of entertainment and opportunities for social interaction have been reduced. Problem gambling has risen to such levels that most people know of either friends or family who have been affected. Corrupt practices regarding the distribution of proceeds from gambling are widespread and gambling is commonly implicated in many fraud cases and in financial scandals involving politicians and community organizations. Despite government and industry rhetoric, many people are progressively troubled by a sense that things are not right and their distrust of government and democratic processes grows.

The alternative to allowing the process of democratic degradation to run its full course is to apply medium-term imaginative foresight in a way that activates a willingness to protect and enables protective measures to be put in place. It is far easier to set up protective mechanisms in a system where the integrity remains relatively intact than it is to respond when systems are falling apart. The next chapter further explores specific opportunities for establishing protective responses, and also explores the prospect of transnational and global responses.

10 Strategies for Change:
Three Ways Ahead

A focus on the ethics of gambling industry funding is new territory and research and intervention will take time to evolve. As commercialized gambling proliferates throughout Western democracies and as it begins to engage developing nations and nations in transition, the challenges posed by moral jeopardy in community–industry relationships will become increasingly apparent. This chapter is devoted to exploring in more detail three different but interlinked approaches that could be adopted, or at least partially adopted, to help protect social and political ecologies from distorting influences. The first approach examines the use of harm minimization strategies for managing subtle degradation and moral jeopardy. The second approach outlines a framework and guidelines for self-assessment of moral jeopardy as a means of promoting a proactive ethical approach to the risks inherent in industrial relationships. The third approach examines the development of an international charter as a means of promoting benchmark ethical standards that guide governments in their duty of care when they opt to participate in the global expansion of commercial gambling. The approaches examined are by no means exhaustive of what could be advanced. They are intended to provide initial examples that, along with other approaches, could be incorporated into an overall strategy aimed at protecting democratic systems from the subtle degradations associated with gambling.

GAMBLING AND HARM MINIMIZATION

Mood-altering substances or processes with the potential to foster dependency will lead to harm at multiple levels. The term *dependency* can be interpreted in a number of ways, but is understood here to refer in a general fashion to the emergence of an intense reliance on one relationship that overshadows the potential contribution of a range of other relationships. Such reliance can occur at an individual level where an intensified relationship to, for example, alcohol eclipses the benefits of relationships with family members and friends. This amplifies the reliance, which over time emerges with features we identify as addiction. Dependency can also occur at social and societal levels. Groups, organizations, and even whole societies can find themselves on a path of increasing reliance on one aspect of their development. For instance, taxation on tobacco could grow in such importance to state revenue that it is seen as a necessary part of state income (Godfrey & Maynard, 1988). The diversity and resilience of the economy is diminished and this further intensifies the dependence. Although an organization or state can benefit from the income, it carries with it associated harms that include the loss of other opportunities, losses in autonomy, and distortions in business and community relationships.

Tobacco, alcohol, and gambling comprise the major dependency-forming consumptions legally supported in most Western-style democracies. Each of these consumptions confronts the host state with a common spectrum of harms, spanning across physical, psychological, interpersonal, and broader social impacts. Tobacco use has social and cultural impacts by, for example, linking its promotion with the emerging identity of younger people (Pechmann & Shih, 1999). However, tobacco's main impact is unquestionably on physical health as evidenced by the high number of people who die from smoking-related illnesses (Doll et al., 1994; Lopez & Peto, 1996). Alcohol has significant impacts on physical health (see Edwards et al., 1994), but it differs from tobacco in contributing more to harm at the level of psychological impacts and social relationships (see Clark & Hilton, 1991; Devlin, Scuffham, & Bunt, 1997). For example, the impacts of alcohol dependence on family members, particularly children, can lead to enduring disruptions of psychological and social functioning (Cuijpers & Smit, 2001; West & Prinz, 1987). Gambling shares the potential for impacts on health and psychological well-being. For example, prolonged and intense episodes of gambling are accompanied by associated anxiety, stress, depression, and deteriorating self-care (Becona, Del, Lorenzo, & Fuentes, 1996; Crockford & el-Guebaly, 1998; McCormick, Russo, Ramirez, & Taber, 1984). The psychological processes of problem gambling lead to distortions in thinking and disrupted relationships (Blaszczynski & Silove, 1995; Lorenz & Yaffee, 1986; Williams, 1996). In addition to these, when it comes to comparing the impact of gambling with that of alcohol and tobacco, gambling stands out with a stronger zone of potential harm derived from its impact on social and political systems (see Doughney, 2002; Goodman, 1995). As explored throughout this book, the money that is generated from gambling and the potential for governments to develop a strong interest in its capacity to generate revenue creates environments where the integrity of social and democratic systems is at risk. Consequently, one of the key challenges for countries that embark on liberalizing commercial gambling is to find ways to minimize these types of impacts.

The principles of harm minimization have provided a high-level framework for governments to respond to alcohol, tobacco, and other drug problems (Single, 1995). The principles are embedded in the alcohol and other drug strategies in Canada, Australia and New Zealand, the United Kingdom, and other European Union nations. Harm minimization philosophy remains neutral on the morality of drug use, but recognizes that because most societies accept the regular use of some form of mood-altering drug, policy efforts need to focus on ways to identify harm and reduce it to tolerable levels.[1] If a society chooses to accept, for example, alcohol as a part of daily life, the task then becomes one of finding ways of keeping predictable harms to a minimum. For example, alcohol intoxication is known to increase the probability of road injuries; accordingly, authorities might choose to minimize such harm by recording the circumstances in which injuries are occurring, designing pragmatic prevention strategies (e.g., designated drivers, low-alcohol beer, media campaigns, etc.), and then evaluating the impact of strategies to see if they actually do reduce the frequency and severity of alcohol-related injuries. In this way the two key elements to a harm minimization approach can be seen as a pragmatic focus on harms as they are occurring and an emphasis on measuring whether or not what is implemented actually makes a difference.

A harm minimization approach can also usefully be applied to gambling. In preparing populations for high-intensity gambling, the challenge is to find ways to enjoy the benefits from gambling while at the same time reducing the likelihood of widespread negative impacts. Gambling brings with it a range of predictable harms. For example, the move into high-intensity gambling typically leads to increases in problem gambling, along with increases in associated harms such as marital conflict, property crime, and mental health problems (Brown, 1987; Lesieur, 1999; Volberg, 1996). In a harm minimization framework, the first task involves setting up ongoing and reliable ways of measuring the occurrence of these harms. The next task is to devise intervention strategies that look likely to lead to reductions in harm. Initially these strategies might be transferred from successful applications with other consumptions such as with alcohol and tobacco. Typical examples include improved consumer information at point of sale, modification to the design of products (e.g., slower reel spins or forced breaks on EGMs) and public education on the risks and false beliefs associated with gambling (see Korn & Shaffer, 1999). The next step involves evaluating whether or not the chosen intervention does actually lead to reductions in problems, with the expectation that the more effective strategies will be more widely implemented.[2]

According to this book, one of the predictable harms from widespread commercial gambling is an increase in moral jeopardy and the consequent degradation of democratic structures and processes. It is arguing that for a nation to embrace high-intensity gambling it also needs to embrace a range of strategies that will effectively reduce harms to its democratic systems. Despite recognition of gambling-related harm at an individual level, the broader harms gambling inflicts on social systems have so far attracted scant attention. This zone of predictable harm requires closer examination with the aim of devising appropriate prevention and remedial responses.[3] The following material touches briefly on three strategies that could be developed to advance a harm minimization approach to issues of moral jeopardy: The first strategy involves targeting interventions according to the stage a person or organization is at in terms of readiness to embrace ethical understandings; the second strategy explores the use of awareness training as a way of advancing ethical readiness; and the third strategy examines ways in which governments might reduce the overall levels of moral jeopardy.

Advancing Ethical Readiness

The notion of "readiness" is a familiar and widely used construct in intervention programs across all dangerous consumptions. It acknowledges that it would be unrealistic to expect individuals or organizations to move suddenly from having no or very little awareness of ethical dilemmas to a position where they were actually ready to implement policy. Change takes time, and a range of milestones need to be attained before full implementation becomes possible. For instance, awareness of ethical issues might initially occur with only one or two individuals within an organization, and they are unlikely to influence policy until they can engage a wider circle of supporters. Even with wider support, concerns about viability and external perceptions can provide enough of a barrier to restrict change. The idea that change involves a process in which readiness emerges over time is captured usefully in the widely used transtheoretical model of change (or "wheel of

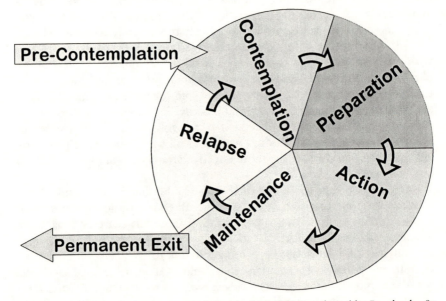

Figure 10.1 Stages of Change "Transtheoretical Model" Developed by Prochaska & DiClemente (1986)

change"). This model identifies several levels of readiness as illustrated in Figure 10.1 (developed by Prochaska & DiClemente, 1986). Community and other public good organizations that remain unaware of the ethical risks ("precontemplation") will require assistance in shifting to a point where they are capable of considering the risks ("contemplation") then onto a point where they are proactively involved in planning, resource development, and implementation of a change process ("action"). The following sections highlight three of the identified stages and apply them to difference stages of ethical readiness.

Action

During the action stage, individuals and organizations are proactively involved in planning, accessing resources, and implementing a change process. For example, in losing weight, a person can be seen to have moved from merely thinking and preparing for change to actually implementing a program of diet and exercise. Similarly, action with ethical readiness is demonstrated when an organization moves beyond discussion and debate and begins behaving in new ways; that is, they are actively devising and implementing appropriate preventive policies or processes. Recent developments in the tobacco control sector illustrate this transition. Although ongoing debate continues on the morality of tobacco industry links, increasing numbers of organizations have implemented restrictive policies regarding tobacco manufacturer associations and are willing to back up their position with consequences for those who do not comply. In comparison, when reviewing gambling sources, very few organizations have created policies, let alone considered the issues associated with links to gambling industry providers.

Contemplation

An individual or an organization would be considered to be in contemplation when there are clear signs of genuine and concerned debate regarding whether to change or to remain the same. Contemplation is often characterized by a state of uneasy ambivalence and strategies that promote change attempt to make the most of this ambivalence to propel people into some form of commitment (Miller & Rollnick, 1991). For example, when people consider losing weight, they typically spend considerable time reviewing the pros and cons of whether they will lose weight before they are ready for some form of commitment. The alcohol sector could arguably be seen as closest to contemplation in that the ethical issues are being widely debated but are as yet unlikely to be converted into actual policy. With regard to gambling, few organizations are demonstrating genuine concern about receiving industry funding. Although some will acknowledge uneasiness regarding this source of funds, the concern is expressed in a fleeting, often joking manner, and most around them are willing to receive the money in an uncritical and unconcerned way.

Precontemplation

The stage of precontemplation is characterized by low awareness or token concern regarding a particular at-risk behavior. The issues might simply have never been thought about. Alternatively, the issues might be acknowledged but in a fairly cursory manner; that is, with little evidence of genuine concern. For example, in considering weight gain, a person might acknowledge that continued increases could have negative impacts on health, but the concern might be insufficient for serious consideration and it is shrugged off to think about another day. Currently precontemplation is the stage that best categorizes the ethical readiness of most organizations regarding their acceptance of gambling funds. There is practically no published literature on these issues with regard to gambling, transnational organizations lack any clear policies, and very few people show signs of debating the issues, let alone formulating prevention strategies. Discussions with members of sports, charity, and government organizations tend to reveal difficulties recognizing the ethical and perceptual risks and those raising the issues are a minority and are frequently marginalized.

The main advantage of looking at organizational change in terms of stages of change is that it recognizes that the goal of such interventions will be different depending on the extent of readiness. For example, there is little point discussing how to start dieting with a person who is unconcerned about his or her weight; what that person really requires is access to information and opportunistic moments to reflect on the issues. Similarly with the majority of agencies and organizations at the precontemplation stage of ethical readiness, the goal of engaging them in implementing policies is unlikely to meet with success. A more realistic goal would be to develop strategies that assist them in moving from precontemplation to contemplation. Such strategies could involve the development of educational packages, discussion workshops, booklets, and promotional materials that engage people within organizations in thinking about the issues. As with assisting people in other areas of behavior change, the opportunities for reflection need to be engaging, matter-of-fact, and nonjudgmental (Rollnick, Butler, & Hodgson, 1997).

Ethical Awareness Training

Chapter 9 emphasized the critical role ethical awareness will play in the current environment for reducing the prevalence of risky industry involvements. One approach that could assist in this process would involve the development of educational packages that aim at helping individuals and organizations in understanding the risks of industry associations. Such packages could incorporate a range of resource materials that could include some of the content from the current chapter, fact sheets, discussion scenarios, and a guide on assessing moral jeopardy (see next section). These items could be incorporated into discussion exercises that engage participants regarding topics such as the pros and cons of receiving gambling funds and how to respond to situations that discourage openness. These materials could then be delivered—contingent on funding support[4]—in the form of facilitated workshops offered in various forms to groups of people operating at the levels of governance, management, service delivery, and service consumption. Ideally, initial workshops should focus on people at the level of governance. Members of governance boards and councils, owners of organizations, and ultimately governments, have a special duty both on behalf of their organizations and on behalf of consumers and other stakeholders, to minimize immediate and longer term risks to their organizations. Next, with governance support, management could be engaged in similar workshops adapted to their level of interest. Management and governance intentions are difficult to implement when staff are opposed or ambivalent about the intent. For example, although a governance board for a gambling service might have decided not to accept funds from gambling sources, the staff might continue to pursue industry relationships with a view to pressuring their board to accept these funds. Staff workshops could be used to both increase staff awareness of moral jeopardy issues and as a means of including them more in critical decisions.

In the delivery of such awareness packages, facilitators with advanced skills in conducting workshops and engaging precontemplating participants would be required to organize and convene discussions and to undertake the running of the workshops. Each session would need to be tailored to suit the context in which it is delivered. For example, governance boards might prefer 1-day workshops, whereas staff might prefer workshops broken into several shorter weekly sessions. The delivery would also require mechanisms that enable improvement and refinement. One mechanism could involve independent evaluation examining the responsiveness of participants within organizations to the process and assessment regarding whether their participation has in effect improved their awareness of the ethical issues. Another mechanism that could add to awareness and monitor impacts would be to conduct consumer surveys of ethical awareness. Service consumers (variously identified as clients, patients, the public, and citizens) have a critical interest in the manner in which a service is provided. For example, consumers of addiction counseling services might be interested in whether the funding for the service they attend bears any relationship to the source of their woes. As part of regular client satisfaction surveys, items could be included that enquire into consumer views on industry relationships. Again the activity of thinking about it increases awareness and for some creates choice points in terms of whether and where they connect with dangerous consumption industries.

Low Moral Jeopardy Environments

A nation that values its democracy and the part community organizations play in it will appreciate the link between moral jeopardy and levels of participation in democratic processes. In responding to the fourth principle for prevention discussed in Chapter 9 ("government duty of care"), government agencies in collaboration with organization governance boards are in an excellent position to examine how environments could be created that encourage low-risk industry involvements and consequently assist in reducing the extent to which community organizations are exposed to moral jeopardy. An environment in which large amounts of gambling-generated community benefit funds are circulating will, without any other measures, entice organizations into relationships involving rising levels of reliance on those funds and thereby expose them to higher moral jeopardy. In such circumstances, governments have a special duty to set up mechanisms to protect organizations from this higher risk exposure. It falls on them because it is the policies and regulations they pursue that will largely determine the environment and because it is hard to see where else the role of public protection is best implemented.

In contexts where governments have opted for an environment of high gambling consumption and high community sector reliance on gambling funding,[5] special efforts are required to minimize the harms associated with this. To work out how best to tackle these harms, government-mandated working groups could be convened with the purpose of examining more closely how environments could be changed to reduce the likelihood of high gambling industry dependence. Such working groups could look more closely at the effectiveness of the various prevention options listed earlier. For example, they could oversee the evaluation of establishing independent broker agencies in moderating industry connectedness, or they could explore whether restricting the visibility of industry associations for promotional purposes has an impact on levels of industry involvement. They might also explore the effects of fostering alternative funding for community organizations as has occurred in many countries with state-funded alternatives to tobacco industry sponsorship. At all stages, these initiatives would require systems for regularly monitoring and evaluating their effect on overall levels of moral jeopardy. These could involve methods such as assessing the proportion of organizational funding that is derived from gambling and surveying organizations on their awareness of risk and their difficulties in making changes.

GUIDELINES FOR ASSESSING MORAL JEOPARDY

As part of the development of a strategy for preventing moral jeopardy and associated degradation of democratic systems, individuals and organizations will require access to practical ways in which they can gauge the risks they are taking and in which they can explore alternatives.[6] Community and other public good organizations confront decisions on whether to receive funding from gambling sources with increasing regularity. For example, in contexts with less community support from government, the decision on whether or not to accept such funding and on what terms can have implications for survival. The following sections explore the development of guidelines and a framework to assist organizations in reaching an informed position on receiving such funds.

A Continuum of Moral Jeopardy

A binary way of looking at the world involves slotting key aspects of one's reality into category pairs: The weather is either fine or wet, people are either good or bad, and patients are either compliant or disruptive. Thinking in binary categories is tempting and powerful. Their use helps organize a complex picture and facilitates decisive action, such as when needing to know who to trust in a crisis situation. However, despite these benefits, their use also runs the risk of oversimplifying and stereotyping the subject material. For example a common binary related to alcohol is the division of drinkers into "social" and "dependent" drinkers. The distinction is useful in helping to identify people who require some form of assistance, but it also oversimplifies the diversity of possible relationships to alcohol and runs the risk of stigmatizing dependent drinkers as weak and qualitatively different than those who drink in other ways. The consequent negative stigma discourages people from discussing pertinent issues, thereby making it less likely that they reflect on their own vulnerability. An alternative to interpreting things in terms of binary categories is to see them in terms of a continuum or spectrum of multiple positions. A continuum interpretation involves looking at the world less in terms of fixed categories, and more in terms of gradations of intensity across a particular dimension.[7] When practitioners and their clients shift from thinking in terms of binaries and seeing themselves as positioned more along a continuum of risk, the activities of self-reflection and discussion are legitimized. For example the relationship a person chooses to have with alcohol is now seen as moving dynamically across a range of positions between no relationship and a very intense relationship. In this frame conversations about drinking become less uncomfortable because they are no longer tied to all-or-nothing categories and their implied negative associations. A person's current relationship to alcohol is positioned on a continuum that will naturally vary over time, and that regular review of one's position is a normal and legitimate activity.

A binary interpretation of the morality of receiving money from the profits of gambling divides the world into those who are willing to accept such funding and those who are unwilling. Either an organization buys into industry involvement or it does not; either it is morally sound or it is not.

This oversimplified perspective can play a strategic role in putting pressure on organizations to consider rejecting funding, but in the longer term it runs many of the risks of binary categorization discussed earlier. It discourages people from thinking about the ethics of their involvement and discourages them from talking about it because to question such involvements is tantamount to accusing someone of ethical cowardice.

The concept of a continuum of moral jeopardy avoids these pitfalls. Instead of distancing those who are ambivalent, it recognizes that the extent to which a person or organization engages with gambling industries can vary in intensity and that it is less a case of whether or not to accept the funding, but more a question of at what level of intensity someone deems the relationship unsustainable. Furthermore, as the profits from gambling circulate more into the economy, it becomes increasingly difficult for public good organizations to avoid such connections. In a larger organization such as a hospital or a university, one part of the organization might have little influence over or might be unaware that other parts have entered into direct funding relationships with industry sources. The continuum perspective recognizes a range of potential relationships with gambling funds, and in so doing promotes ongoing discussion and review of the extent of these involvements.

A Framework for Self-Assessment

The process of self-assessment can help community organizations clarify their position on the continuum of moral jeopardy and thereby enable them to incorporate it into their planning. For example, the board for a private accident and emergency service might be trying to decide whether or not to take up a generous offer of funding from a local casino. Members of the board might differ strongly on the wisdom of striking up such a relationship and their discussions could often deteriorate into repetitive arguments. To move forward they now require a more organized framework on which to assess and deliberate on their views. For the purpose of self-assessment, the following breaks down the discussion on moral jeopardy into five subcontinuums: Purpose, Extent, Relevant harms, Identifiers, and Links (PERIL). These together can be used to assist individuals and organizations to assess their level of overall risk. The following sections examine each in turn.

Purpose (Degree to Which Purposes Between Funder and Recipient Diverge)

As outlined in Chapter 4, gambling has widespread impacts in terms of harm to individuals, families, and communities. If a primary purpose of the recipient organization is the advancement of public good, particularly benefits related to social well-being, health, and welfare, then receiving funds from a dangerous consumption industry will conflict with this purpose. For example, a child health organization will have credibility difficulties in commenting on child poverty when it is seen to be receiving significant funding from gambling sources. A sports or an arts organization might perceive itself as less affected, but if it identifies its activity as important to promoting the health and well-being of the community, it too could be challenged as to the consistency between its funding source and its stated purpose.

Extent (Degree to Which the Recipient Is Reliant on This Source)

As the proportion of income increases, it becomes more difficult to separate from expectations associated with the source and more likely that disagreements would be avoided to ensure the relationship remains positive. An organization that relies heavily on industry funding will carry higher vulnerability to the dictates and the terms and conditions imposed by the funding provider. The organization will be aware that disagreements with the funder could jeopardize the relationship, which in turn could put the whole organization at risk. Special efforts need to be made to ensure the relationship remains on a positive footing, and as a result industry funders are likely to enjoy high levels of acknowledgment and compliance. For example, a tennis club that derives the majority of its revenue from EGMs in a local hotel is likely to make special efforts to maintain that sponsorship. This might involve members wearing its insignia on their clothing and other apparel, thanking them for their backing at public events, and drinking and celebrating whenever possible within its venue. An organization that receives only a small proportion of income from industry sources is less likely to be influenced by the wishes of the funder, and more likely to pull out of the relationship when additional expectations are imposed.

Relevant Harms (Degree of Harm Associated With This Form of Consumption)

The level of harm generated by different forms of gambling will vary and the risk to an organization of forming associations with gambling industry sources will increase according to the salience of the product. Continuous forms of gambling with high odds of winning and high jackpots (e.g., casino EGMs) are currently the most likely form to be associated with problem gambling and its related harms. Noncontinuous forms of gambling such as raffles and lottery products are less likely to lead to problem gambling and other harms related to excessive gambling.[8] For example, receiving funds from a local EGM provider to assist in the construction of a community hall might lead community members severely affected by problem gambling to experience dilemmas regarding whether to make use of that facility. Because fewer people are affected by less salient forms (e.g., lottery products) financing the hall from these sources is likely to involve fewer people being troubled by such dilemmas.[9]

Identifiers (Degree to Which the Recipient Is Visibly Identified With the Funder)

Gambling providers are unlikely to willingly contribute anonymously to a community organization because the visible association with public good has an important role within their business. From the recipient's perspective, anonymous contributions tend to involve less risk because the recipient is not openly connected to the source. However the option on anonymous contributions is less likely to occur because a key motive for the industry funder is likely to be the positive public perception derived from an identifiable association with recognized public good. Nonetheless, there are degrees of visible association, from high visibility with prominent branding on signage, stationary, staff clothing, prizes, and so on, to very discrete acknowledgments, which for many will pass unnoticed.

Links (Nature and Directness of Links Between Recipient and Donor)

The more direct the link between funder and recipient, the stronger the potential influence and the more visible the association. For example, receiving funds directly from a casino involves more exposure than receiving that funding via an independent intermediary agency, such as a government department. As long as there are no major conflicts of interest for the intermediary agency, the separation reduces the likelihood that recipients will feel obligations—perhaps coercion—for their activities to comply with the interests of the donor. Another possibility includes protecting the organization's independence through clauses and contractual provisions and the involvement of governance boards in mediating influences.

Application of the Framework

Community and other public good organizations can incorporate these five subcontinuums into a process of assessing how far along the continuum of moral jeopardy they wish to traverse. The procedure for application would involve the following steps: First, the criteria for assessing the intensity of involvement are worked out for each subcontinuum. Next, discussion needs to occur regarding where on each subcontinuum members would like to see their organization positioned. The overall extent of moral jeopardy would then vary from very high levels, as indicated by high ratings on all five subcontinuums, to very low levels, as indicated by consistently low ratings. Decisions regarding future industry relationships are made accordingly. As with any continuum (e.g., the continuum of colors in a rainbow) the grades of distinction between one position and another are difficult to identify; when exactly, for example, does blue turn into green and green into brown? For ease of application, and as applies with the colors of the rainbow, a continuum can be divided into convenient but arbitrary divisions. In Figure 10.2 each subcontinuum is graded across four levels of intensity: low, medium,

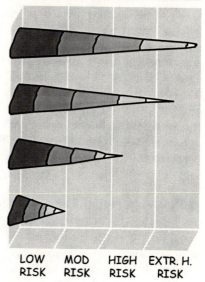

| ■ Purpose | ■ Extent | ■ Relevant-harm | ■ Identifiers | □ Links |

1: A problem gambling counselling service relying exclusively on receiving funds directly from EGM provider sources in a publicly visible way.

2: A sports club receiving half its income from its own limited number of EGMs

3: A church charity providing emergency housing that receives a small amount of funding from track racing sponsorship.

4: A performing arts organisation receiving a small grant anonymously from a government run lottery distribution mechanism.

| LOW RISK | MOD RISK | HIGH RISK | EXTR. H. RISK |

Figure 10.2 Moral Jeopardy Estimates in Four Sample Contexts

high, and extremely high. To illustrate their application, four examples of different situations have been listed alongside rough estimates of risk. This graphic presentation can assist participants in identifying levels of risk and help them decide to what extent along the continuum of moral jeopardy they are willing to traverse. Presumably for most organizations when their level of combined exposure is consistently at the high or extremely high level (as with examples 1 and 2), this should signal to them the need to consider making changes.

The use of these subcontinuums in reviewing exposure to moral jeopardy could be applied in a variety of ways. They could be incorporated into the educational packages as discussed earlier in the chapter. For example, workshop participants could be asked to review their own contexts or engage in discussions that review common scenarios. An alternative application could involve the development of self-help resources in which individuals or groups of individuals within an organization move through a series of questions that lead them through a process of self-assessment of their level of industry reliance. This approach could initially be developed in booklet form and evaluated with a variety of users. In the long term its accessibility as a resource would work best as an interactively designed Internet resource. Another application could involve incorporating it as part of the framework on which managers provide their reports to governance boards. For example, the chief executive in a regional health service could be required in quarterly reports to provide assessment of exposure across each subcontinuum.

The governance board then has an ongoing source of information upon which to make decisions regarding when the risks are too high and when to adjust accordingly. Finally, in line with developing a strategy for protecting low moral jeopardy environments, proactive governments could fund relevant independent agencies to adapt the domains into auditing tools for use in independently assessing levels of moral jeopardy. Once the auditing agency identifies those organizations at the high or extremely high end of the moral jeopardy continuum, they could be invited to participate in a program of educational and governance guidance aimed at awareness raising and negotiating change. In the long term, assistance might also involve the option of transition funding to enable the organization time to seek alternative sources.[10]

SETTING INTERNATIONAL BENCHMARK STANDARDS

With the two approaches recommended so far (harm minimization and self-assessment of moral jeopardy) emphasis has been placed on engaging individuals and agencies in recognizing risks and then engaging them in reviewing their links to industry funding as a way of preventing further democratic degradation. This next approach shifts the focus onto the behavior of governments and the role they play in the global proliferation of commercial gambling. The transition between the phases of regulation and liberalization (see Chapter 3) is a significant period. Low gambling consumption during the regulation phase keeps levels of associated problems to a minimum. People are likely to perceive gambling as benign enjoyment with few negative consequences. They have grown accustomed to a government that enforces tough regulations and takes a direct role in restricting gambling to less potent forms. The public does not need to know too much about gambling because associated problems are minimal. Any changes to the regulatory environment are assumed to have been implemented for the correct reasons and with the public interest at heart. When the government orientation shifts from regulation to liberalization, the government's previous role as public protector is tipped on its head. With the public continuing to assume high standards of protection, governments begin to explore the potential of gambling to generate easy tax revenue. They might begin with introducing state-run lotteries, then move on to license gambling machines in controlled environments, then perhaps allow the first casino license, and so on. The public, naive to the risks, tolerates each progressive liberalization, assuming that governments have fully examined potential harms and that negative consequences will continue at previous tolerable levels. The public is unaware that their government is taking them on a new adventure with very little understanding of its long-term consequences.

The time lag between the beginning of liberalization and public recognition of the social and economic downsides creates a window of opportunity for gambling providers to gain a foothold for high-intensity gambling into the economies of those nations naive to its effects. As with the logging of primeval forests, operations reach full swing before public attention is fully aroused regarding what is happening around them. This lack of awareness is massaged further by deploying some of the profits into media campaigns that highlight the benefits of gambling. People's anxieties are calmed with reassurances that gambling proliferation has only minor negative consequences and that it is on balance a positive activity within a community. It might not be until well into the normalization phase that sufficient public concern is expressed to worry governments, but by this time the commercial base for high-intensity gambling is well established and public health advocates have little chance of introducing significant changes. The momentum of gambling is now well underway and its impetus is difficult to stop, consequently the expansion continues until markets reach saturation. The key concern then becomes what to do when gambling reaches saturation in one place. What can be expected when a specific population reaches saturated levels of gambling? As with tobacco, once initial markets reach saturation, commercial imperatives drive gambling industries to seek out new opportunities and to realize new markets. These new markets tend to span out in two directions: first, new markets within the current population and, second, untapped markets in foreign locations.

The task of engaging new consumers within the current population often relies on the development and marketing of a new product. In many contexts, during the regulation phase, the typical gambler is a middle-aged man with a passion for horse betting. During liberalization and normalization, a greater range of products have become available that appeal specifically to populations such as youth, older people, women, and people of different ethnicities. For instance, the increasing presence of casinos in major urban centers is drawing in higher numbers of immigrant Chinese to play on casino tables.[11] Increased availability of gambling machines in clubs and casinos has engaged more women in regular gambling, and the introduction of interactive game technologies and sports betting are increasing the participation of young people. These new users understandably have little awareness of the risks associated with these new products.

The marketing of new forms of gambling to targeted populations has been particularly damaging to First Nation peoples. Indigenous communities in North America and the South Pacific have had little previous exposure to commercial gambling and typically have low awareness of the risks. For Maori (the indigenous people of New Zealand) during the regulation phase their communities have made use of noncontinuous forms of gambling, such as cards and housie or bingo, to fund communal projects like the building of *marae* (meeting houses).[12] Locally organized gambling events also provided important opportunities for families and communities to reconnect in an atmosphere of enjoyment and sharing. During the current phase of liberalization, the availability of continuous forms of gambling is enticing gamblers away from local events in favor of bulk gambling in larger commercial establishments. The investment of time and money is drawn out of the community with little benefit filtering back to local groups. With Maori families having a poorer capital base than the remainder of the population, coupled their little previous experience of continuous forms of gambling, negative impacts have rapidly emerged. For example, national statistics on problem gambling services recorded as high six times the proportional rate of Maori to non-Maori women seeking services than rates among the remainder of the population (Problem Gambling Committee, 2003). A similar pattern of poor preparedness, asset loss, and increased problem gambling can be observed for other First Nations people and can also be observed with people migrating from nations with lower to higher gambling intensity.

Formulating International Standards

The proliferation of gambling occurs as a global phenomenon, so part of the response to associated harms needs to involve measures that address issues at a global level. It is unrealistic to expect extractive industries in the midst of a boon period to restrain their own activities. It has not happened with other extractive industries (e.g., the logging of primeval forests) and it is unlikely to happen with a commercial product that is as profitable as the new forms of continuous gambling. The drivers for competition are far too strong to expect all sectors of gambling in all countries to display restraint. Similarly it is unrealistic to expect governments who are first experiencing the benefits of expanded gambling revenues to willingly constrain this easy form of income. It would make no sense, particularly in contexts where other forms of revenue are difficult to obtain. To moderate both industry and government appetites for revenue, nations considering or undergoing rapid gambling proliferation have a strong need for an external reference point on which they might assess any change. More importantly, in a new environment of high-intensity gambling, people require a means to gauge the performance of their governments, a measuring stick that can assist in telling whether or not the rhetoric of change is concealing or distorting what internationally would be viewed as real social and political responsibilities. One strategy for setting agreed-on standards across countries is the development of international charters and conventions that set international benchmark standards regarding how governments should behave. Many examples of such international conventions exist, including the Ottawa and Bangkok Charters for Health Promotion, the Universal Declaration of Human Rights, the Convention on the Rights of the Child, the International Covenant on Civil and Political Rights, the Convention on the Political Rights of Women, and so forth. Signatories might not always conform to them, but they provide an important reference point on which to gauge ethical standards.

One such charter with closer relevance to gambling is the European Charter on Alcohol (WHO, 1995), which emerged during the 1990s from negotiations between participant European Union countries concerned about the impacts of alcohol-related harm. It has formed the base of a number of initiatives that include collaborative projects coordinated by Eurocare and the development of the European Alcohol Action Plan 2000–2005 (WHO, 2000), which provides a framework for European Union member states to implement strategies that are most likely to reduce alcohol-related harm in their respective countries. The harmful outcomes of problem gambling and inappropriate use of gambling are not dissimilar to the abuse of alcohol. Accordingly, the European Charter provides a model for defining minimum standards and advocating a bottom line of social and ethical considerations regarding the sale, marketing, promotion, and accessibility of gambling.

Development of an International Charter for Gambling

I have over the last 10 years been involved in various attempts to adapt the European approach to alcohol into formulating an international charter for gambling (the "Auckland Charter"[13]). The development of this charter involved several versions of a document processed with various combinations of people. Its development into its current form took place in three stages.

Draft 1: Adapting the European Charter on Alcohol

In 1997 I copresented the original draft of an international charter at the Tenth Conference on Gambling and Risk Taking in Montreal. Our idea was prompted by exposure to the European Charter on Alcohol (WHO, 1995)[14] that is built up from a framework of seven ethical principles that stipulate clearly expectations for responsible governments in preventing and managing harms associated with alcohol consumption. Borrowing heavily from this Charter,[15] our first version of a gambling charter was based on an overarching guiding principle:

> All people have the right to a family, community and working life protected from violence, property crime, and other negative consequences of the consumption of gambling.

Following on from this overarching principle were seven other principles that included two that were specifically designed to minimize impacts on democratic systems:

> *Principle 5:* All people have a right to participate in a democratic process in deciding the amount and type of gambling that occurs in their communities.

Principle 6: Governments have a duty to provide regulatory frameworks and social policy responses on behalf of citizens to maximize the enjoyment of and limit the harm from the provision of all gambling.

We continued to present the idea of an international charter at national and international forums that included conferences in Australia[16] and at the second international conference on gambling, "Understanding and Minimizing Harm," held in Auckland in July 2001.[17]

Draft 2: Incorporating Public Health Perspectives

In the second phase, the first draft was reedited with the input of two colleagues: John Raeburn (with a long-term involvement in empowerment-based approaches to health promotion and community development) and Lorna Dyall (with a background in public health and approaches to improving the well-being of indigenous populations). Together the three of us embarked on a series of lively discussions that focused on preparing a second draft of the charter to be presented for discussion at an upcoming international conference in Auckland.[18] The combination of gambling expertise with public health and community development expertise helped strengthen the conceptual base for the charter. During our discussions, there was considerable tension between the bottom-up health promotion approaches advanced by Raeburn and my interest in more top-down harm minimization approaches. Tension also existed between the needs of more specific cultural and indigenous contexts and the need to address issues on a global basis. Despite these tensions we managed to produce a document to form the basis of discussion at the conference.

Draft 3: Integrating Multiple Perspectives

The third draft emerged as a central output of the 2003 conference. The conference was a 3-day event attended by more than 300 registrants, many attending from overseas. We had allocated the whole second day for everyone at the conference to discuss the formulation of the Charter. The first part of the day consisted of brief presentations on information and issues that were relevant to the Charter. Attendees then broke into specific discussion groups to focus on key aspects of the Charter. The outcomes of these discussions were then fed back into a plenary discussion. Later in the day further groups were formed to discuss population-related issues (e.g., its relevance to indigenous populations, Pacific peoples, gambling industries, government agencies, etc.). The day ended with a plenary discussion, following which Raeburn redrafted the Charter to incorporate all the key recommendations from the day's discussions. The revised version was then presented to the conference for approval on the following day.

The Auckland Charter on Gambling

The following lists seven key principles as they emerged from the discussions at the July 2001 conference.[19] Under each heading, the principle is described with a brief comment following to provide further elaboration.

Principle 1: Enjoyment of Gambling and Freedom From Harm

➤ All people have the right to enjoy responsible gambling, in the context of a family, community, and national life protected from the negative consequences of gambling.

➤ All people have the right to be enabled to take self-determined action individually and collectively to ensure their own and their community's well-being with regard to gambling, and a right to be heard and to participate in a democratic fashion when it comes to the creation of policy by governments in the area of gambling.

➤ All people have the right to have gambling issues communicated and dealt with in terms of their own culture and worldview. This includes people from indigenous groups, immigrants and refugees, those who are less well off, youth, older people, and other groups who are especially at risk or significant with regard to the impacts of gambling in a modern society.

This guiding principle lays down the primary purpose of the Charter. It recognizes the main function of gambling as a form of entertainment but at the same time acknowledges unambiguously that gambling has the capacity to impact seriously on the social ecology of communities and societies. It states that, as a fundamental human right, people need to be able to live their lives in ways that are not restricted by these impacts. It also links in the contribution of research in ascertaining whether people are adequately protected from gambling-related harms. If it can be shown that gambling is having significant impact on families, communities, or workplaces, the onus is then on public bodies to pursue policies that minimize these harms.

Principle 2: Government Duty of Care and Protection

➤ Gambling should be recognized by governments as a public health issue.

➤ Governments have a duty to provide regulatory frameworks and social policy responses on behalf of all their citizens to allow enjoyment and limit harm in the provision of all gambling, within a framework of independence from parties with a financial interest in the provision of gambling. They need to ensure that regulations are enforced. Supply of gambling products known to be harmful should be controlled.

> ➤ Governments also have a duty to enable communities to take action with regard to gambling on their own behalf, and to have a decisive influence on relevant policy and legislation.
> ➤ Governments need to ensure that appropriate consumer and product information is supplied with regard to gambling products and practices, and that the promotion of gambling is not unduly exploitative or manipulative.

This statement places the duty of care squarely on the shoulders of government. What body, other than government, is adequately positioned to protect the public from harms associated with gambling? Although governments will remain interested in the substantial revenues gained from gambling, they still have a primary responsibility to establish and enforce laws that effectively discourage hazardous participation in gambling. They are required to lead the way in fostering awareness of ethical and legal responsibility among those involved in the marketing or provision of gambling, in ensuring strict control of product safety, and in implementing appropriate measures against illicit provision.

Principle 3: Community Empowerment

> ➤ All people have a right to effective participation in a democratic process of deciding the amount and type of gambling. Where possible, this process should be guided by research.
> ➤ Where appropriate, extra consideration must be given to the rights of indigenous populations who have original occupant status in their own countries.

By way of a counterbalance to the power of governments, communities themselves require some leeway to influence gambling behavior in their midst. As with drinking, gambling behavior is deeply embedded within a social context. Its meaning and value varies according to dimensions such as culture, age, prior experience, and levels of awareness. It also varies considerably over time. Some communities are prepared for a more liberal approach to regulation, whereas some communities require more controls. To enhance the capacity of any people to find effective and appropriate ways to manage gambling, each community requires the power to determine what types and how much gambling it is able to sustain.

Principle 4: Informed Consent and Education

> ➤ All people have the right to valid, accurate, detailed information about gambling and education consonant with their language, culture, and values, and about the consequences of gambling to health, family, community, and society. This should start early in

life. All people also have the right to information and resources that enable them to take effective self-determined and responsible action in the area of gambling at the community, regional, and national levels.

In preparing a population for a lifelong involvement with gambling, consumers need to be equipped with a clear appreciation of the risks associated with that behavior. Such an understanding will emerge from exposure to a variety of public information strategies. These might include programs such as media campaigns, gambling content within school curriculum, point-of-sale information, and product labeling. The delivery of this information needs to vary according to characteristics of the target population. For example, older people tend to respond to different messages and images than younger people. The outcome of such strategies will be consumers who recognize not only the overall risks, but also the relative risks of different products and different environments.

Principle 5: Protection of Populations From the Negative Effects of Gambling

➤ All people have the right to an environment protected from the harmful effects of gambling, and where vulnerabilities are not exploited in the provision of gambling. This is particularly so for population groups such as young people, older people, women, minorities, immigrants, and indigenous peoples.

➤ They also have the right to develop their own resilience and action with regard to the potentially damaging consequences of gambling. This includes the development of partnerships with experts, governments, and nongovernment organizations as is deemed appropriate by those people.

On the flip side of strengthening consumer understanding is protecting those who remain vulnerable. Younger people are continually being introduced to the world of gambling and from their first encounters they emerge through to settle on their long-term relationship. During this initial period of learning, their lack of experience places them at risk of engaging in behaviors that might restrict their development in other ways. They require some means by which to grade their exposure while they learn to manage their response to risk. Similar protections are required for other groups in transition: people and communities first encountering a new form of gambling; people in developing economies; and people migrating, separating, and retiring. Protections might consist of controls on the price of gambling products, their availability, and the levels of promotion. For example, governments could introduce strict controls on direct and indirect advertising of gambling and ensure that no form of advertising is specifically addressed to young people, for instance, through the linking of gambling to sports, wealth, or sexual prowess.

Principle 6: Access to Care and Effective Resources for Those Affected by Problem Gambling

> ➤ All those adversely affected by gambling have the right to accessible professional treatment, care, and support, which acknowledges their culture, gender, and sexual preference. They also have the right to community support and information resources that enable them to determine their own process of recovery and to improve their own quality of life. In the context of indigenous peoples, these processes involve recognition of those people's inherent right to self-determination.

A society that moves beyond prohibition to a permanent acceptance of gambling will need also to accept the presence of problem gambling in all its manifestations. At its core stand individuals and family members who are struggling with repeated challenges to their finances and relationships. To ameliorate the immediate suffering and avoid the longer term intergenerational impacts, these people will require resources to affect change. The proceeds from gambling should, therefore, contribute to ensuring the accessibility of effective and appropriate treatment and rehabilitation services.

Principle 7: Right to Abstain or Limit Consumption

> ➤ All people who do not wish to gamble, or to gamble at only modest levels, have the right to be safeguarded from pressures to gamble, to be supported in their nongambling lifestyle if that is their choice, and to have access to information and resources that facilitate choices and action related to such abstinence or low-level participation in gambling.

In contexts of high gambling consumption, heavy gambling can end up normalized to such an extent that people are expected as a matter of course to participate in gambling. As with alcohol use, such normalization will impact negatively on two major groups: those who make a moral choice not to gamble and those making lifestyle changes in response to problem gambling. Changes in social awareness are required that endorse the possibility that some people will choose not to gamble. This will require supportive strategies such as restrictions on normalizing content in advertising, social marketing campaigns acknowledging the right to abstain, and the creation of nongambling zones in entertainment venues.

The Charter's Future

The Charter as currently formulated is intended as a constructive guide to governments in a global environment of gambling liberalization and normalization. Its principles are part of an evolving process. As more interested parties participate, it is anticipated that definition of the principles will be further refined and that they will begin to be employed as a basis for formulating strategies for action that individual countries can then employ in devising their gambling action plans. However, its future is highly dependent on the extent to which people begin recognizing the global threats to democracy posed by unfettered expansion of commercial gambling. In the current climate, this looks likely to take considerable time. In the meantime the groundwork for international conventions can continue because, in their absence, it is difficult to see how governments will adequately protect their structures from degradation and the need for international benchmarks is only going to get stronger. The interest governments have in gambling revenue will continue to distort what they understand as responsible management in this area. As tax revenue increases, motivation to adequately monitor systems decreases. This book has provided many illustrations of how gradual distortions to democratic systems can be difficult to spot; consequently any remedial response is likely to come too little too late. There is, therefore, a role for external agencies to assist governments in identifying when their management of gambling is likely to compromise public interests. International bodies, such as the WHO or the United Nations, could perform an important function in sponsoring the further recognition of threats to democracy and then seeking member country endorsement of its principles as a guide to public policy on gambling. It is unclear at what point the interest of these organizations will be sufficient for them to consider playing a role.[20]

MONITORING FUTURE STRATEGIES

This chapter has developed three paths forward that advance the goal of protecting democratic systems from distortions imposed by high-frequency commercial gambling. The first approach explored the application of harm minimization principles in reducing democratic degradation and presented three examples of how this might be done. The second approach delved into the development of a self-assessment tool for individuals and organizations to assess levels of moral jeopardy as a basis for calibrating their links to profits from gambling. The third approach explored the development of an international charter to guide governments in their responsibilities during the expansion of commercial gambling. With all three approaches, successful application will require the development of systems for monitoring their impact and effectiveness. For example, those countries that adopt the Charter as a reference point for managing harm from gambling will also need to build up a research infrastructure that is capable of providing the required monitoring. The Charter's ethical principles could provide a basis for specifying clear targets and identifying compliance indicators with which to monitor the performance of individual governments. International organizations are then able to provide independent monitoring by taking the compliance indicators and developing audit processes for evaluating government compliance. The publication of the outcome of such audits will provide a reference point for governments that wish to expand gambling opportunities while preventing harm to democratic institutions. Similarly, with harm minimization and self-assessment approaches, the evolution of systems for monitoring and the levels of independence built into those monitoring processes will play a crucial role in justifying and refining their application.

11 Facing the Future

This book began with a discussion of the effects on freedom associated with the distortions of political ecologies that result from the proliferation of high-intensity commercial gambling. I argued that the modern expansion of gambling can be likened to primary extractive industries such as native logging, large-scale mining, or other commercially driven extractive industries in which resources are tapped without needing to exchange resources in return. Whereas the target for logging and other primary extractive industries is the bounty offered by the natural world, the target for commercial gambling is the bounty offered within the systems of social and financial interchange. One is derivative of naturally occurring cycles of birth and death, whereas the other is derivative of processes for interchanging resources and values within social and economic systems. The book explored how, in accessing both these forms of bounty, the triple alliance among governments, multinational business interests, and local entrepreneurs creates a development momentum that is difficult to contain. As the scale of activity grows and the methods of extraction are refined, more and more people are drawn into roles derived from this industrial complex and they become embedded as an integral part of its social and political structures. Reliance on gambling activities grows incrementally and involvements disperse into strands of intensifying dependency that entangle themselves around larger societal structures, local communities, and individuals with key social responsibilities. The book focuses particularly on the subtle degradations of roles that occur for individuals (e.g., politicians, researchers, and reporters) who occupy critical positions in the maintenance of democracy. It concludes that for those nations choosing to embrace the new world of high-intensity gambling, they will need to consider strenuous and proactive measures that protect their democratic systems from moral and political degradation.

Using the material outlined in this book, what can we expect with commercial gambling and its effects on democracy in the future? Some major developed economies (e.g., Australia, Japan, and parts of the United States) have enabled rapid increases in gambling consumption. Other nations have taken a more measured approach (e.g., the United Kingdom, Canada, and Germany). Whether fast or slow, in both circumstances the capacity for further growth in consumption still has a long way to go. For example, per-capita consumption in the United Kingdom would need to almost double before it reaches levels similar to those recorded in parts of Australia, and countries in Latin America and European countries in transition are only just beginning to flirt with gambling liberalization. Because commercial gambling introduces levels of consumption that were unfamiliar in previous historical periods, it is difficult to see clearly where this will lead. Besides, the future remains determinedly elusive and often defies the most informed predictions. For example, 30 years ago the modernist dream of an ordered rational utopia and cynics' depictions of overpopulated chaos were both wide of the mark. Accordingly, it would be foolhardy at this early stage to attempt to sketch in any detail a picture of this unfamiliar territory. Nonetheless, although it might be difficult to feel confident about any predictions, in a general way, this book has identified a range of reasons for justifiable concern about the way gambling and democracy are becoming intertwined.

VISIONING THE FUTURE

Perhaps, in time, nations that participate in rapid proliferation will find ways of correcting the excesses associated with expansion and will construct their own systems and processes that enable them to keep benefits and harms in balance, but this seems unlikely. Historically gambling has involved either highly regulated forms of wagering or low-salience forms that generate only peripheral interest and concern. These high-intensity gambling environments are a new phenomenon and the incentives that drive them appear far too strong to rely on self-correction. So, although the way this pans out is uncertain, I am still going to hedge my bets and explore the future through the aperture of four separate scenarios.

Direction 1: Open Season

In this scenario governments continue to experience pressure to reduce taxation and view revenue from gambling as a means to expand key social and other development programs without burdening personal and other forms of income tax. They progressively reduce constraints on gambling and allow new forms of betting along with their associated improved technologies. They also enable increases in gambling availability and promotion. As a result the levels of commercial gambling rise sharply with resultant negative impacts on local businesses, increased social harms, and rising levels of problem gambling. With rising tax revenue from gambling, government interest and dependence on it continues to increase and accordingly any emerging harms are responded to using strategies that aim to play down the negative impacts, keep the public ill informed, silence critics, and, together with the industry, celebrate the gains. Although there are some business casualties (particularly for the less potent noncontinuous forms of gambling such as horse racing), the gambling industry overall grows rapidly in size and gambling technologies (both electronic and psychological) become more potent. Leading gambling providers generate large surpluses, which enables them to consolidate both the resources and intelligence they need to partner with government in silencing dissent.

Direction 2: Graded Expansion

In this scenario governments become sensitized to the negative impacts of gambling perhaps through public moral outcry or because their own monitoring is picking up signs of increased crime, corruption, and social dislocation. They are still primarily interested in commercial gambling for its revenue potential but are mindful that in the long term this potential could be at risk if the negative impacts are not moderated. Established gambling providers too are concerned about long-term effects of negative perceptions and they team up with government to discipline the more blatantly exploitive practices of fringe and aspiring providers. Between them, the rougher edges of the business are trimmed away and all activities proceed lawfully with little outward signs of antisocial activities. A small but conspicuous commitment is made to supporting problem gambling services as well as funding host responsibility programs and public education campaigns but, underneath these positive displays, regulations continue to be loosened and consequently consumption continues to rise. The main protagonists remain suspicious of both independent research and public health initiatives and seek to ensure these activities are steered away from enquiries that might question continued expansion.

Direction 3: Managed Expansion

In this scenario public outcry regarding the effects of gambling reaches sufficient levels for governments to question the desirability of some forms of commercial gambling and to become weary of their own increasing reliance on the revenue. Accordingly they actively curtail certain forms (particularly the highly salient continuous forms such as EGMs) and adopt a pathway of controlled and managed expansion. They set up independent mechanisms for assessing harms from gambling and are responsive to subsequent recommendations. They regularly monitor changes in consumption patterns and closely examine their implications for both their social and political ecologies. They also maintain vigilance regarding points of reliance and compromise that creep into their systems and the autonomy of community organizations. They set in place robust and independent systems that establish high standards of host responsibility in gambling venues and ensure providers comply with ethical codes. Established gambling providers recognize that their opportunities for expansion are contingent on demonstrating that increased consumption will incur only minor harms. Consequently they have a strong interest in supporting systems that assess impacts and help moderate community reliance. As a result of these measures, consumption rises very slowly in ways that are acceptable to the public and incur relatively few problems. The public also becomes progressively accustomed to and comfortable with slow increases in gambling consumption and perceives governments as responsible guardians. In the long term, this could entail accepting high availability of gambling, similar to the way alcohol has gradually entwined itself as a common feature of everyday life.

Direction 4: Abiding by International Standards

In pursuing this final direction, governments have recognized the potential of commercial gambling to cause widespread harm and have acknowledged that the drivers are not only happening within their own domain but also as a result of global pressures. They openly acknowledge their conflicts of interest in receiving gambling revenue and are actively seeking ways to reduce moral jeopardy. Accordingly, they commit the shaping of their gambling environment to guidance from a set of internationally endorsed ethical principles that define obligations and mechanisms they would need to abide by to prevent further degradation (see the example given in Chapter 10). They adopt these principles to help constrain the influence of transnational gambling interests in promotion of global gambling expansion. This global orientation also enables them to assist nations that have recently embraced gambling expansion and, help them recognize social and political hazards, and set in place (early on) mechanisms that reduce political degradation and moral jeopardy. Gambling providers recognize that their future will depend on assisting governments in conforming to ethical standards and they become active in promoting standards both within their businesses and with businesses in connected jurisdictions. Independent research becomes a cornerstone of both government and industry planning and research of high standards is conducted on ethical dilemmas, social impacts, cognitive behavioral dynamics, product testing, and venue host responsibility.

In current circumstances, it looks likely that various combinations of the first three directions are set to continue. Nations that are new to the expansion of commercial gambling and relatively naive to the risks will be easily persuaded by the revenue potential and will tend to embrace variations of Direction 1 ("open season"). This is particularly worrying in large rising economies (e.g., Brazil, Russia, India, and China), where their progressive attitude to economic development presents the ideal circumstances for gambling to proliferate. In contexts where commercial gambling has already proliferated, Direction 2 ("graded expansion") is the most probable outcome. In such circumstances the rapid embracing of high-intensity gambling generates nodes of high reliance on gambling revenue and, as documented throughout the book, leads to increases in moral jeopardy and associated degradations in democratic roles. The strongest examples of this are occurring in parts of Australia, Canada, and the United States. Unfortunately, when state and community reliance on gambling revenue consolidates, it is difficult to see these locations progressing to Direction 3 ("managed expansion"). On top of their revenue dependency, these systems have already enabled gambling industries to attain substantial surpluses, which they are then able to invest into linking up internationally and exerting collective pressure on governments to further extend their gambling markets. Nonetheless, some nations, which have opted wisely for slow expansion, are looking as though they are heading for Direction 3. Most notable is the Netherlands, where they have adapted their harm minimization framework for alcohol and drug consumption and applied its principles to gambling.

With regard to Direction 4 ("conforming to international standards"), despite it being the safest option, it appears unlikely to emerge as an orientation for a long time to come. In the first place, discussion on the international ethical standards has yet to find its way onto the agendas of international relations and international bodies. In the second place, people in most countries around the world remain naive to the likely impacts of high-intensity commercial gambling and the damage might need to intensify before it registers sufficiently. In the third place, international gambling interests are gathering momentum and, as occurred with tobacco, they will understandably endeavor to influence international opinion in ways that promote gambling expansion. Finally, the infrastructure required for conducting independent academic enquiry into commercial gambling is a long way from forming. A critical literature on gambling expansion has yet to emerge and current research activities are heavily influenced by expansion priorities.

FUTURE MORAL JEOPARDY

In January 2006 newspapers reported that after long periods of rain, many people had been killed in a series of flash floods in Indonesia:

> Environmentalists say that much of the forest cover in the area—which would normally absorb some of the rain and prevent the hillsides from slipping—has been cut down in recent years, contributing to the disaster. ("Dozens Killed in Indonesian Floods," 2006)

Erosion of deforested land led to silt being washed down and deposited in rivers, causing them to clog up and resulting in widespread flooding. The degradation caused by deforestation clearly contributed to this disaster and, although it was a natural event, it was a series of events that occurred in the political ecology that really enabled this tragic sequence to proceed. More specifically, the deforestation was a result of alliances among government agencies, international logging interests, and local entrepreneurs who pursued a course of rapid logging expansion with minimal attention to strategies that might rectify disruptions to the natural ecology. Their efforts also contributed to less dramatic impacts that include loss of animal species, effects to the atmosphere, dislocation of people, and the spread of corrupt practices. What is of fundamental concern here for the future of gambling expansion is that a parallel process of stripping and denuding of the financial networks will lead to similar disruptions and dislocations and that the increases in moral jeopardy and the subtle degradations in democratic duties will, downstream, expose societies to wider problems. These exposures will reduce a society's capacity to deal with crises and diminish its longer term resiliency in responding to future challenges.

Banks (2002), a leading figure in the Australian Productivity Commission's beacon report on gambling, presented a paper that analyzes changes in Australia 3 years after their landmark review. He concluded his presentation by stating:

> This brings me to the *last* and, in my view, *highest* priority: the need to reform policy-making and regulatory governance arrangements. Ensuring the substantive independence of the core regulator in each jurisdiction is central to this. It has demanding requirements, which the Commission spelt out in its report. In most jurisdictions those requirements have not yet been met. (p. 40)

His comments signal that despite a range of regulatory changes that followed from their review, the central issue of government dependence had not been addressed. His words signal a critical concern. Once a governance body buys into receiving substantial revenue from gambling, it then faces enormous difficulties in protecting levels of independence in its policymaking and regulatory processes. When governance is compromised there is little to prevent that compromise from spreading through the systems it governs. In a way he was suggesting that Australian state governments appear to have crossed the line in terms of their ability to manage their conflicts of interest; they appear to be at a loss as to how and where they can establish points of independence and integrity within their systems.

Throughout this book, discussion has sought to identify possible locations of independence within political ecologies that could act as reliable points of reference that would ensure moral integrity in a world of expanding commercial gambling. However, stable points of reference were difficult to find. Governments are influenced by revenue potential, researchers are swayed by funding opportunities, the public is manipulated by industry marketing, the media are swayed by promotional potential, and community organizations are captured by funding arrangements. Looking ahead, I have difficulty imagining one place that could provide an independent reference point that is impervious to the influence of gambling revenue interests. As

I ventured deeper into the world of gambling I grew more convinced that these points of independence were unlikely to emerge. Instead, I am beginning to consider the possibility that a solid and reliable reference point is not the only means of countering moral degradation. It might be possible to envisage a time when instead of one solid independent reference point, a system of multiple points of partial independence could make a difference. This could be likened to laying foundation poles into a bottomless swamp where no one particular pole rests on solid ground but where each pole is set into the mud deep enough to become fixed. Standing alone they are not stable, but bound together the poles have enough collective strength to hold a platform in place. Similarly, each person who plays a significant role in determining a particular gambling environment, as he or she is subjected to the forces of moral degradation, standing by himself or herself is likely to sink. However, where procedures are in place that ensure awareness and open discussion regarding issues of moral jeopardy and where systems are in place that enable some degree of transparency and surveillance, then when one party begins to sink there is enough collective strength in the system to either correct or compensate for this degradation.

Chapter Notes

NOTES ON CHAPTER 1: INTRODUCTION

1. Good discussions on the variable ways expenditure figures are calculated are provided in the Australian Productivity Commission's (1999) *Australia's Gambling Industries: Final Report,* as well as in Azmier's (2001) *Gambling in Canada 2001: An Overview.*
2. Saul (2005) claimed, "Worldwide, some $900 billion is spent by citizens on gambling" (p. 130). He provided little information on how he arrived at this figure, and it seems likely it is a rough guess. (Throughout this book, currency is converted into current U.S. dollars; that is, the amounts have been calculated according to relative values in 2006).
3. It is difficult to find estimates of total expenditure in the United States, but this estimate was provided by Eadington (2005).
4. Figures are also in Canadian Partnership for Responsible Gambling (2004; converted to current U.S. dollars).
5. This combines the New Zealand 2004 figure of $1.4 billion (Department of Internal Affairs, 2005) with the Australian 2003–2004 figure of $12.8 billion (ANU Centre for Gambling Research, 2005).
6. This is the amount retained by operators after the payment of winnings but before the deduction of the costs of operation. This is 20% higher than income 4 years earlier.
7. For example, in New Zealand in 2004, expenditure on EGMs (outside casinos) accounted for about half the total gambling expenditure of $1.4 billion, whereas 10 years before it was only one quarter of the total expenditure (New Zealand Department of Internal Affairs, 2006).
8. See Horbay's (2004) presentation on behalf of Game Planit, where he explored how in EGMs the processes of virtual reel mapping can lead to false impressions for players of a near win.
9. Reith (1999) discussed this in more detail.
10. For example, without government pressure, casinos typically commit small amounts of money to community benefit funds relative to the size of their profits.
11. Australian Productivity Commission (1999) provides an overview of gambling and employment in Australia.

NOTES ON CHAPTER 2: SUBTLE DEGRADATION

1. Substantial portions of this chapter were published in the Adams (2004). I am grateful to the *Journal of Gambling Issues* (and the Centre for Addiction and

Mental Health, Toronto) for their kind permission to incorporate this material into this chapter.

2. Two books that have explored the close alliance between governments and gambling providers in the expansion of commercialized gambling are, with reference to Australia, Costello and Milar's (2000) *Wanna Bet? Winners and Losers in Gambling's Luck Myth;* and with reference to the United States, Goodman's (1995) *The Luck Business: The Devastating Consequences and Broken Promises of America's Gambling Explosion.*

3. These oppositions have occurred particularly with the licensing of casinos, and a description of these in New Zealand is covered by Adams (1999). In an examination of EGM expansion in Australia, Doughney (2002) discussed how justifications for market economies have engaged governments and obscured the public from appreciating the true impacts of gambling.

4. Jernigan (1997) looked in detail at some of the methods global alcohol industry networks use to expand into new liquor markets. In a similar discussion, Studlar (2002) explored similar processes with government and tobacco industry relationships.

5. For example, Tobin (1997) discussed their use with sensitive topics.

6. The examples used in the chapter are composites contrived for the purpose of illustration. They point out possibilities in our current systems, and any resemblances to real people or situations are purely coincidental.

7. The moral dilemmas for researchers are discussed more fully in Chapter 7, and in an article by Adams, Raeburn, et al. (2003) and in Adams and Rossen (2006).

NOTES ON CHAPTER 3: GOVERNMENTS

1. Reith (1999) provided an excellent account of the early origins of European concepts of luck and chance and their links with early forms of gambling.

2. For example, the Romans recognized potential harms and prohibited gambling during Saturnalia, and in medieval times specific legislative prohibitions were enforced by rulers (Reith, 1999).

3. The emergence of the regulatory and prohibitionist approaches to gambling are documented by Dixon (1991; particularly for England), Kavanagh (1993; for continental Europe), and Morton (2003; for more recent changes in Canada).

4. For example, the United Kingdom introduced its first draw of the National Lottery in 1994, followed a year later by instant scratch cards, a second weekly draw in 1997, and Thunderball in 1999, as described by Orford, Sproston, Erens, White, and Mitchell (2003).

5. The general expansion of gambling in the United States is described by Grinols (2004) and First Nation gambling by Zitzow (2003).

6. The spread of EGMs throughout Australia is well described by Doughney (2002) and Costello and Milar (2000).

7. Based on consumption figures provided by the Department of Internal Affairs (all figures converted into current U.S. dollars). The per capita calculations include the whole population rather than just the adult population because evidence indicates that adolescents under the age of 18 years can be frequent gamblers.

8. For example, see Cayuela and Guirao (1991) and Becona, Labrador, Echeburua, and Ochoa (1995), who indicated a fivefold increase in gambling consumption in Spain during the 1980s. Large increases in participation have also been described in Germany by Meyer (1992), in the Netherlands by Hermkens

and Kok (1991), in Sweden by Ronnberg et al. (1999), and in Russia by Kassinove, Tsytsarev, and Davidson (1998).

9. Detailed in Azmier (2001; all figures converted into current U.S. dollars). Over these periods (1992–2000), although expenditure on lottery products remained reasonably stable, the main drivers for the increase were derived from greater consumption in casinos or with EGMs.

10. The emergence of this type of gambling in the United Kingdom is documented in books by Clapson (1992) and Dixon (1991).

11. In the United Kingdom, the 1960 Gaming Act relaxed constraints on casino gambling, but soon led to what officials later described as "an uncontrolled proliferation of casinos and other gaming with attendant malpractices and criminal involvement" (Gaming Board, 2000, p. 63). They soon realized their mistake and reintroduced constraints in the 1968 Gaming Act. Similar links to organized crime occurred with the initial liberalization of casino gambling in Nevada as described by Goodman (1995).

12. The major part of gambling expansion in New Zealand occurred as a result of the introduction of EGMs, which were progressively deregulated in a complex series of amendments to previous acts, none of which had considered the underlying purposes and principles of an environment of high-intensity gambling.

13. For example, in the United Kingdom, Australia, and New Zealand, the advertising of national lotteries dominates television advertising and has played a major role in normalizing gambling as a common form of family entertainment.

14. This is particularly obvious in the Australian states of Victoria and New South Wales, where in 2005 gambling contributes to over one seventh of their tax revenue. Even for politicians opposed to widespread commercial gambling, it is likely to be political suicide to pursue policies that would lead to significant increases in personal income tax.

15. In the few countries that do allocate funds, these are usually in the range of less than 0.5% of expenditure on gambling.

16. In New Zealand during the 1990s, one agency of government, the Department of Internal Affairs, for many years played the roles of leading policymaker, regulator, enforcer, and manager of remedial responses, and at times engaged in promotion activities for gambling expansion. Despite fundamental clashes in role, officials were adamant that they had enough systems within the agency to ensure these roles were not confused.

17. In a survey of public attitudes to gambling, Azmier (2000) concluded that "In a number of policy areas, current provincial regulations run counter to prevailing public attitudes. In particular government policies towards VLTs (video lottery terminals), charitable gambling, First Nations gambling, public accountability, and the negative impact of problem gambling do not reflect the prevailing attitudes or desires" (p. 31).

18. The *Responsibility in Gambling Trust* moved in 2005 to being a public–private partnership with statutory independence that is realized through a governance board of half industry representation and half "independent" representation from organizations such as churches, helping agencies, and experts. The arrangement resembles the now defunct *Problem Gambling Committee* that operated between 1998 and 2003 in New Zealand. The two key issues in both arrangements is the extent to which the industry half of the committee can exercise greater power and influence over decisions and the extent to which they are equipped to decide on funding arrangements for problem gambling services and research.

19. This Ministry of Health reluctantly adopted this role in 2004, prior to which the Problem Gambling Committee—with links into the Department of Internal Affairs—managed remedial responses. Interestingly, when the remedial and preventive response to gambling moved to the Ministry of Health, it was positioned in its Public Health Directorate with support from the Mental Health Directorate.

20. It would be interesting to contrast the evolution of gambling regulations in countries such as the United States, United Kingdom, and Australia, particularly the transitions from the earlier phases of regulation to the later phases of liberalization and normalization. Early stages are likely to involve more frequent merging of roles, then a slow separation of duties. These could be observed in action in countries new to gambling expansion such as Poland, China, and Brazil.

21. In several states in Australia (e.g., Queensland and Victoria), it is their state treasuries that have adopted leadership roles in the area of gambling policy, regulation, harm minimization, and remediation. A treasury's clear interest in protecting the revenue income from gambling challenges its ability to credibly implement these other roles.

22. An interesting example of this is occurring in the Australian state of Queensland, where the Community Investment Fund has been created and is administered by the state treasury for the purpose of responding to gambling-related harm. The treasurer is guided and advised in its investment of this fund by a Responsible Gambling Advisory Committee made up of representatives from state government, the community, and gambling industries. The treasury here is in a conflicted position in that it has a clear interest in gambling tax revenue, it is trying to manage the harm, and it is strongly advised in this duty by government and industry representatives with a strong interest in increases in gambling consumption (see http://www.responsiblegambling.qld.gov.au/).

23. Such as those mentioned earlier with regard to casino expansion in Nevada during the 1950s and in the United Kingdom during the 1960s.

NOTES ON CHAPTER 4: COMMUNITIES

1. The prevalence of problem gambling in North America is summarized by Ladouceur, Boisvert, Pepin, Loranger, and Sylvain (1994) and Shaffer, Hall, and Vander Bilt (1997).

2. The most commonly used manual for identifying mental disorders, the fourth revised edition of the *Diagnostic and Statistical Manual of Mental Disorders* (*DSM–IV–R*; American Psychiatric Association, 2000) categorizes "pathological gambling" as a "disorder of impulse control" but relies heavily on criteria similar to those used to identify alcohol and drug dependence. For a critical overview of issues associated with these classifications see Orford et al. (2003).

3. The position that increases in consumption are linked to increases in problem gambling is a controversial topic, challenged by gambling providers and by research such as a New Zealand repeat prevalence study that suggests that despite significant increases in gambling consumption, the level of problem gambling dropped (see Abbott & Volberg, 2000). However, overall, despite some anomalies, the overall trend is for the two to coincide. For example, see Gernstein et al. (1999).

4. The impacts of frequent parental gambling on the development of children were detailed by Williams (1996) and the broader effects on the social coherence and connectedness of communities were examined by Raeburn (2001).
5. In a study of the seven local authorities of Auckland, we found statistically significantly higher concentrations of EGMs in low-income neighborhoods (Census Area Units) than in high-income neighborhoods (Adams et al., 2004; see also similar studies reported by Costello & Milar, 2000; Doughney, 2002).
6. For accounts of the expansion in the United States, see books by Goodman (1995) and Grinols (2004). For Australia, see Doughney and Kelleher (1999). For Canada, see Azmier (2001).
7. Dyall (2002) explored the issue of how commercialized gambling has impacted negatively on Māori communities. See also Dyall and Hand (2003).
8. For instance, the relationship of Asian migrants in New Zealand was discussed by Tse, Wong, and Kim (2004) and Tse et al. (2005).
9. For example, ACIL Consulting (1999) detailed a broad range of economic benefits to communities for gambling.
10. For example, these are apparent in industry-supported reports such as Centre for International Economics (2001) and ACIL Consulting (1999).
11. His calculations made allowances for aspects such as contributions to charities and reductions in unemployment.
12. For accounts of these histories see O'Sullivan and Christoffel 1992) on New Zealand, Reith (1999), on the United Kingdom, and Morton (2003) on Canada.
13. Exact figures are difficult to ascertain, but during the years from 2000 to 2004, approximately $90 million came from the national lottery, more than $250 million from EGMs outside casinos, and an undisclosed amount distributed by casinos and track betting organizations (amounts converted into current U.S. dollars).
14. This was the conclusion of the economic analysis of gambling in the Australian study of Bendigo as reported by Pinge (2000).
15. Goodman (1995) argued that reservations were used to construct progressively larger casinos close to population centers.
16. For example, in June 2006 the state government in the province of Saskatchewan relaxed their regulations by allowing charitable organizations to raise extra money by holding poker tournaments and gaming nights.
17. This position that charitable gambling is a doubly regressive tax is very controversial but supported by work such as Clotfelter and Cook (1989) and Pickernell et al. (2004).
18. In New Zealand, I served for 5 years on a committee similar to the RIGT, the Problem Gambling Committee, which administered a voluntary levy from the industry for the purpose of helping problem gamblers. In its early years, we were continually reminded by the independent chair that "He who pays the piper, calls the tune."
19. Versions of the following discussion have also been published in articles in the *Journal of Gambling Issues* and *Addiction*.
20. For a more detailed discussion on these issues see Adams, Raeburn, et al. (2003) and Adams (2004).

NOTES ON CHAPTER 5: FREEDOM IN THE MEDIA

1. In compiling material for this chapter, I am grateful for access to newspaper and other media collections provided by the Problem Gambling Foundation of

New Zealand and also supplied by Dave McPherson at GamblingWatch New Zealand.

2. For example, Goodman (1995) detailed the expansion of the U.S. casino industry in destination venues (e.g., Las Vegas), riverboats, and First Nation reservations. He documented how, with each advance, the casino industry adapted its public communications to facilitate incremental allowances in gambling liberalization.

3. Constructions in media forms such as newspapers have been studied closely on a broad range of topics. Examples include depictions of retirement (Rudman, 2005), global warming (Antilla, 2005), drug fatalities (Forsyth, 2001), and farmers (Reisner, (2003).

4. A description of these proceedings is described in the *GamblingWatch* newsletter (March 2001, available at http://www.gamblingwatch.org.nz/index.asp?pageID=2145822110.

5. Maureen Waaka also distinguished herself in standing up to the leadership of her own *Iwi* (tribe) in contesting their active promotion of a casino for Rotorua.

6. Doughney (2002) provided a detailed and thought-provoking discussion of the notions of harm and rights with regard to the expansion of gambling. The discussions in Chapters 3 and 4 of that book are particularly relevant, especially Doughney's discussion of utilitarian ethics relating to individual and collective well-being.

7. These figures (converted to U.S. dollars) are derived from data provided by the Department of Internal Affairs in 2002. Figures here are reported as expenditure, meaning the amount spent minus winnings. Gross turnover (including winnings) is often used, and tends to be 5 to 10 times the expenditure, depending on the average rate of return.

8. These data are taken from the national statistics on problem gambling collected by the Problem Gambling Committee (2003) and the following year by Paton-Simpson, Gruys, and Hannifin (2004).

9. For example, in line with research from North America summarized by Gupta and Derevensky (1998), adolescent problem gambling rates in New Zealand are two to three times that of adult gamblers (F. Rossen, personal communication, 2006).

10. The suggestion that problem gambling is being managed is a bold assertion, particularly when research into effective ways to assist problem gamblers is in its infancy and few approaches currently in use can demonstrate strong effectiveness (Pallesen, Mitsem, Kvale, Johnsen, & Molde, 2005; Raylu & Oei, 2002).

11. Instant Kiwi is a scratch lottery product widely available throughout New Zealand.

12. The contribution of the leaders of major U.S. corporations to philanthropic causes is well known and forms a base for the many charitable organizations that operate in the United States. For example, according to a 2004 *Forbes* magazine article, Microsoft mogul Bill Gates gave away over $29 billion to charities from 2000 onward.

13. For example, as reported in Gambling Expenditure Statistics by the Department of Internal Affairs, for all of New Zealand, net expenditure in casinos rose from $230 million in 2000 to $325 million in 2004. An even stronger increase occurred for EGMs outside of casinos, from $302 million in 2000 to $694 million in 2004.

14. For larger firms it is now commonplace to engage public relations companies in devising and implementing public communication strategies. Many firms

also engage prominent media personalities as spokespersons to front public promotions, debates, and media controversies.

NOTES ON CHAPTER 6: GAMBLING ADVERTISING

1. As recorded in Australian Bureau of Statistics (2002). Again all these figures have been converted into current U.S. dollars.
2. Data reported by Korn, Reynolds, and Hurson (2006), and extracted from the Ontario Lottery and Gaming Corporation's Annual Report, 2004 (amounts converted to current U.S. dollars). The data were collated from annual reports, with the amount of "promotional allowances" difficult to identify.
3. The role of classical conditioning is discussed in Orford et al. (2003). Sharpe, Tarrier, Schotte, and Spence (1995), in a study of autonomic arousal, were able to demonstrate that people in stronger relationships to gambling were more likely to respond physiologically to watching images of gambling.
4. A helpful description of the ways in which social and psychological identities interact is provided by Turner (1987).
5. Tajfel (1981) researched this by demonstrating how subjects would allocate resources (money, points, etc.) according to how they are categorized socially.
6. Tajfel's (1978) "prisoner dilemma" studies, involving subjects allocating points to other people according to nominal group affiliations, indicated that people tend to choose to maximize differences over choosing collective good. This suggests that membership of the immediate social category is stronger than larger social identities.
7. A detailed and comprehensive examination of the various ways in which delivery influences the ways a message is received was provided by Perelman (1982) and Perelman and Olbrechts-Tyteca (1958/1969).
8. As outlined in 333 B.C. by Aristotle in *The Rhetoric of Aristotle* and by Quintilian in 88 A.D. in *The Institutio Oratoria of Quintillian*.
9. As outlined by Corbett (1971), the study of figures of speech was formulaic artifact of the significantly more vibrant and academically challenging forms of rhetoric.
10. For example, Feyerabend (1975) argued that science actually progresses in very different and unpredictable ways than the standard modernist accounts lead us to believe. Lakoff (1987) also challenged the perspective that communications in science reduce rhetorical elements to a minimum.
11. A collection of papers on this topic has been compiled by Enos and Brown (1993).
12. For accounts of the relationship between rhetoric and the linguistic turn that underlines postmodernism, see Antaki (1994) and Pavel (1986). For broader discussions, see Shotter and Gergen (1990) and White and Epston (1990).
13. Referred by some as mastertropes (see Eco, 1985 and Ricoeur, 1978).
14. The everyday importance of metaphors is examined by Lakoff and Johnson (1979) and McCloskey (1985).
15. Soyland (1994) particularly focused on the widespread use of metaphors in psychology.
16. I have developed applications of these to understanding communications concerning mystical experience and violence against women (Adams, 1991; Adams, Towns, & Gavey, 2003).
17. I was intrigued during a visit to the casino in Amsterdam in 2000 to see a series of sacks of money with wings had been suspended across the ceilings. It

was presumably meant to signal the ease with which money could be acquired, but it also is suggestive of the ease with which it disappears.

18. Leymore (1975) explored the use of binaries in advertising. Other relevant discussions can be found in Sicher (1986) and in Vorlat (1985).

NOTES ON CHAPTER 7: RESEARCHERS

1. To which I promptly replied by referring to her as a member of the "evil empire." In a similar situation, following a presentation at an Australian conference, the conference organizer chose in his closing address to refer obliquely to me and a group of colleagues (who had previously presented on gambling as a public health issue) as "Talibanists," likening our advocacy for a public health approach to the violent activities of Muslim fundamentalists who were at that time plaguing Afghanistan.

2. For example, we opened our Centre for Gambling Studies in 2001, but since then, despite strong public interest in gambling, government investment in research was negligible (except for prevalence studies) up until 2005, during which time we relied on seeking funding support for very small projects from a variety of other sources.

3. A version of this dialogue was published as an editorial entitled "Should Gambling Researchers Receive Funding Directly From Gambling Industries? Editorial and Commentaries." in Harvard University's *WAGER: Weekly Addiction Gambling Education Report* (February 2003). This article appears to be no longer available on the journal's website. All characters in the dialogue have been fictionally contrived as composite characters and any resemblance to any actual person is entirely unintentional and coincidental.

4. The idea for such a dialogue was fashioned on Galileo's *Dialogues,* in which he chose a similar device to discuss issues of controversy regarding the rotation of the earth, without necessarily positioning himself as challenging the prevailing views of the Church. When the preceding dialogue was published in Harvard's *WAGER*, members of the editorial board were invited to provide commentaries. The five responses (including the editor's) varied from severe criticism to praise.

5. See Chapter 4 for a fuller discussion on ethical, reputational, and other forms of risk associated with receiving industry funding.

6. For background research on the following section, I am grateful for funding support from the Problem Gambling Foundation of New Zealand and the work of Fiona Rossen in finding relevant literature. For a fuller discussion, see Adams and Rossen (2005).

7. The issue of refusing outright to publish research that is funded by dangerous consumption industries was contested by Davies, Drucker, and Cameron (2002), who argued that there might be considerable merit in some of this research and a blanket ban denies public access.

8. The Marin Institute provides material for monitoring the behavior of the alcohol industry. See their Web site (Marin Institute, 2006).

9. I have done my best to raise these issues in articles such as Adams (2004), and Adams and Rossen (2006).

10. Fiona Rossen and I scanned for published literature in major databases (SCOPUS, MedLine, etc.) and on the Internet. Most material we encountered focused on tobacco, with some discussion of alcohol and pharmaceutical issues.

11. Volberg (2004) discussed 15 years of gambling prevalence studies in North America, Europe, and Australasia. In her article she referred to more than 22

such prevalence studies, several of which were national surveys. In a systematic review, Shaffer and Hall (2001) synthesized the results from 146 such studies. All other areas of research pale in comparison to investments into this type of research.

12. The other "low inconvenience" areas similarly pose few challenges. For example, in the alcohol field there is a long history of both the alcohol industry and governments supporting ongoing alcohol and drug education research focusing on adolescents. This has continued despite 20 years of consistent literature that challenges its effectiveness. A similar trend appears to be happening with gambling. For both areas, adolescent education provides the opportunity of maximizing public kudos and minimizing the chance that findings would inconvenience business as usual.

13. In my 5 years on a similar committee in New Zealand, the Problem Gambling Committee, I found government officials, industry representatives, and community representatives maintained a well-formed indifference to research, which ensured that little was invested in research projects. The research that did occur posed few threats to ongoing expansion.

14. Quoted from an ABC Stateline radio interview with Linda Hancock and John Pandazopoulos, Broadcast October 15, 2004, reporter Kathy Bowlen (http://www.abc.net.au/stateline/vic/content/2003/s1221108.htm, accessed March 2007).

15. Hancock also provided a detailed overview of processes that led to the demise of the Panel in a plenary address in the Third Annual Dangerous Consumptions Symposium, held at the University of Melbourne in December 2005.

16. Victorian Minister of Gaming press release: http://www.ghsouthern.org.au/gurublog/gamcouncil.pdf (accessed March 2007).

17. Quoted from an ABC Stateline radio interview with Linda Hancock and John Pandazopoulos, Broadcast October 15, 2004, reporter Kathy Bowlen (http://www.abc.net.au/stateline/vic/content/2003/s1221108.htm, accessed March 2007).

NOTES ON CHAPTER 8: HELPING PROFESSIONALS IN THE FRONTIER TOWN

1. The authors admitted that putting together data like these is very difficult across so many states and with different ways of calculating data. They also claimed it to be a gross underestimate because they could not capture the intrafamilial costs of divorce and family disruption.

2. They noted that the wide range reflects the difficulty of putting dollar values on the intangible but important emotional impacts.

3. For example, in Canada's largest province of Ontario, the majority of services are provided as adjuncts to alcohol and drug services.

4. This information was provided in a personal communication by the Clinical Head of Services at GamCare in November 2006. He also indicated they have had difficulties maintaining consistency in how data are reported between their service and other providers and with the National Helpline.

5. The Problem Gambling Purchasing Agency administered a voluntary levy from gambling industries under the auspices of the Problem Gambling Committee. This arrangement was dismantled during 2004 as the new Gambling Act came into effect, empowering the Ministry of Health to take over the responsibility of service funding.

6. Following new omnibus legislation that was enacted by the New Zealand government in 2003 (and slowly came into effect during 2004), regulations on

availability were tightened, curbing the rate of increase in consumption and leading to a subsequent drop in people seeking help in 2005.

7. This colorful time was described by Brinkley (2004). The Wild West is described as a natural extension of the continual western expansion in the United States that began from when the British first settled along the eastern coastline and led to a constant frontier zone that moved steadily westward.

8. I was heavily involved in New Zealand with the formation of what we understood at the time as the world's largest service, a national service that employed more than 60 staff members throughout the country and with specific services in counseling, health promotion, public health, education, and policy.

9. When a news story broke, the glory seekers I worked alongside could be engaged with more than 10 interviews in 1 day, which included television appearances, live radio interviews, and major newspaper articles.

10. A common area of diversification is with host responsibility. It is also particularly important to have funding from sources other than their main funders, because other activities (e.g., advocacy) can be attributed to profits from this source.

11. The gender-specific reference here is constrained by common usage, but reference to *medicine men* is intended to refer to both men and women.

12. Examples of applications of psychotherapy to gambling are presented in papers such as Victor and Krug (1967), Lester (1980), and Schaap (1988).

13. The most influential paper on this approach was presented as a whole special issue by Korn and Shaffer (1999). Also see Korn, Gibbins, and Azmier (2003). Personally I am a strong supporter of these applications and have participated with enthusiasm in their development. However, they have been developed in other contexts and the major proponents have brought their approaches in from applications elsewhere.

14. In reflecting on my own involvement, I can identify myself as motivated by missionary zeal, but I also admit the prospects of trade and glory were also enticing. I suspect that like myself, the initial motives are multilayered, and it might not be until being in the pioneer environment for some time that one motive eclipses the others.

15. One context that springs to mind that illustrates this relationship is the Problem Gambling Committee, which was formed to administer a voluntary contribution from the gambling industries for services for problem gambling. It was comprised of equal representation from helping services and senior industry executives. I served on this committee for 5 years during a key central period in the frontier expansion of gambling in New Zealand. The committee was a turgid affair. On one side of the table, gambling industry executives were working hard to ensure their contribution was both contained and gave them maximal positive public exposure. On the other side, helping services worked to maximize funding support. In 1997 the interchanges flowed into conflict, which led to legal action. Government agencies also retained a strong presence and their involvement could also lead to hostilities. On one occasion a government official threatened to curtail my career prospects unless I adopted a softer line on gambling issues.

16. I had direct exposure on the New Zealand Problem Gambling Committee to the extent to which gambling industry executives invested in intelligence and strategizing and the way in which they built strong links to government agencies in pursuing their interests.

17. Although the different forms of gambling (e.g., casinos, racing, lotteries, EGMs in bars) competed for their share of gambling money, on issues of government regulations and responding to critics they still ensured a level of cooperation.

18. An interesting example of this occurred in Melbourne where, led by the efforts of Tim Costello, an interchurch coalition has been at the forefront of challenging the expansion of EGM gambling in the state of Victoria.
19. To illustrate this with two examples: Nick Xenophon has been voted in twice for 8-year terms in the Upper House of the Parliament of South Australia on the basis of a "No Pokies" campaign and Tom Grey in the United States has for many years pursued a high profile anticasino campaign.
20. Indeed, in Australia and New Zealand casinos have recruited a number of helping professionals to front their harm minimization initiatives. Their recruits are people familiar with the language and practices of the helping sector and able to present credibly in health and government contexts to explain the merits of their initiatives.
21. The strongest examples of this that I have observed have occurred in the Australian states of Victoria and New South Wales and in the Canadian province of Ontario. In these places, gambling services have remained relatively small and either set up alongside other small agencies or embedded in larger, broader services. In both arrangements, the agencies have difficulty participating in open health advocacy.
22. In Canada this perception is further complicated by the government owning all legalized gambling. To criticize the expansion is to criticize the government, the very people who determine an agency's funding.
23. For example, best practice might favor cognitive or behavioral approaches because they are more established in other fields and have been subject to a small amount of research with gambling.
24. The New Zealand Problem Gambling Committee between 1997 and 2003 sought to restrict its funding to three main nationally based organizations, the Problem Gambling Foundation, the Gambling Problem Helpline, and the Salvation Army.
25. The organization I chaired, the New Zealand Problem Gambling Foundation (1998–2002), grew rapidly during that period, increasing its income tenfold within 5 years. During that time we were faced with having to simultaneously develop governance structures, develop operational systems, recruit (or create) an appropriate workforce, and set up a range of different services from scratch.

NOTES ON CHAPTER 9: PROTECTING INDEPENDENCE

1. See the discussion on subtle degradation in Chapter 2.
2. As discussed in the next chapter, harm minimization is a high-level approach used as a basis for responding to the negative consequences of dangerous consumptions. It forms the basis for drug policies in many countries (e.g., Australia, Netherlands, Canada, New Zealand), the principles for which are being gradually incorporated into policy on gambling.
3. Chapter 7 briefly explored relationships between the tobacco industry and researchers and concluded that such relationships involve such high degrees of moral jeopardy that the relationships need either to be strongly supervised or not occur at all.
4. Details on a public health approach to gambling are summarized in Brown and Raeburn (2001) and Korn et al. (2003).
5. In many situations it works the opposite way. During liberalization and normalization, those governments with a dominant interest in gambling for its revenue potential tend to put in place mechanisms and systems where independence is questionable.

6. This favored relationship status between government and gambling industries is explored by Goodman (1995) and Costello and Milar (2000).

7. In Australia in 1998, these concerns led the Federal Treasurer, Peter Costello, to admit that the gambling spending is having serious economic and social planning implications for Australia, hence the need for the high-level and thorough Productivity Commission Review. See Australian Productivity Commission (1999).

8. As discussed in Chapter 3, these include inducements such as receiving shares in race horses, contributions to overseas trips, supporting conference expenses, and so on.

9. The Australian Productivity Commission (1999) placed strong emphasis on the concept of "consumer sovereignty" and the need for consumers to be protected from exploitation through the use of measures that enable informed consent and adequate choice at the point of sale. They pointed out that for EGM players little accessible information is provided on risks or on details such as the odds of winning.

10. Experiences with voluntary advertising codes of practice with other dangerous consumptions, such as alcohol and tobacco, have on the whole resulted in weak responses to advertising promotional strategies and often functioned as a distraction in the further advancement of product promotional techniques.

11. For example, in North America, Europe, and Oceania there has been an abundance of large-scale population studies that use telephone interviewing to monitor patterns of gambling consumption and the prevalence of problem gambling. High levels of investment in this narrow and basic form of research contrast with the minimal investment in the range of other forms of research that could assist in understanding more pressing concerns such as impacts on communities, moderating the potency of new gambling technologies, and understanding the key drivers for problem gambling.

12. For example, from 2001 onward, the Problem Gambling Foundation of New Zealand developed a division of its services that focused entirely on public health initiatives with gambling. It began initially with public communication activities involving brochures and posters. As funding was made available, the organization extended its activities into forming a community development team that adopted an empowerment-based health promotion strategy. This team focused on activities in local communities, with youth and with special populations such as Maori, Pacific, and Asian peoples. It later developed advice and advocacy services targeting local government and central government. By 2006 all these activities were firmly embedded in the operations of the organization.

13. During the late 1990s, gambling counselors in Australia repeatedly related to me how they had been muzzled by government officials from speaking out in the media about harm from gambling.

NOTES ON CHAPTER 10: STRATEGIES FOR CHANGE: THREE WAYS AHEAD

1. An outline of the various ways of applying harm minimization principles to drug use are provided by Hamilton, Kellehear, and Rumbold (1998).

2. Interestingly, proof of effectiveness does not guarantee that authorities will abide with the results. With harm reduction around drug use, didactic

education in schools has been evaluated consistently as one of the least effective strategies, and yet despite the strength of this research, governments continue to invest consistently in this type of program.

3. Ideally this process should involve setting up mechanisms for measuring these impacts, but because the general recognition of threats to democracy is low, effort is required for more consciousness raising rather than properly formed harm minimization strategies.

4. Presumably the funding would not come directly from industry sources.

5. The strongest examples of this are in New Zealand and Canada.

6. Aspects of this section have been extended to use with all dangerous consumptions and have been submitted for publication as an article in the journal *Addiction*.

7. The importance of a continuum of risk approach to all aspects of health is presented by Rose (1992) and Ioannou (2005).

8. See discussion of the idea of a continuum of salience in Berdahl & Azmier (1999).

9. Unfortunately in a liberalized gambling environment, the more potent the forms of gambling are, the higher the earnings and therefore the opportunities for funding might be easier to access. Furthermore, as more organizations adopt ethical stances on gambling funds, the decreased number of potential recipients increases the availability of funding to those less ethically inclined.

10. Government provision of transition sponsorship is commonly provided to organizations to help them find alternatives to tobacco sponsorship.

11. An exploration of the experiences of Asian immigrants and gambling in New Zealand is provided in Tse et al. (2004) and in Tse et al. (2005).

12. Dyall detailed these broader effects on Maori as a First Nation people whereby gambling expansion contributes further to their ongoing colonization by Europeans (see Dyall, 2002; Dyall & Hand, 2003).

13. So named because it was instigated in Auckland and went through two iterations at international conferences in Auckland.

14. I had previously been part of a collaborating research team in a multicountry project developing brief interventions for risky drinking in primary health settings. Because most of the 15 collaborating countries were European, I had a chance to observe the manner in which different countries had been influenced by their adherence to the European Charter on Alcohol.

15. At this stage I was working closely with Ralph Gerdelan, who was executive director of the Compulsive Gambling Society of New Zealand (later to become the Problem Gambling Foundation) and we were thinking the Charter could form the founding base for the formation of an international NGO concerned with gambling (Adams & Gerdelan, 1997).

16. Such as a plenary presentation on "Development of an International Charter for Sustainable Gambling" at the First International Gambling Impact Conference, Adelaide, South Australia (April 2000), as well a discussion at the Australian National Association of Gambling, Sydney (November 2001).

17. This conference was attended by more than 500 registrants. Other presentations of this version of the Charter included three national workshops on gambling policy held in Taupo (April 2000), Wellington (March 2001), and Auckland (March 2002).

18. The Third International Conference on Gambling, "Gambling Through a Public Health Lens," held in Auckland in September 2003.

19. During the conference, Raeburn synthesized the recommended changes into this version, which he subsequently published in our special issue from the conference (Raeburn, 2004).

20. I have at various times spoken with people in key positions within the WHO on the need for international gambling conventions. They stated unofficially that their work currently on dangerous consumptions is focused more on alcohol and tobacco and that gambling has yet to reach sufficient levels of concern to warrant specific attention.

References

Abbott, M. W., & McKenna, B. (2000). *Gambling and problem gambling among recently sentenced women prisoners in New Zealand* (Rep. No. 4 of the New Zealand Gambling Survey). Wellington, New Zealand: Department of Internal Affairs.

Abbott, M. W., & Volberg, R. A. (2000). *Taking the pulse on gambling and problem gambling in New Zealand: A report on phase one of the 1999 national prevalence survey.* Wellington, New Zealand: Department of Internal Affairs.

ACIL Consulting. (1999). *Australia's gambling industries: Submission to the Productivity Commission Inquiry.* Melbourne, Australia: Author.

Adams, P. J. (1991). *A rhetoric of mysticism.* Unpublished doctoral dissertation, University of Auckland, Auckland, New Zealand.

Adams, P. (1999). Introduction. In P. Adams & B. Bayly (Eds.), *Problem gambling and mental health in New Zealand: Selected proceedings of the National Conference on Gambling 1999.* Auckland: Compulsive Gambling Society of New Zealand.

Adams, P. J. (2004). Minimising the impact of gambling in the subtle degradation of democratic systems. *Journal of Gambling Issues, 11,* 1–8.

Adams, P. J., & Gerdelan, R. V. (1997). *The need for international health protocols to moderate the negative social impact of boom-and-bust growth in sunrise target markets such as New Zealand.* Paper presented at the Tenth International Conference on Gambling and Risk Taking, Montreal, Canada.

Adams, P., & Hodges, I. (2005). Understanding dangerous consumptions: Moving forward with a national strategy for research on tobacco, alcohol, other drugs and gambling. *Social Policy Journal of New Zealand, 26*(November), 17–42.

Adams, P., Raeburn, J., Brown, R., Lane, L., Tse, S., Manaia, W., et al. (2003). Should gambling researchers receive funding directly from gambling industries? Editorial and commentaries. *WAGER: Weekly Addiction Gambling Education Report, February.*

Adams, P., & Rossen, F. (2005). *The ethics of receiving funds from the proceeds of gambling.* Auckland, New Zealand: Centre for Gambling Studies, University of Auckland.

Adams, P. J., & Rossen, F. (2006). Reducing the moral jeopardy associated with receiving funds from the proceeds of gambling. *Journal of Gambling Issues, 17,* 1–21.

Adams, P., Rossen, F., Perese, L., Townsend, S., Brown, R., Brown, P., et al. (2004). *Gambling impact assessment for seven Auckland territorial authorities: Part 1. Introduction and overview.* Auckland, New Zealand: Centre for Gambling Studies, University of Auckland.

Adams, P. J., Towns, A., & Gavey, N. (2003). Dominance and entitlement: The rhetoric men use to discuss their violence towards women. In M. Talbot, K. Atkinson,

& D. Atkinson (Eds.), *Language and power in the modern world* (pp. 184–198). Edinburgh, UK: Edinburgh University Press.

American Psychiatric Association. (2000). *Diagnostic and statistical manual of mental disorders* (4th ed., text revision). Washington, DC: Author.

Antaki, C. (1994). *Explaining and arguing: The social organization of accounts.* London: Sage.

Antilla, L. (2005). Climate of scepticism: US newspaper coverage of the science of climate change. *Global Environmental Change, 15,* 338–352.

ANU Centre for Gambling Research. (2005). *Fact sheets 2005.* Canberra, Australia: Author.

Australian Bureau of Statistics. (2002). Service industries special article: Gambling in Australia. In *Year book Australia.* Canberra, Australia: Author.

Australian Casino Association. (2006). Casino contribution to communities. Retrieved November 2006, from http://www.auscasinos.com/economicContribution.cfm?EconomicContribution_ID=4&session.validated=no

Australian Productivity Commission. (1999). *Australia's gambling industries: Final report.* Canberra, Australia: Author.

Azmier, J. J. (2000). *Canadian gambling behavior and attitudes: Summary report* (Gambling in Canada Research Rep. No. 8). Calgary, AB, Canada: Canada West Foundation.

Azmier, J. J. (2001). *Gambling in Canada 2001: An overview* (Gambling in Canada Research Report No. 13). Calgary, AB, Canada: Canada West Foundation.

Baker, R., & Hannan, E. (2005, April 6). *The Melbourne Age.*

Baldwin, C. S., & Clark, D. L. (1939). *Renaissance literary theory and practice.* New York: Macmillan.

Bandura, A. (1977). *Social learning theory.* Englewood Cliffs, NJ: Prentice-Hall.

Bandura, A., & McDonald, F. J. (1963). Influence of social reinforcement and the behavior of models in shaping children's moral judgments. *Journal of Abnormal and Social Psychology, 67,* 274–281.

Bandura, A., Ross, D., & Ross, S. A. (1963). Vicarious reinforcement and imitative learning. *Journal of Abnormal and Social Psychology, 67,* 601–607.

Bandura, A., & Walters, R. H. (1963). *Social learning and personality development.* New York: Holt, Rinehart & Winston.

Banks, G. (2002, November). *The Productivity Commision's gambling inquiry: 3 years on.* Paper presented at the 12th Annual Conference of the National Association for Gambling Studies, Melbourne, Australia.

Banks, G. (2003). The Productivity Commission's gambling inquiry: 3 years on. *Gambling Research, 15,* 7–27.

Barr, C., & Setiono, B. (2003). Writing off Indonesia's forestry debt: How the IMF, the Indonesian Bank Restructuring Agency and Bank Mandiri are financing forest destruction. *Multinational Monitor, 24*(11).

Becona, E., Del, M., Lorenzo, C., & Fuentes, M. J. (1996). Pathological gambling and depression. *Psychological Reports, 78,* 635–640.

Becona, E., Labrador, F., Echeburua, E., & Ochoa, E. (1995). Slot machine gambling in Spain: An important and new social problem. *Journal of Gambling Studies, 11,* 265–286.

Benveniste, E. (1985). The semiology of language. In R. Innes (Ed.), *Semiotics.* London: Hutchinson.

Berdahl, L. Y., & Azmier, J. (1999). *Summary report: The impact of gaming upon Canadian non-profits: A 1999 survey of gaming grant recipients.* Calgary, AB, Canada: Canada West Foundation.

Billig, M. (1987). *Arguing and thinking: A rhetorical approach to social psychology.* London: Cambridge University Press.

Bland, R. C., Newman, S., Orn, H., & Stebelsky, G. (1993). Epidemiology of pathological gambling. *Canadian Journal of Psychiatry, 38,* 108–112.

Blaszczynski, A., & Silove, D. (1995). Cognitive and behavioral therapies for pathological gambling. *Journal of Gambling Studies, 11,* 195–221.

Bolgar, R. R. (1954). *The classical heritage and its beneficiaries.* Cambridge, UK: Cambridge University Press.

Brinkley, A. (2004). *The unfinished nation: A concise history of the American people* (4th ed.). Boston: McGraw-Hill.

Brown, R. (2001). The harm minimisation strategy: Policy overview. In R. Brown & J. Raeburn (Eds.), *Gambling, harm and health: Two perspectives on ways to minimise harm and maximise health with regard to gambling in New Zealand* (pp. 50–57). Auckland, New Zealand: Problem Gambling Committee/Gambling Studies Institute.

Brown, R. I. (1987). Pathological gambling and associated patterns of crime: Comparisons with alcohol and other drug addictions. *Journal of Gambling Behavior, 3,* 98–114.

Brown, R., & Raeburn, J. (Eds.). (2001). *Gambling, harm and health: Two perspectives on ways to minimise harm and maximise health with regard to gambling in New Zealand.* Auckland, New Zealand: Problem Gambling Committee/Gambling Studies Institute.

Burke, K. (1969a). *A grammar of motives.* Berkeley: University of California Press. (Original work published 1945)

Burke, K. (1969b). *A rhetoric of motives.* Berkeley: University of California Press. (Original work published 1950)

Canadian Partnership for Responsible Gambling. (2004). *Canadian gambling digest.* Toronto: Author.

Casino Community Benefit Fund Trustees. (2005). *CCBF trustees report 2004–2005.* Sydney: Author.

Cayuela, R., & Guirao, J. L. (1991). Characteristics and situation of gambling addiction in Spain. In W. R. Eadington & J. A. Cornelius (Eds.), *Gambling and public policy: International perspectives.* Reno: University of Nevada.

Centre for International Economics. (2001). *Gaming machine revenue at risk: The impact of three proposed modifications to gaming machines in New South Wales.* Sydney: Author.

Clapson, M. (1992). *A bit of a flutter: Popular gambling and English society, c.1823–1961.* Manchester, UK: Manchester University Press.

Clark, W. B., & Hilton, M. E. (1991). *Alcohol in America: Drinking practices and problems.* Albany: State University of New York Press.

Clotfelter, C. T., & Cook, P. J. (1989). *Selling hope: State lotteries in America.* Cambridge, MA: Harvard University Press.

Cohen, J. E. (2001). Editorial: Universities and tobacco money. *British Medical Journal, 232*(7), 1–2.

Cohen, J. E., Ashley, M. J., Ferrence, R., & Brewster, J. M. (1999). Institutional addiction to tobacco. *Tobacco Control, 8*(Spring), 70–74.

Corbett, E. P. J. (1971). *Classical rhetoric for the modern student* (2nd ed.). New York: Oxford University Press.

Costello, T., & Milar, R. (2000). *Wanna bet? Winners and losers in gambling's luck myth.* Melbourne, Australia: Allen & Unwin.

Crockford, D. N., & el-Guebaly, N. (1998). Psychiatric comorbidity in pathological gambling: A critical review. *Canadian Journal of Psychiatry, 43,* 43–50.

Cuijpers, P., & Smit, F. (2001). Assessing parental alcoholism: A comparison of the family history research diagnostic criteria versus a single question method. *Addictive Behaviors, 26,* 741–748.

Cunningham-Williams, R. M., Cottler, L. B., Compton, W. M., & Spitznagel, E. L. (1998). Taking chances: Problem gamblers and mental health disorders—Results from the St. Louis epidemiological catchment area study. *American Journal of Public Health, 88,* 1093–1096.

Dauvergne, P. (1997). *Shadows in the forest: Japan and the politics of timber in southeast Asia.* Cambridge, MA: MIT Press.

Davies, J. B., Drucker, E., & Cameron, D. (2002). Editorial: The Farmington consensus. Guilt by association. *Addiction Research and Theory, 10,* 329–334.

de Sassure, F. (1959). *Course in general linguistics* (A. Sechehaye, Trans.). New York: Philosophical Library. (Original work published 1959)

Devlin, N., Schuffham, P., & Bunt, L. (1997). The social costs of alcohol abuse in New Zealand. *Addiction, 92,* 1491–1506.

Dixon, D. (1991). *From prohibition to regulation: Bookmaking, anti-gambling and the law.* Oxford, UK: Clarendon.

Dixon, R. M. (1982). *Rhetoric.* London: Methuen.

Doll, R., Peto, R., Wheatley, K., Gray, R., & Sutherland, I. (1994). Mortality in relation to smoking: 40 years observations on male British doctors. *British Medical Journal, 309,* 901–910.

Doughney, J. R. (2002). *The poker machine state: Dilemmas in ethics, economics and governance.* Melbourne, Australia: Common Ground.

Doughney, J., & Kelleher, T. (1999). *The impact of poker machine gambling on low-income municipalities: A critical survey of key issues.* Victoria, Australia: Workplace Studies Centre, Victoria University.

Dozens killed in Indonesian floods. (2006, January). *BBC News.*

Drope, J., & Chapman, S. (2001). Tobacco industry efforts at discrediting scientific knowledge of environmental tobacco smoke: A review of internal industry documents. *Journal of Epidemiological Community Health, 55,* 588–594.

Dyall, L. (2002). Kanohi ki te Kanohi: Face to face. A Maori face to gambling. *New Ethicals: New Zealand's Journal of Patient Management, 5,* 11–16.

Dyall, L., & Hand, J. (2003). Maori and gambling: Why a comprehensive Maori public health response is required in New Zealand. *International Journal of Community Health and Addiction, 1*(1), 1–16.

Eadington, W. R. (2005). Paper presented at the NASPL conference, Current Trends in Gambling Industries Worldwide, Minnesota.

Eco, U. (1985). The semantics of metaphor. In R. Innes (Ed.), *Semiotics.* London: Hutchinson.

Edwards, G. (1998). If the drinks industry does not clean up its act, pariah status is inevitable. *British Medical Journal, 517,* 336–337.

Edwards, G., Anderson, P., Babor, T. F., Casswell, S., Ferrence, R., Giesbrecht, N., et al. (1994). *Alcohol policy and the public good.* New York: Oxford University Press.

Enos, T., & Brown, S. C. (Eds.). (1993). *Defining the new rhetorics.* Newbury Park, CA: Sage.

Feyerabend, P. K. (1975). *Against method: Outline of an anarchistic theory of knowledge.* London: Verso.

Fields, N., & Chapman, S. (2003). Chasing Ernst L Wynder: 40 years of Philip Morris' efforts to influence a leading scientist. *Journal of Epidemiological Community Health, 57,* 571–578.

Forsyth, A. J. M. (2001). Distorted? A quantitative exploration of drug fatality reports in the popular press. *International Journal of Drug Policy, 12,* 435–453.

Gaming Board. (2000). *Report of the Gaming Board for Great Britain 1999/2000.* London: Her Majesty's Stationary Office.

Gergen, K. J. (1990). Toward a postmodern psychology. *The Humanist Psychologist, 18,* 23–34.

Gergen, K. J., & Gergen, M. (1987). Narratives of friendship. In R. Burnett, P. McGhee, & D. Clarke (Eds.), *Accounting for relationships*. London: Methuen.

Gernstein, D., Murphy, S., Toce, M., Hoffman, J., Palmer, A., Johnson, R., et al. (1999). *Gambling impact and behavior study: Report to the National Gambling Impact Study Commission*. National Opinion Research Center.

Godfrey, C., & Maynard, A. (1988). Economic aspects of tobacco use and taxation policy. *British Medical Journal, 297,* 339–343.

Goodman, R. (1995). *The luck business: The devastating consequences and broken promises of America's gambling explosion*. New York: The Free Press.

Grant, J. E., & Kim, S. W. (2002). Effectiveness of pharmacotherapy for pathological gambling: A chart review. *Annals of Clinical Psychiatry, 14,* 155–161.

Grinols, E. L. (2004). *Gambling in America: Costs and benefits*. Cambridge, UK: Cambridge University Press.

Grinols, E. L., & Mustard, D. B. (2006). Casinos, crime, and community costs. *Review of Economics and Statistics, 88,* 28–45.

Gu, Z. (2000). The impact of the Asian financial crisis on Asian gaming activities: An examination of Las Vegas strip casino drops. *Current Issues in Tourism, 2,* 354–365.

Guggenheim, D. (Director) & Gore, A. (Writer/Presenter). (2006). *An inconvenient truth* [Motion picture]. United States: Paramount Classics.

Gupta, R., & Derevensky, J. (1998). Adolescent gambling behavior: A prevalence study and examination of the correlates associated with problem gambling. *Journal of Gambling Studies, 14,* 319–345.

Hamilton, M., Kellehear, A., & Rumbold, G. (Eds.). (1998). *Drug use in Australia: A harm minimisation approach*. Melbourne, Australia: Oxford University Press.

Hermkens, P., Kok, I. (1991). Gambling in the Netherlands: Developments, participation and compulsive gambling. In W. R. Eadington & J. A. Cornelius (Eds.), *Gambling and public policy: International perspectives*. Reno: University of Nevada.

Holenstein, E. (1976). *Roman Jakobson's approach to language: Phenomenological structuralism* (C. T. Schelbert, Trans.). Bloomington: Indiana University Press.

Horbay, R. (2004). *EGM transparency: An essential element of product safety & consumer protection*. Paper presented at the Insight Nova Scotia International Conference on Problem Gambling, Halifax, NS, Canada.

Howes, R. F. (1961). *Historical studies of rhetoric and rhetoricians*. New York: Cornell University Press.

Hulme, V. (2005). Gambling on China's edge. *China Business Review, 32*(2), 20–23.

Human Rights Watch. (2003). New Order forestry policy and the roots of the crisis. Retrieved May 2004, from http://www.hrw.org/reports/2003/indon0103-02.htm

Ioannou, S. (2005). Health logic and health-related behaviors. *Critical Public Health, 15,* 263–273.

International Society of Addiction Journal Editors. (2005). Web site of International Society of Addiction Journal Editors. Retrieved January 7, 2005, from http://www-users.yourk.ac.uk/~sjp22/isaje/farmington.htm

Jackson, A. C., Thomas, S. A., Thomason, N., Bowell, J., Crisp, B. R., Ho, W., et al. (2000). Literature review on therapeutic effectiveness. In *Longitudinal evaluation of the effectiveness of problem gambling counseling services, community education strategies and information products: Vol. 2. Counseling interventions*. Melbourne, Australia: Victorian Department of Human Services.

Jacobs, D. F. (2000). Juvenile gambling in North America: An analysis of long term trends and future prospects. *Journal of Gambling Studies, 16,* 119–152.

Jakobson, R. O. (1974). Mark and feature. In S. Rudy (Ed.), *Selected writings VII*. Berlin: Mouton.

Jernigan, D. H. (1997). *Thirsting for markets: The global impact of corporate alcohol.* San Rafael, CA: Marin Institute for the Prevention of Alcohol and Other Drug Problems.

Kassinove, J. I., Tsytsarev, S. V., & Davidson, I. (1998). Russian attitudes toward gambling. *Personality and Individual Differences, 24,* 41–46.

Kavanagh, T. M. (1993). *Enlightenment and the shadows of chance: The novel and the culture of gambling in eighteenth-century france.* Baltimore: Johns Hopkins University Press.

Korn, D., Gibbins, R., & Azmier, J. (2003). Framing public policy towards a public health paradigm for gambling. *Journal of Gambling Studies, 19,* 235–256.

Korn, D. A., Reynolds, J., & Hurson, T. (2006). *Commercial gambling advertising: Exploring the youth connection.* Paper presented at the 13th International Conference on Gambling and Risk-Taking, Lake Tahoe, NV.

Korn, D. A., & Shaffer, H. J. (1999). Gambling and the health of the public: Adopting a public health perspective. *Journal of Gambling Studies, 15,* 289–365.

Labonte, R. (1990). Empowerment: Notes on professional and community dimensions. *Canadian Review of Social Policy, 26,* 64–75.

Ladouceur, R., Boisvert, J., Pepin, M., Loranger, M., & Sylvain, C. (1994). Social cost of pathological gambling. *Journal of Gambling Studies, 10,* 399–409.

Ladouceur, R., & Walker, M. (1996). A cognitive perspective on gambling. In P. M. Salkovskis (Ed.), *Trends in cognitive and behavioral therapies* (pp. 89–120). Chichester, UK: Wiley.

Lakoff, G. (1987). *Women, fire, and dangerous things: What categories reveal about the mind.* Chicago: University of Chicago Press.

Lakoff, G., & Johnson, M. (1979). *Metaphors we live by.* Chicago: University of Chicago Press.

Laverack, G. (2001). An identification and interpretation of the organizational aspects of community empowerment. *Community Development Journal, 36,* 40–50.

Ledgerwood, D. M., & Petry, N. M. (2005). Current trends and future directions in the study of psychosocial treatments for pathological gambling. *Current Directions in Psychological Science, 14,* 89–94.

Lesieur, H. R. (1999). Policy implications and social costs of problem gambling. In P. Adams & B. Bayly (Eds.), *Problem gambling and mental health in New Zealand: Selected proceedings from the National Conference on Gambling, July 1999.* Auckland: Compulsive Gambling Society of New Zealand.

Lester, D. (1980). The treatment of compulsive gambling. *International Journal of the Addictions, 15,* 201–206.

Levi-Strauss, C. (1966). *The savage mind.* London: Weidenfeld & Nicolson.

Leymore, V. (1975). *Hidden myth: Structure and symbolism in advertising.* London: Heinemann.

Lim, D., & Sellman, D. (2004). Pathological gambling: Neurobiology and pharmacological treatment. In R. Tan & S. Wurtzburg (Eds.), *Problem gambling: New Zealand perspectives on treatment.* Wellington, New Zealand: Steel Roberts.

Lopez, A., & Peto, R. (1996). The future effects of current smoking patterns: Assessing the magnitude of the pandemic. In R. Richmond (Ed.), *Educating medical students about tobacco: Planning and implementation.* Paris: International Union Against Tuberculosis and Lung Disease.

Lorenz, V. C. (1990). State lotteries and compulsive gambling. *Journal of Gambling Studies, 6,* 383–396.

Lorenz, V., & Yaffee, R. (1986). Pathological gambling: Psychosomatic, emotional and marital difficulties as reported by the gambler. *Journal of Gambling Behavior, 2,* 40–49.

Macarte, P. (1970). A new approach in advertising research. *Advertising Quarterly, 7,* 36–43.

Marin Institute. (2006). Alcohol industry. Retrieved November 2006, from http:// www.marininstitute.org/alcohol_industry/watch.htm

Marshall, K., & Wynne, H. (2004, June). Against the odds: A profile of at-risk and problem gamblers. *Canadian Social Trends*, 25–29.

Massaro, D. W. (1986). The computer as a metaphor for psychological inquiry: Considerations and recommendations. *Behavior Research Methods, Instruments & Computers, 18*, 73–92.

Mayor, S. (2004). UK universities agree to protocol for tobacco company funding. *British Medical Journal, 329*(3), 9.

McCall, M. H. (1969). *Ancient rhetorical theories of simile and comparison.* Cambridge, MA: Harvard University Press.

McCloskey, D. N. (1985). *The rhetoric of economics.* Sussex, UK: Harvester Press.

McConaghy, N., Armstrong, M. S., Blaszczynski, A., & Allcock, C. (1983). Controlled comparison of aversive therapy and imaginal desensitisation in compulsive gambling. *British Journal of Psychiatry, 142*, 366–372.

McCormick, R. A., Russo, A. M., Ramirez, L. F., & Taber, J. I. (1984). Affective disorders among pathological gamblers seeking treatment. *American Journal of Psychiatry, 141*, 215–218.

McGowan, V., Droessler, J., Nixin, G., & Grimshaw, M. (2000). *Recent research in the socio-cultural domain of gaming and gambling: An annotated bibliography and critical overview* (literature review). Edmonton, AB, Canada: Alberta Gaming Research Institute.

McLuhan, M. (1965). *Understanding media.* New York: McGraw-Hill.

Meyer, G. (1992). The gambling market in the Federal Republic of Germany and the helpseeking of pathological gamblers. *Journal of Gambling Studies, 8,* 11–20.

Miller, W. R., & Rollnick, S. (1991). *Motivational interviewing: Preparing people to change addictive behavior.* New York: Guilford.

Morton, S. (2003). *At odds: Gambling and Canadians 1919–1969.* Toronto: University of Toronto Press.

Murphy, J. J. (1974). *Rhetoric in the middle ages.* Berkeley: University of California Press.

Murphy, P. J. (1997, 7 June). Army thrives on problems. *Waikato Times*, Edition 2, p. 6.

Namrata, R., & Oei, T. P. S. (2002). Pathological gambling: A comprehensive review. *Clinical Psychology Review, 22,* 1–53.

National Opinion Research Center, Gemini Research, The Lewin Group, & Christiansen/Cummings Associates. (1999). *Gambling impact and behavior study: Report to the National Gambling Impact Study Commission.*

New Zealand Department of Internal Affairs. (2006). Gambling expenditure statistics 1981–2005. Retrieved from http://govinfo.library.unt.edu/ngisc/reports/ exsum_1-7.pdf

Orford, J., Sproston, K., Erens, B., White, C., & Mitchell, L. (2003). *Gambling and problem gambling in Britain.* New York: Brunner-Routledge.

Osgood, D. (1994). Government failure and deforestation in Indonesia. In K. Brown & D. W. Pearce (Eds.), *The causes of tropical deforestation: The economic and statistical analysis of factors giving rise to the loss of the tropical forests.* UCL Press.

O'Sullivan, J., & Christoffel, P. (1992). The development of gambling policy in New Zealand. In C. Scott (Ed.), *Lotteries, gambling and public policy* (pp. 61–69). Wellington, New Zealand: Institute of Policy Studies.

Pallesen, S., Mitsem, M., Kvale, G., Johnsen, B. H., & Molde, H. (2005). Outcome of psychological treatments of pathological gambling: A review and meta-analysis. *Addiction, 100,* 1412–1422.

Pan America Health Association. (2004). *Strategies promoting access to medicines: The role of supply management.* Retrieved November 2006.

Paton-Simpson, G. R., Gruys, M. A., & Hannifin, J. B. (2004). *Problem gambling counseling in New Zealand: 2003 national statistics.* Palmerston North, New Zealand: Problem Gambling Purchasing Agency.

Pavel, T. G. (1986). *Fictional worlds.* Cambridge, MA: Harvard University Press.

Pavlov, I. P. (1927). *Conditioned reflexes.* New York: Oxford University Press.

Pechmann, C., & Shih, C. (1999). Smoking scenes in movies and antismoking advertisements before movies: Effects on youth. *Journal of Marketing, 63*(3), 1–13.

Pepperell, S. (1997, 14 June). The casino experience. *Waikato Times*, Edition 2, p. 13.

Perelman, C. (1982). *The realm of rhetoric* (W. Kluback, Trans.). Sounth Bend, IN: University of Notre Dame Press.

Perelman, C., & Olbrechts-Tyteca, L. (1969). *The new rhetoric: A treatise on argumentation.* South Bend, IN: University of Notre Dame Press. (Original work published 1969)

Petry, N. M., Ammerman, Y., Bohl, J., Doersch, A., Gay, H., Kadden, R., et al. (2006). Cognitive-behavioral therapy for pathological gamblers. *Journal of Consulting and Clinical Psychology, 74*, 555–567.

Petry, N. M., Armentano, C., Kuoch, T., Norinth, T., & Smith, L. (2003). Gambling participation and problems among South East Asian refugees to the United States. *Psychiatric Services, 54*, 1142–1148.

Pickernell, D., Brown, K., Worthington, A., & Crawford, M. (2004, June). Gambling as a base for hypothecated taxation: The UK's national lottery and electronic gambling machines in Australia. *Public Money & Management*, 167–174.

Pinge, I. (2000). *Measuring the economic impact of electronic machines in regional areas: Bendigo, a case study.* Bendigo, Australia: Centre for Sustainable Regional Communities, La Trobe University.

Pountney, M. (2005, January 4). Costello reverses gaming donor rule. *Herald Sun.*

Problem Gambling Committee. (2003). *Problem gambling counseling in New Zealand: National statistics.* Palmerston North, New Zealand: Problem Gambling Purchasing Agency.

Prochaska, J. O., & DiClemente, C. C. (1986). Towards a comprehensive model of change. In W. R. Miller & N. Heather (Eds.), *Treating addictive behaviors: Processes of change* (pp. 3–27). New York: Plenum.

Pugh, P., & Webley, P. (2000). Adolescent participation in the U.K. national lottery games. *Journal of Adolescence, 23*, 1–11.

Raeburn, J. (2001). Towards healthy gambling: A health promotion approach to gambling in New Zealand. In R. Brown & J. Raeburn (Eds.), *Gambling, harm and health: Two perspectives on ways to minimise harm and maximise health with regard to gambling In New Zealand.* Auckland, New Zealand: Problem Gambling Committee/Gambling Studies Institute.

Raeburn, J. (2004). An international charter for gambling: The Auckland conference and beyond. *Journal of Gambling Issues, 10.*

Raylu, N., & Oei, T. P. S. (2002). Pathological gambling: A comprehensive review. *Clinical Psychology Review, 22*, 1009–1061.

Reisner, A. (2003). Newspaper construction of a moral farmer. *Rural Sociology, 68*(1), 46–63.

Reith, G. (1999). *The Age of chance: Gambling in Western culture.* London: Routledge.

Ricoeur, P. (1978). *The role of metaphor: Multi-disciplinary studies in the creation of meaning in language.* London: Routledge & Kegan Paul.

Rollnick, S., Butler, C., & Hodgson, R. (1997). Brief alcohol intervention in medical settings. *Addiction Research, 5*, 331–342.

Ronnberg, S., Volberg, R., Abbott, M. W., Moore, W. L., Andren, A., Munck, I., et al. (1999). *Gambling and problem gambling in Sweden* (Series on Gambling, Rep. No.2). Stockholm, Sweden: National Institute of Public Health.

Rose, G. (1992). *The strategy of preventive medicine.* Oxford, UK: Oxford University Press.

Rubenstein, R., & Scafidi, B. (2002). Who pays and who benefits? Examining the distributional consequences of the Georgia lottery for education. *National Tax Journal, 55,* 223–238.

Rudman, D. L. (2005). Understanding political influences on occupational possibilities: An analysis of newspaper constructions of retirement. *Journal of Occupational Science, 12,* 149–160.

Saul, J. R. (2005). *The collapse of globalism and the reinvention of the world.* New York: Penguin.

Schaap, G. E. (1988). Treatment and rehabilitation of pathological gamblers: A chance or a realistic goal. *Tijdschrift voor Alcohol, Drugs en Andere Psychotrope Stoffen, 14,* 191–199.

Searle, J. (1984). *Minds, brains and science.* Cambridge, MA: Harvard University Press.

Shaffer, H. J., & Hall, M. N. (1996). Estimating the prevalence of adolescent gambling disorders: A quantitative synthesis and guide toward standard gambling nomenclature. *Journal of Gambling Studies, 12,* 193–214.

Shaffer, H. J., & Hall, M. N. (2001). Updating and refining prevalence estimates of disordered gambling behavior in the United States and Canada. *Canadian Journal of Public Health, 92,* 168–172.

Shaffer, H. J., Hall, M. N., & Vander Bilt, J. (1997). *Estimating the prevalence of disordered gambling behavior in the United States and Canada: A meta-analysis.* Boston: Presidents and Fellows of Harvard College.

Shaffer, H. J., Hall, M. N., Vander Bilt, J., & George, E. M. (Eds.). (2003). *Futures at stake: Youth, gambling and society.* Reno: University of Nevada Press.

Sharpe, L., Tarrier, N., Schotte, D., & Spence, S. H. (1995). The role of autonomic arousal in problem gambling. *Addiction, 90,* 1529–1540.

Sherif, M. (1967). *Group conflict and co-operation: Their social psychology.* London: Routledge & Kegan Paul.

Shotter, J., & Gergen, K. J. (1990). *Texts of identity.* London: Sage.

Sicher, E. (1986). Binary oppositions and spatial representation: Toward an applied semiotics. *Semiotica, 60,* 211–224.

Simons, H. W. (1989). *Rhetoric in the human sciences.* London: Sage.

Single, E. (1995). Defining harm reduction. *Drug & Alcohol Review, 14,* 287–290.

Soyland, A. J. (1994). *Psychology as metaphor.* London: Sage.

Specker, S. M., Carlson, G. A., Edmonson, K. M., Johnson, P. E., & Marcotte, M. (1996). Psychopathology in pathological gamblers seeking treatment. *Journal of Gambling Studies, 12,* 67–81.

Star City Casino. (2006). Casino Community Benefit Fund. Retrieved November 2006, from http://www.starcity.com.au/dir013/internetpublishing.nsf/Content/BenefitFund

Statistics Canada. (2005). *Perspectives on labour and income: Fact-sheet on gambling* (Catalog No. 75-001-XIE, 2005). Ottawa, ON, Canada: Author.

Studlar, D. T. (2002). *Tobacco control: Comparative politics in the United States and Canada.* Peterborough, ON, Canada: Broadview.

Tajfel, H. (1978). *Differentiation between social groups: Studies in the social psychology of intergroup relations.* London: Academic.

Tajfel, H. (1981). *Human groups and social categories.* Cambridge, UK: Cambridge University Press.

Tajfel, H. (1982). *Social identity and intergroup relations*. Cambridge, UK: Cambridge University Press.

Taylor, G. (2002, 20 July). We reserve the right to gamble with our future. *Waikato Times*, p. 7.

Tobin, J. J. (1997). Playing doctors in two cultures. In J. J. Tobin (Ed.), *Making a place for pleasure in early childhood education*. New Haven, CT: Yale University Press.

Tse, S., Abbott, M., Clarke, D., Townsend, S., Kingi, P., & Manaia, W. (2005). *Examining the determinants of problem gambling*. Auckland, New Zealand: Health Research Council of New Zealand, Auckland UniServices Ltd., University of Auckland.

Tse, S., Wong, J., & Kim, H. (2004). A public health approach for Asian people with problem gambling in foreign countries. *Journal of Gambling Issues, 12*, 1–15.

Turcotte, F. (2003). Editorial: Why universities should stay away from the tobacco industry. *Drug & Alcohol Review, 22*, 107–108.

Turner, J. C. (1987). *Rediscovering the social group: A self-categorization theory*. Oxford, UK: Basil Blackwell.

Vickers, B. (1988). *In defence of rhetoric*. Oxford, UK: Clarendon.

Victor, R. G., & Krug, C. M. (1967). "Paradoxical intention" in the treatment of compulsive gambling. *American Journal of Psychotherapy, 21*, 808–814.

Volberg, R. R. (1996). Prevalence studies of problem gambling in the United States. *Journal of Gambling Studies, 12*, 111–128.

Volberg, R. A. (2004, February). Fifteen years of problem gambling prevalence research: What do we know? Where do we go? *Journal of Gambling Issues, 10*, 1–19.

Vorlat, E. (1985). Metaphors and their aptness in trade names for perfumes. In W. Paprotte & W. Dirven (Eds.), *The ubiquity of metaphor*. Amsterdam: John Benjamins.

West, M. O., & Prinz, R. J. (1987). Parental alcoholism and childhood psychopathology. *Psychological Bulletin, 102*, 204–218.

White, M., & Epston, D. (1990). *Narrative means to therapeutic ends*. New York: Norton.

Williams, A. (1996). *Gambling: A family affair*. London: Sheldon.

Williams, R., & Wood, R. (2003). *The demographics of Ontario gaming revenue*. Toronto: Ontario Problem Gambling Research Centre.

Wong, J., & Tse, S. (2003, October). The face of Chinese migrants' gambling: A New Zealand perspective. *Journal of Gambling Issues, 9*, 1–11.

World Health Organization. (1995). *The European charter on alcohol*. Copenhagen, Denmark: World Health Organization Regional Office for Europe.

World Health Organization. (2000). *European Alcohol Action Plan* (Rep. No. E67946). Copenhagen, Denmark: World Health Organization Regional Office for Europe.

World Health Organization. (2002). *WHO's interactions with civil society and nongovernmental organizations*. Geneva: Author.

World Health Organization. (2004). *Policy for relations with nongovernmental organizations*. Paper presented at the Fifty-Seventh World Health Assembly.

Wunsch, T. (1998). Evidence to the Productivity Commission enquiry into Australia's Gambling Industries.

Yeo, R. R. (1986). Scientific method and the rhetoric of science in Britain, 1830–1917. In J. Schuster & R. Yeo (Eds.), *The politics and rhetoric of scientific method: Historical studies*. London: Collier-Macmillan.

Zitzow, D. (2003). American Indian gaming. In H. J. Shaffer, M. N. Hall, J. Vander Bilt, & E. M. George (Eds.), *Futures at stake: Youth, gambling and society* (pp. 39–48). Reno: University of Nevada Press.

Index